FEB   1990

914.436
Han   Hansen, Arlen J.

        Expatriate Paris

DATE DUE

12 June			
			Stat

EXPATRIATE PARIS

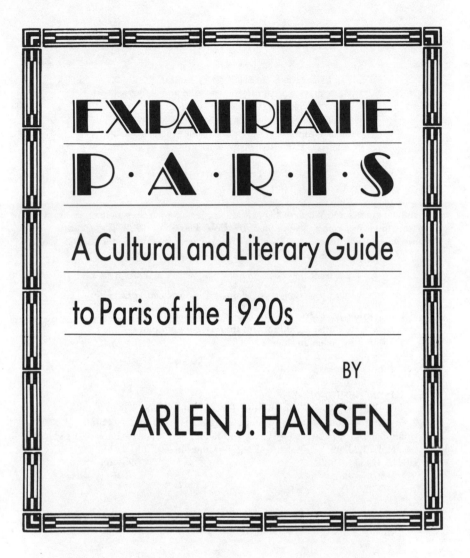

EXPATRIATE
P·A·R·I·S

A Cultural and Literary Guide

to Paris of the 1920s

BY

ARLEN J. HANSEN

Arcade Publishing·New York
Little, Brown and Company

FIRST EDITION

The author is grateful to Warner/Chappell Music, Inc., for permission to reprint excerpts from the following songs: "Omnibus" by Cole Porter © 1928 Warner Bros. Inc. (renewed). All rights reserved. "You Don't Know Paree" by Cole Porter © 1929 Warner Bros. Inc. (renewed). All rights reserved.

Excerpts from this book originally appeared in *Paris Review*.

Library of Congress Cataloging-in-Publication Data

Hansen, Arlen J., 1936–
    Expatriate Paris: a cultural and literary guide to Paris of the
    1920s / by Arlen J. Hansen.
        p.   cm.
    Bibliography: p.
    Includes index.
    ISBN 1-55970-018-1
    1. Paris (France) — Intellectual life — 20th century.
2. Authors — 20th century — Homes and haunts — France — Paris —
Guide-books.   3. Artists — Homes and haunts — France — Paris — Guide-
books. 4. Walking — France — Paris — Guide-books.   I. Title.
DC715.H334 1989   89-6963
914.4'361 — dc20   CIP

Published in the United States by Arcade Publishing, Inc., New York,
a Little, Brown company

10   9   8   7   6   5   4   3   2   1

Design by Marianne Perlak
FG

*Published simultaneously in Canada
by Little, Brown & Company (Canada) Limited*

PRINTED IN THE UNITED STATES OF AMERICA

For the two DLHs —
the one for the first two decades,
the other for the remainder

"Paris has, of course, the tradition
of guarding the exile."

— Ludwig Lewisohn

CONTENTS

FROM SAINT-GERMAIN TO THE LUXEMBOURG 69

MONTPARNASSE: THE HEART 117

THE SEVENTH ARRONDISSEMENT 179

ALONG THE CHAMPS-ELYSEES 195

PASSY 229

MONTMARTRE AND CLOCKWISE 257

LIST OF MAPS

Mais ce qui les séduisait, c'était cette vie de café, de terrasse, cette liberté de moeurs qu'ils ne connaissaient ni à Londres, ni dans aucune ville de la libre et austère Amérique; c'était cette kermesse internationale de *La Rotonde*, du *Dôme*, du *Parnasse*, où l'on pouvait indistinctement, et quelle que fût l'heure, travailler, boire, jouer du piano, même le dimanche, et danser même avec des filles que l'on ne connaissait pas, et qui venaient volontiers faire connaissance, pour le plaisir de voir de près des Américains artistes, car il n'y avait point de filles vénales dans cet endroit, ou si peu vénales: du lait quand elles avaient faim, deux gouttes d'alcool quand elles s'ennuayaient. . . .

— Michel Georges-Michel, *Les Montparnos* (1923)

Freely translated:
"What seduced them [the Montparnos] was the café life and cafe-sitting, a free and open style of living that they didn't know either in London or anywhere in Puritanical America; it was an international bazaar, a county fair, a round-robin dance of the Rotonde, the Dôme, the Parnasse where all hours of the day a person could indiscriminately work, drink, play the piano (on Sunday, no less), and dance — even with women one didn't know, who freely offered to make one's acquaintance simply for the fun of seeing an American artist up close, or, if they weren't quite so spontaneously free, then some milk for their hunger, a couple shots of liquor for their boredom. . . ."

ACKNOWLEDGMENTS

This book would not have been possible without the assistance of a great number of people and organizations: the University of the Pacific, its library staff and Faculty Research Committee; the "Travel to Collections" Program of the National Endowment for the Humanities; the Princeton University Library, particularly Ms. Jean Preston, Curator of Manuscripts, and her assistant Ann Van Arsdale; Professor Michel Fabre of Sorbonne III; and three gifted physicians who became my daily companions and my friends: Peter Garbeff, David White, and Prasad Dighe.

I was also blessed by the steady encouragement and support of my family and friends: Lynn, Laura, Kip, James, Tess, Eddie, Charles, John, Kate, Bob C. (*juglar por excelencia*), Jim B., Jeff, and hundreds more. Finally, this book benefited immeasurably from the counsel and practical wisdom of my editor, Dick Seaver, and Peggy Freudenthal, who is surely one of the finest copyeditors in captivity. Even with all this assistance and my own compulsion for perfection, however, I have probably still managed to make mistakes, oversights, and errors of judgment. For them I apologize.

How does one acknowledge a thousand sources of information? The manifold and various works where I found and confirmed facts and uncovered the details and the gossip? How does one indicate that his was the easy job, collecting the products of others' labors — and acknowledge that the fundamental effort belongs to those who wrote or compiled the memoirs, histories, literary studies, biographies, editions of letters that perforce precede a work like this? I suspect that true indebtedness can never be fully or properly acknowledged. I know that such a task is, sadly, beyond the limits of my ability.

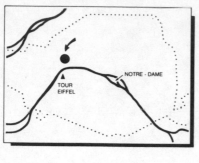

MAP 1

includes addresses from ...

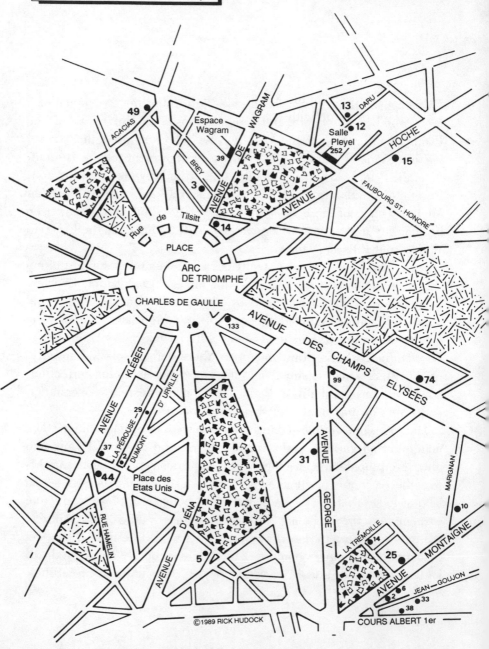

©1989 RICK HUDOCK

INTRODUCTION

Composing lyrics for his 1929 musical, *Fifty Million Frenchmen*, Cole Porter came up with a verse that cautioned the casual visitor to Paris:

> You come to Paris, you come to play;
> You have a wonderful time, you go away.
> And, from then on, you talk of Paris knowingly,
> You may know Paris, you don't know Paree.

Porter knew "Paree," for he himself lived on the Left Bank, and he was right about the elusive, hidden side of Paris, especially during the twenties.

In those years Paris hosted a vast assortment of transplanted artists: the hardworking young rookie Ernest Hemingway; the gregarious sculptor Constantin Brancusi; zany Tristan Tzara; the brilliant, beautiful, and brave Kay Boyle; James Joyce, an enigmatic genius; music's "bad boy," George Antheil; the rebellious André Breton; the ebullient Josephine Baker; lanky James Thurber; timid Anaïs Nin. . . .

But if expatriate life evaded the cursory tourist of the twenties, its legacy — the music, poetry, paintings, and fiction — is palpable today. Looking back, we can sense the unusual and rich mix that constituted Expatriate Paris: a unique period, a special place, and extraordinary people.

Only, *expatriate* is not the word exactly. Most of the writers, painters, sculptors, dancers, musicians, celebrities, and assorted hangers-on who are mentioned in this book were not, strictly speaking, "expatriates." Only a very few might be thought of as having abandoned their native country and taken France as a new homeland. Those who did were probably Russians associated with the deposed czar, frustrated revolutionaries from any number of unsettled postwar countries, or people from other parts of Europe whose money had been fueling a skyrocketing inflation at home.

Hardly any American visitor, short-termer or long, could be considered to be forsaking the United States — neither Edna Ferber passing through, nor Scott and Zelda Fitzgerald, who in their extended stays in Paris displayed no desire whatsoever to become "Parisian." The concept of "expatriate" does not apply, even, to someone like Natalie Barney, who frequently wrote in French and made Paris her principal residence for half a century. Barney was simply an American living in Paris. Or consider the Hemingways. When Hadley's child was due, she and Ernest returned to North America so the baby would have either U.S. or Canadian — but emphatically not French or European — citizenship. No, these were not "expatriates" in the pure sense of the word.

So, why use it? If literally inaccurate, at least the term is handier than the cumbersome "member of the lost generation," another classification that doesn't fit everyone. When Gertrude Stein first reported the use of this phrase, she was referring to the younger generation who'd been disillusioned by the Great War. Having abandoned the values and the codes of conduct of their Victorian and Georgian predecessors, the younger generation seemed rootless and lost to people like Stein. Thus, she, Picasso, and others who had come to Paris before the war were not of the "lost" generation.

Howsoever inappropriate, *expatriate* is less misleading than *exile*, another word that is sometimes used. *Exile* implies banishment and connotes punishment. *Exiled* to Paris indeed. Nor could the expatriates be considered "self-exiles," for few severed their ties with home. Most of the Americans, for example, made frequent trips back and forth, and virtually all of them depended on financial support from stateside friends, family, patrons, or buyers.

The designation "expatriate" is meet and fit, however, insofar as it implies a deliberate, freely made decision to leave Chicago or Chelsea and move, at least temporarily, to Paris. In the twenties Sisley Huddleston described the expatriates' situation this way:

We expatriates — as it is now the fashion to call Americans and English writers and artists who live in Paris — are not cut off from home. . . . The visitor comes, sees us in our daily haunts, and invariably regrets that he cannot stay: life seems to him so much easier than at home. So indeed it is in many respects. That is why many of us, who are not absolutely compelled by the exigencies of our profession, choose to stay abroad.

The choice to go to Paris was a conscious surrender to its magnetism. Like the beatniks' North Beach of the fifties, or the hippies' Haight-Ashbury of the sixties, Paris of the twenties was where the action was. And for many that was attraction enough.

Paris was also *possible*. Americans could afford it. Although the French economy wasn't as bad off as that of Germany or Austria, where galloping triple-digit inflation was eliminating the middle class, it was nevertheless weak. The franc was worth about 6¢ in 1921, and by 1926 it had dropped to 4¢, a rate of exchange that meant flush times for anyone with dollars to spend.

Janet Flanner's hotel room, for instance, was ideally located and sufficiently comfortable for her to keep it the entire decade. It cost her a dollar a day. In 1925, William Faulkner spent about a dollar a day *total*, including 55¢ for his room. And, according to A. J. Liebling, a journalist who took his dining seriously, if you knew what you were doing you could obtain a substantial dinner, with wine, for under 10 francs (50¢).

The war had made Paris possible in another way, too. The naval battle off Denmark's Jutland peninsula in 1916 convinced England of the merit of destroyers and other ships of that size, which were more mobile and less of a target for U-boats than the big cruisers. British and American shipbuilders tooled up accordingly. So, when the war was over, they were prepared to turn out moderate-sized ocean liners and steamers.

The same sea battle persuaded the Germans to port their surface ships and emphasize submarine warfare. To cope with the German mines and U-boat blockades, the Allies inaugurated the use of escorted convoys to transport goods and troops. This strategy, however, required an abundance of merchant ships, for only large convoys could justify and make efficient use of naval escorts. To meet the resulting increase in demand, shipyard production picked up sharply. In 1916, for example, before the United States entered the war, American shipbuilders turned out 129 steam vessels. In 1919, still filling contracts that had been made during the war, they built nearly seven times as many: 891.

Thus, when the war came to a halt, the Allies were ship-heavy. Obliged by a disarmament agreement, they sank many of their ships, but a surplus remained. Magnates like Cunard and Ellerman, and lesser dreamers, bought what they could and converted them into passenger liners. For the fiscal year 1918–19, *The World Almanac and Encyclopedia* lists 117 "Great Ocean Steamers," including ships from all nations. In 1922–23, after four years of intensified ship-building and the conversion of war surplus, the number of registered "Great Ocean Steamers," nearly tripled to 328. Liners and tramp steamers of varying degrees of comfort, speed, and cost routinely began to ply the Atlantic. Easier and cheaper to get to than, say, Santa Fe, Paris was now "possible" for most anyone.

But why *Paris?* Berlin, with its runaway inflation, was an even less costly place to live and, besides, it was more exotically decadent. Mahler, Wittgenstein, and Freud had given elegant Vienna an intellectual and cultural allure. Florence, too, had its appeal. It was the city celebrated by Bernard Berenson, whose life was dedicated to art, and by Mabel Dodge, a champion of modern art since the 1913 Armory Show in New York. Rome also beckoned, as did Venice and, for that matter, Greenwich Village. So, why Paris?

For one thing, many American soldiers and volunteers had seen Paris during the war, after which it wasn't easy to keep their thoughts down on the farm. To them Paris was synonymous with excitement. Paris meant even more to the aspiring artist, who tended to regard it as a special, virtually holy place. The city carried the reputation not only of tolerating artistic independence and eccentricity but also of actually encouraging it. Leaving its artists alone, Paris nonetheless provided them the accoutrements necessary to art: excellent printers and presses, galleries and bookshops, art schools, social companions and intellectuals, patrons and buyers, concert halls and salons, and an unusually accessible and sympathetic press. The artistic atomic pile in Paris achieved critical mass.

Paris held another attraction, particularly for Americans. The presence of four English-language newspapers in Paris indicated a sizable English-speaking community. It also meant that there would be numerous British and American journalists in town — and, just possibly, work too. Since Paris was hot news back home, virtually every American magazine and newspaper sensitive to its image had a branch in Paris and hired stringers to cover the news. Periodicals as diverse as the *Brooklyn Daily Eagle*, *Vogue*, the *Saturday Evening Post*, and *Vanity Fair* maintained editorial offices in Paris. For the American writer, Paris offered an assembly of fellows, a parliament of peers.

The state of affairs in the United States at the time was quite different. Many American intellectuals and artists had begun to feel uncomfortable at home. A repressive new Puritanism was on the rise, and the Eighteenth Amendment (Prohibition) was only one sign of it. U.S. Attorney General A. Mitchell Palmer opened the decade by authorizing raids on labor headquarters and private homes to stop what he fancied to be a "red menace." On a single night in January 1920, Palmer's men arrested some 4,000 people in thirty-three different cities. In Detroit, to cite a further example, 300 entirely innocent people were brought in and held for a week, presumably to thwart Communist agitation.

The United States Post Office and the recently established New York Port Authority had license to intercept mail and destroy material they felt to be salacious or dangerous. For years James Joyce's *Ulysses*, one of the masterpieces of the twenties — and of the twentieth century — had to be smuggled into the land of the free and the home of the brave. Various Societies for the Suppression of Vice, most notably Boston's Watch and Ward Society, also assumed the role of censor. Such institutions and the attitudes they generate effectively salt the fields of art.

More subtle but also more pernicious attitudes showed up in American society at large. After the New York Armory Show in 1913, which boasted Marcel Duchamp's *Nude Descending a Staircase*, insensitive public officials and the sensational media openly ridiculed artistic innovation. The American public added its hoots of derision. Sherwood Anderson, William Faulkner, and Ernest Hemingway may have appreciated the work of Gertrude Stein, but around the country the mere mention of her name in a newspaper lead or an after-dinner speech was reliably good for a laugh. The American culture, as if having reached adolescence, seemed unusually nervous about any of its citizens who appeared "different."

A precampaign speech by Warren G. Harding in 1920 points up the issue:

America's need is not heroics, but healing; not nostrums, but normalcy; not revolution, but restoration; not agitation, but adjustment . . . ; not experiment, but equipoise; not submergence in internationality, but sustainment in triumphant nationality.

These words ran directly counter to the fundamental beliefs of the expatriate artists, who were disillusioned by the excessive nationalism, or "jingoism," as it was called, rampant during the war years. Artists like Virgil Thomson, John Dos Passos, and E. E. Cummings were calling for radical experimentation, artistic innovation, intellectual stimulation, and internationalism. But the American majority sided with Mr. Harding of Ohio, whom they elected President in November 1920. Not surprisingly, the expatriates elected for Paris.

Mostly, they settled on the Left Bank, in the area known as Montparnasse. As their numbers grew during the first years of the decade, a new vitality and artistic dedication emerged. True, there also appeared the flotsam and jetsam of art: sham, folly, laziness, drunkenness, deprivation, and envy. Nevertheless, the expatriates were shaping their own "Paree." Writing at mid-decade, Huddleston summarized the character of its uniqueness:

The chief attraction of Montparnasse is that there one feels surrounded by young life, with genuine aspirations, and although much that is done is silly, and mistakes are innumerable, yet, in spite of the dealers, and the snobs, and the visitors, and the foolish short-cuts, and the deliberate fakers, and the noxious night-haunts, something big may veritably emerge from this welter of cafés and studios and academies in which artists from many lands meet to understand each other, to stimulate each other, and to — "try."

NOTE TO THE READER

To capture a sense of the real Expatriate Paris, this book offers a mosaic of persons, places, dates, images, incidents, and rumors. The mosaic quality comes from treating the material geographically, spatially. As Marx suggested, geography is history. Geography is also accident, the prismatic stone next to the combustible leaf. Ideally, the mosaic structure will reproduce the motion and lag of people arriving and departing, the repetitions of concert-going and café-sitting, and the richly patterned motifs of quarrels, affairs, and accidental encounters.

This book strives to be accurate but also seeks deliberately to be somewhat gossipy. It contains roughly 1,000 addresses of residences, cafés, hotels, galleries, commercial establishments, and other note-worthy places. Should the reader be in Paris, or simply wish to imagine Paris, these individual addresses have been grouped into thirty-three different clusters or neighborhoods. Insofar as possible each cluster is made up of addresses that are within reasonable walking distance of one another.*

Three indices are provided. The "Index of Streets, Avenues, Boulevards, Etc." simply lists all references to particular streets. The "Index of Noteworthy Places, Infamous Events, and Sundry Things" indicates where one can find information about specific cafés, incidents, concerts, bars, theatres, and exhibitions. And the "Index of Persons Mentioned" directs the reader to all references to a

* The clusters themselves have been grouped into eight major areas that spiral out clockwise from the Right Bank center of Paris. The eight areas are: (1) The Inner Right Bank, (2) The Inner Left Bank, (3) From Saint-Germain to the Luxembourg Gardens, (4) Montparnasse, (5) The Seventh Arrondissement, (6) Along the Champs-Elysées, (7) Passy, and (8) Montmartre.

particular individual. Thus, by checking, say, James Joyce, a reader can follow the Irish novelist's career through the decade.

All of the addresses have been verified as objectively as possible. In most cases, each address was confirmed in at least two different places. When there is some question about the reliability of a bit of information, the doubt is noted. Also noted are any blatant contradictions between two or more "reliable" sources. Whenever possible, verification was made by checking city records in the Bibliothèque Nationale and in the postal and telephone archives.

Of special value was the work familiarly known as le Bottin (*Annuaire du Commerce*, Didot-Bottin) — an "annual of commerce" that lists all business operations for a given year. The telephone books were a great help, as was Jacques Hillairet's *Dictionnaire Historique des Rues de Paris* (Les Editions de Minuit). Another valuable source was the odd little *Franco-American Yearbook*, which contained a "Residential Directory" of Americans living in Paris. The "yearbook" was issued in conjunction with the U.S. Chamber of Commerce in 1921 (no other number has been found). Other city directories, tourist booklets, Baedekers, handbooks, picture books, and travel-and-tour guides were also used to verify the addresses.

The greatest sources of information — though they were sometimes contradictory — were the many memoirs, biographies, and histories of Paris during the twenties. If the test of a period's appeal lies in the quantity and quality of the books written about it, the expatriates' Paris surely must outshine any other period. Numbering well into the hundreds, the works about Paris in the twenties make lively reading.

Readers will be captivated by standard works like Noel Fitch, *Sylvia Beach and the Lost Generation*; George Wickes, *Americans in Paris*; or Malcolm Cowley, *Exile's Return* and *A Second Flowering*. Some may prefer the more subjective memoirs: Ernest Hemingway, *A Moveable Feast*; Alice Toklas, *What Is Remembered*; or Robert McAlmon and Kay Boyle, *Being Geniuses Together*. There are also topic-oriented works, like Matthew J. Bruccoli, *Scott and Ernest* or Morrill Cody and Hugh Ford, *The Women of Montparnasse*, which is enriched by Cody's personal, if sometimes inaccurate, recollections.

One of the most fascinating and readable works to come out recently is William Wiser, *The Crazy Years*, an irresistible survey of the personalities of the period. Notice should also be made of Brian

N. Morton's ambitious *Americans in Paris*, an "anecdotal street guide" that covers all periods and includes many expatriates. Two books in French should be noted: Michel Fabre, *La Rive Noire: De Harlem à la Seine*, which offers a rich guide to the black expatriates, and Alain Jouffroy's study of the period, *La Vie Réinventée: L'Explosion des Années 20 à Paris*.

These works and hundreds more — including, this author hopes, the book you have in your hands — help log the remarkable facts and preserve the splendid stories of Expatriate Paris.

Make that *Paree*.

THE
INNER RIGHT BANK

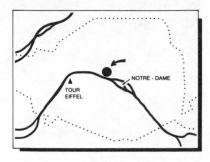

MAP 2

includes addresses from ...

1. The Grand Hotels
2. The Madeleine to the Opéra
3. Italiens to the Louvre

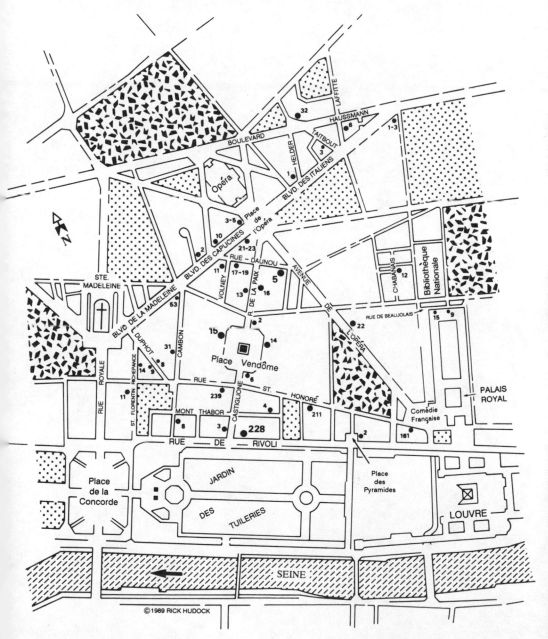

©1989 RICK HUDOCK

THE GRAND HOTELS

PLACE VENDOME

14 · Morgan, Harjes et Cie (now Morgan Guaranty Trust)

Already a free spirit when he started as an apprentice at this bank on 8 May 1922, Harry Crosby became a poet, editor, diarist, publisher, and suicide by the end of the twenties. Crosby's mother, who was a sister of Mrs. J. Pierpont Morgan, had sought the Paris position for Harry, hoping that it would separate him from his latest obsession, Mrs. Richard (Polly) Peabody.

Polly's given name was Mary Jacobs (under which, incidentally, she had patented her own invention — the stayless, wireless brassiere). Although Polly was already married and the mother of two, she and Harry were in love. Polly obtained a divorce, followed Harry to Paris, and took a room at the Hôtel Regina. Back in the States that fall, Harry and Polly were married in the chapel of New York City's Municipal Building on 9 September 1922. Polly eventually changed her name to Caresse, and Harry left the Morgan Bank for good in December 1923.

RUE DE LA PAIX

2 · Shop of Elizabeth Arden

Offering everything from facials to weight-reducing exercises, Elizabeth Arden's shop was popular with the wealthier American women — like Zelda Fitzgerald, who wrote it prominently in her address book of the twenties.

(In addition to the addresses of her friends, Zelda also listed a variety of shops and services, some in the States and some in Paris. For example, under "corsets" and "lingerie" were several Parisian listings. Zelda also made note of the addresses of doctors, dentists, hat shops, shoe stores, servants, rental agencies, cleaners, and toy stores. Under *B* Zelda included several American bootleggers, and under *F* she listed a fur repairer's name. Zelda's address book thus captures a sense of the Fitzgeralds' priorities and requirements during the twenties.)

The Paris office of *Harper's Bazaar*, managed by Joan Taylor, was also located at number 2, as was the headquarters for the American Hearst Publications, run by C. F. Bertell.

PLACE VENDOME

15 · Hôtel Ritz

The most expensive hotel in Paris, the Ritz charged $9 a night for its cheapest single room. The Ritz had two bars. One was a tiny bandbox of a room reserved primarily for women, who could buy the popular new drink of the day — the Champagne Cocktail — for 10 francs (50¢). The second was a large bar with its main entrance on the rue Cambon. This one opened precisely at noon, even though a line of customers usually formed outside well ahead of time. By 12:02, reports say, the place was full. When Hemingway, Fitzgerald, or nearly any other male refers to the Ritz Bar during the twenties, he usually meant this one.

Although it's said that European royalty preferred the Hôtel Meurice, a few stayed here — including Queen Marie of Romania, King Peter of Serbia, the Duke and Duchess of York, and the American version of royalty, Mr. J. Pierpont Morgan — or, as Harry Crosby would call him, "Uncle Jack."

Before World War I, Elinor (Hoyt) and Horace Wylie, the man with whom the poet was living in exile in England (and later married), made occasional "runs" to Paris, putting up at the Ritz under the assumed names of Mr. and Mrs. Waring.

The popular novelist Elinor Glyn stayed at the Ritz during World War I as an American press reporter. She gave up her room only when she was invited to move to even cushier quarters at Versailles to cover the Peace Conference for Lord Riddell's *News of the World*.

In the mid-twenties when Elsa Maxwell brought her considerable talents as a professional hostess to Paris, she moved into the Ritz. Out of fear of offending this woman who had such powerful friends, the Ritz allowed Maxwell to run up sizable bills at will.

Another popular resident of the Ritz in the twenties was Duff Twysden and her consort, Pat Guthrie, when he was in town. Duff was the model for Lady Brett Ashley in Hemingway's novel *The Sun Also Rises*, and Guthrie appeared as Mike Campbell.

F. Scott Fitzgerald's well-known short story "Babylon Revisited" begins and ends at the bar of the Ritz, where he'd spent a small fortune in the twenties.

In 1944 accompanied by a platoon of soldiers whom he'd commandeered, Ernest Hemingway liberated the Ritz from the Nazis. After spending the night, Hemingway and his private army then headed off through small-arms fire to rescue Sylvia Beach and her Left Bank bookstore, Shakespeare and Company.

6 · Hôtel du Rhin

This was the hotel Eugene O'Neill used during his visits to Paris in the late twenties. Deciding to separate from his wife, Agnes, O'Neill left for Europe in February 1928 in the company of Carlotta Monterey, a former actress and the ex-wife of Ralph Barton (plus two other former husbands). Raised in England and France, Carlotta intended "to introduce [O'Neill] to the sophistication of Europe."

Traveling incognito to minimize the scandal of their adulterous relationship, Gene and Carlotta drove from Calais to Paris, arriving on 26 February 1928.

Except for an excursion of a few months to the Far East, O'Neill remained in Europe from 1928 until 1931, spending most of that time in the French countryside. He did visit Paris occasionally. In fact, Gene and Carlotta were married in Paris on 22 July 1929, as soon as he'd learned that his divorce from Agnes had become official. O'Neill also spent July and September 1928 in Paris — in addition to September 1929 and the New Year holidays of 1929–30.

O'Neill's days at the Hôtel du Rhin were not typical of expatriate life. For one thing, he was hiding from attention rather than seeking it. For another, he was spending every moment he could spare on his work — polishing his play *Dynamo* and sketching his first drafts of *Mourning Becomes Electra*. Gene and Carlotta returned to America on 17 May 1931.

Among his dozens (literally) of Paris residences during the twenties, the publisher and writer Robert McAlmon also stayed at the Hôtel du Rhin. There is no evidence that he ever bumped into O'Neill, although McAlmon would likely have known Gene from their days in Greenwich Village. As a rule, however, McAlmon and most other American expatriates preferred Montparnasse life and Left Bank hotels.

RUE SAINT-HONORE

239 · Hôtel de France et Choiseul

The American writer Fanny Hurst stayed here on her return from her celebrated trip to Russia. And the world-famous actor Otis Skinner preferred this hotel during his visits to Paris. Accompanying him on his 1920 trip was his daughter, Cornelia, who later gained fame as an actress and a writer.

211 · Hôtel Saint-James-et-d'Albany (the old Hôtel de Noailles)

When F. Scott and Zelda Fitzgerald roared through Paris in May and June 1921, they stayed at the Saint-James-et-d'Albany. The hotel management did not appreciate Zelda's habit of blocking the elevator door open so it would be available whenever they wanted it. The Fitzgeralds disliked Paris during this first trip, but their affection for the City of Light grew during their second visit in 1925 and the subsequent years.

This may also be the hotel that Harold Stearns recalls as "The Oxford and Cambridge," where he and Sinclair Lewis stayed when Lewis first brought the young social critic to Paris in August 1921. In any case, when Sinclair and Grace Lewis (and their son) came to Paris that October, they took rooms here. Lewis at the time was flush from the success of *Main Street*. Although Lewis returned to Paris several times in the twenties, his experiences were never very pleasant. In a word, he was not the lion in Montparnasse that he was in The Village.

161 · Café de la Régence (now gone)

In addition to the Taverne Royale on the rue Royale, the Régence was one of Thomas Wolfe's favorite cafés. Several pages of the Paris material that Wolfe incorporated into his second novel, *Of Time and the River,* are designated as having been drafted "At La Régence." From this café on the place du Théâtre-Français, Wolfe could watch "the streams of traffic up and down the whole avenue de l'Opéra" and study "the delicate, plain, and beautiful facade of the Comédie [Française] across the Square."

PLACE DES PYRAMIDES

2 · Hôtel Regina

As they had planned, Mrs. Polly Jacobs Peabody (later, Caresse Crosby) followed Harry Crosby to Paris in 1922 and took a tiny room on the top floor of this hotel for a few weeks. They met in secret and on their most spirited evenings tossed champagne bottles down onto the statue of Jeanne d'Arc in the center of the *place.* To the consternation of both families, Harry persuaded Polly, who'd just gotten a divorce, to marry him.

Lincoln Steffens made this hotel his residence from July to November 1922 while he was working for Hearst's Universal Service. Steffens left the Regina in November when he went to an economic conference in Lausanne, where he met — and made a considerable impression on — Ernest Hemingway. Steffens returned to Paris that winter and took a room in what became his favorite hotel, the Richepance.

Havelock Ellis, the psychologist, and Arthur Symons, the critic, stayed in this hotel during their brief visit to Paris in 1924.

AVENUE DE L'OPERA

22 · Hôtel des Deux Mondes (now gone)

In May 1924, Scott and Zelda Fitzgerald arrived in Paris and stayed in the Deux Mondes. This was their second trip to Europe.

Unaccustomed to European life (or hotels), they used the bidet as a baby bath for Scottie, their 1½-year-old daughter.

During this brief stopover, they looked up Scott's friend from Princeton, the poet John Peale Bishop, who was living on the outskirts of Paris. They may also have checked in with Gerald and Sara Murphy, whom they'd never met before. Gerald was the elder brother of the Fitzgeralds' New York friend Esther Murphy. Gerald and Sara became true and loyal friends of Scott and Zelda (and, loosely, the models for characters in Fitzgerald's novel *Tender Is the Night*).

RUE DE RIVOLI

228 · Hôtel Meurice

Although technically on the rue de Rivoli, the registration entrance to the Meurice was (and is) on the Mont-Thabor side. Along with such hotels as the Ritz, Crillon, and Continental, the Meurice provided luxurious accommodation for the European aristocracy.

Among its royal guests were the Prince of Wales, former King George of Greece, the King and Queen of Belgium, and the King of Italy. The King of Spain had a suite named after him, so frequently did he stay at the Meurice.

When Lady Ellerman and her husband, Sir John, the English shipping magnate, came to Paris to visit their daughter, Bryher, they usually stayed here, directly across from the Tuileries Gardens. Such visits were few, however, since Bryher — when she wasn't in England herself — preferred to spend her days near Montreux, Switzerland, with the poet H. D. (Hilda Doolittle), rather than in Paris with her husband, Robert McAlmon.

In the early twenties Igor Stravinsky used the Meurice as his Paris mailing address, since his residence was a house on the beach near Biarritz. "Write to me," Stravinsky told a friend, "at the Hotel Meurice. I go by there to pick up my mail, which is care of Madame Sert. . . ."

Misia Sert and her (third) husband, the painter José-Maria, had a suite of rooms in the Meurice, before taking an apartment at 252 rue de Rivoli. Misia was a friend of the Belle Epoque artists — she'd been painted by Vuillard, Toulouse-Lautrec, Vallotton, Renoir, and Bonnard — as well as expatriates of the twenties like Stravinsky and Diaghilev.

248 • W. H. Smith and Son

This English bookstore offered standard English publications, unlike Sylvia Beach's Shakespeare and Company, which carried the little magazines and the experimental, if suspect, works of new writers like James Joyce, Djuna Barnes, and Ernest Hemingway.

RUE DE CASTIGLIONE

3 • Hôtel Continental

This luxurious hotel was the primary residence of Sergei Diaghilev, the manager of the Ballets Russes, whose debut production of Stravinsky's *Sacre du Printemps* shocked its audience in 1913. Boris Kochno, a seventeen-year-old poet and aristocrat fleeing Bolshevik Russia, sought out Diaghilev at this hotel, became his lover, and was eventually named secretary to the Russian ballet.

When Scofield Thayer, co-owner and editor of the *Dial*, came to Paris in July 1921, he stayed at the Continental. The day Ezra Pound called on Thayer, he met another young man with Thayer: painter-poet E. E. Cummings. (Eventually Cummings had a child by and married — in that order — Thayer's wife, Elaine Orr.)

George Moore, the English writer who was a close friend of Nancy Cunard (she sometimes thought he might be her real father), stayed alternately at the Continental and the Foyot during his visits to Paris. This hotel was also the Paris residence of Jeritza, the prima donna.

RUE MONT-THABOR

4 • Hôtel Mont-Thabor

When Edmund Wilson arrived in Paris on 20 June 1921, he took a room at this hotel for a few days. Then, he moved to a pension on the rue du Four where he was closer to his principal object for coming to Paris: the poet Edna St. Vincent Millay.

Two days after Wilson's arrival, Millay and Scott and Zelda Fitzgerald, who were on their first (and disappointing) visit to Paris, searched the city for their mutual friend, Bunny Wilson. They knew he'd arrived, but they didn't know where he was staying. Ironically, Scott and Zelda were at the Saint-James-et-d'Albany, just a couple blocks from Wilson's hotel.

RUE CAMBON

8 · Hôtel Métropolitain (now gone)

When he first came to Paris to work in the Morgan Bank in May 1922, Harry Crosby supposedly shared a room with a young man named Lou Norrie in this hotel on the corner of Mont-Thabor and Cambon. Actually, Harry spent most of his time at the Hôtel Regina with Polly Peabody until she returned home. When Harry raced back to the States to marry Polly that fall, he won a $100 bet from Norrie for beating him to New York.

In May 1927, the elusive Dorothy (Dolly) Wilde — Oscar's eccentric niece — lived in the Métropolitain briefly before taking a flat on Vaugirard and then moving on to the Hôtel Montalembert and then disappearing from Paris for a couple years and then returning and then . . .

2

FROM THE MADELEINE
TO THE OPERA

RUE DUPHOT

8 · Hôtel Burgundy

Heading back to the United States in July 1928, Thomas Wolfe stopped off in Paris and stayed briefly in this hotel.

On 20 May 1930 Wolfe registered at the Hôtel Mondial and apparently spent the following week there. However, according to a journal entry in which he spells the name "Burgendy," Wolfe seems to have stayed one night during that week at this hotel — probably with a prostitute. Moreover, his letter of May 24 to Aline Bernstein was written on Hôtel Burgundy stationery.

Wolfe's behavior during this period (spring 1930) was somewhat erratic. Having published *Look Homeward, Angel* in 1929, he was now trying to break off relations with Mrs. Bernstein, his devoted patron and lover. Unable to shake her, Wolfe often resorted to disguising his exact whereabouts. Thus, it's possible that Wolfe spent a night at the Burgundy with a prostitute and took some of its stationery on which to write Mrs. Bernstein, even though he was in fact registered at the Mondial.

9 · Prunier's

Specializing in seafood, Prunier's was an expensive restaurant, but one of the best in Paris. Thomas Wolfe and Aline Bernstein ate there frequently, as did others who preferred the Right Bank to Montparnasse or who came over for the oysters. It was a sad day in Paris when Emile Prunier died in 1925. Referring to him as a "great server of the French palate," Janet Flanner noted that "his Portuguese oysters were one of the modest-priced tasty traditions of France, and his American clientele so numerous that he planted for them local beds of Cape Cod clams and blue points. . . ."

RUE RICHEPANCE

14 • Hôtel Richepance

The more Lincoln Steffens visited Paris, the more he seemed to prefer this hotel. Steffens had stayed in the Hôtel Chatham with sculptor Jo Davidson in 1919, and occasionally thereafter he opted for the Hôtel Regina. When he came to Paris in the winter of 1922–23, however, Steffens took a room here, and it was the Richepance ever after.

Steffens returned to the Hôtel Richepance in February 1924 when he was about to marry Ella Winter, who was nearly six months pregnant with his child.

After living two years on the Italian Riviera, Steffens once again returned to the Richepance in June 1926 for a few weeks. And he was back in February 1927 for a couple months while working on his *Autobiography*.

RUE SAINT-FLORENTIN

11 • Residence of Bernard Faÿ

Faÿ was a young history professor whose family owned this flat in Paris. Having studied at Harvard, Faÿ was in a position to bring together Parisian artists and American expatriates. He thus introduced Virgil Thomson to the composers Darius Milhaud, Francis Poulenc, Georges Auric, and Arthur Honegger — that is, two-thirds of Les Six. And Thomson in turn brought the young Missouri painter Eugene McCown (Thomson's spelling) to the Faÿs, where McCown met Jean Cocteau and Erik Satie.

RUE CAMBON

31 • House of Chanel

Gabrielle "Coco" Chanel's original establishment is still here, east of La Madeleine. During the boom years, Chanel's twenty-six Parisian sewing shops alone employed 2,400 workers and her perfume laboratories and looms hundreds more. In a piece written around 1940, Janet Flanner observed that whereas the "other establishments indulge in tapestries and objets d'art as furnishings, serve cocktails to buyers, and display their mannequins on a stage, No. 31 rue Cambon looks neither like a museum, a bar, nor a revue. It looks what it is, a shop — deluxe and glassy, but still a shop [and its doorman] is a pink-cheeked fellow in wooden-soled shoes and a green ulster who looks as if he'd be handy with spring lambs."

53 • Paris office of the *Brooklyn Daily Eagle* (now gone)

Operating out of his apartment here and occasionally the Anglo-American Press Club, Guy Hickok was the Paris correspondent for the *Daily Eagle*. By all accounts, Hickok and his wife, Mary, were an amiable, helpful couple who'd come to Paris prior to the big influx of Americans in the twenties. The Hickoks were close friends and supporters of Ernest and Hadley Hemingway during their first years in Paris.

RUE DE CAUMARTIN

8 and 10 • Studios of Madame Egorova (Princess Troubetskoy)

The celebrated ballet instructor Madame Egorova was a good friend of the Murphys, whose daughter, Honoria, studied with her. For five months in 1928, Egorova also gave lessons to Zelda Fitzgerald, whose preoccupation with dance during this time became virtually obsessive. According to changes Zelda made in her address book that year, Egorova's studio was first at number 10, then at number 8, and finally at number 27 rue des Petits-Hôtels in the Tenth Arrondissement.

RUE EDOUARD-VII

2 · Offices of *Vogue* and *Vanity Fair*

In addition to Joan Boyle, the writer Kay Boyle's older sister, Virginia ("Jinny") and Pauline Pfeiffer worked for *Vogue*. After meeting Ernest Hemingway in the winter of 1924–25, Pauline resolved to supplant Hadley and become the second Mrs. Hemingway, which she did in 1927.

Lewis Galantière, to whom Sherwood Anderson wrote in 1921 introducing Hemingway, worked for a while in an adjacent office as an editor for *Vanity Fair*.

BOULEVARD DES CAPUCINES

10 · Paris office of the *Chicago Daily News* (now gone)

In the middle of the decade, young John Gunther was sent over to head up the Paris office of the *Chicago Daily News*. Besides his success as a journalist, Gunther would later gain fame as a novelist and author of sociopolitical exposés like *Inside Europe*.

The chief correspondent for the *Daily News* during the decade was Paul Scott Mowrer. According to the 1921 *Franco-American Yearbook*, Mowrer used number 10 as his mailing address, although he lived on the rue du Bac. He married Hadley Hemingway in 1933.

Between 21 and 23 · Le Trou dans le Mur (Hole in the Wall)

Jimmy Charters, the celebrated British bartender, signed on as assistant bartender here when he first came to Paris in the early twenties. "It was in this bar," he recalled, "that I first developed any personal friends among my clients." Jimmy was so popular that his clients followed him as he moved from bar to bar — the Dingo, the Jockey, the Falstaff, the Trois et As, and his own Bec de Gaz. With Jimmy catering to English-speaking expatriates, the Hole in the Wall became, in his words, "an alternate drinking stop to the New York Bar around the corner."

In *A Moveable Feast*, Ernest Hemingway describes this tiny bar after it had grown somewhat disreputable, and he places it on the "rue des Italiens." (The boulevard des Capucines becomes the boulevard des Italiens nearby.)

By the mid-twenties, the Hole in the Wall had become a virtual drug shop, where opium or cocaine was easily obtained and a joint of hashish cost around a dollar. Presumably, there was a secret escape out the back into the famous Parisian sewers. Today, but probably not for long, the slim door is marked "Restaurant Oriental."

PLACE DE L'OPERA

3–5 · Café de la Paix

Kay Boyle arrived in Paris for a brief visit in September 1923. When she called on her friend Harold Loeb at ten in the morning, he appeared at his door "a bit put out" — since "he had been still asleep with his current lady." Loeb arranged to meet Kay at this famous café later that day. She arrived to find "a young man in a grey suit" with Loeb. This man was writer-publisher Robert McAlmon, whose friendship and support Boyle would always cherish.

RUE VOLNEY

11 · Henry's Bar (now gone)

Having opened in 1890, Henry's was the second-oldest American bar in Paris. Only the Chatham was older, but purists claimed that it wasn't, strictly speaking, "American" in its set-up.

Situated near the corner of Volney and Daunou, the bar occupied the ground floor of Henry's Hotel. Henry, the founder, got his start tending bar at the Chatham. After his suicide in 1917, Henry's wife ran the bar for a while. Wisely, in the early twenties she decided to turn it over to two astute barmen, who made Henry's once again a successful operation.

According to a contemporary account, Henry's was "the only place in Paris where the ancient and honorable profession of domino playing still survives the assaults of a mahjongistic civilization." In the twenties, Henry's customers tended to be genteel businessmen, as opposed to the louder patrons at Harry's New York Bar.

RUE DE LA PAIX

16 • Office of the *New York Times*

Reputed to be particularly luxurious, the *Times*'s quarters were headed by European Director Edwin L. James.

13 • Hôtel Westminster

Aline Bernstein, Thomas Wolfe's patron and lover, took a room in this hotel in 1928 and, most likely, on her other visits to Paris as well. Based on its location — near Harry's and the Grand Boulevards — it seems likely that Wolfe also stayed here during his visits in 1927 and 1928 (and perhaps in 1926 too). Wolfe's journals for the period specify no hotel, but the places he frequented and the itineraries of his walks make this address a likely one. These were, of course, the years of his close relationship with Mrs. Bernstein.

RUE DAUNOU

Between 17 and 19 • Chatham Hotel and Bar
(now only Chatham Bar)

Like Harry's and Henry's, the bar at the Chatham was a touter's hangout. One patron noted that "its dark drinking-rooms, cool in the summer . . . , are filled twice a day by the strong and heady tide of men going to and coming from the races."

Lincoln Steffens made the Chatham Hotel his primary residence from January 1919 to January 1920, although he traveled considerably during that year, including a celebrated visit to the Soviet Union and a trip back to America.

In November 1919, Steffens crossed from New York to Paris in time for the Armistice. With him was the sculptor Jo Davidson, and both men sought rooms at the Chatham, which was fully booked. They ended up renting the bridal suite together, but Davidson soon found suitable quarters on the avenue du Maine. Steffens remained at the Chatham to cover various postwar peace and economic conferences.

5 · Harry's New York Bar

Still in operation at "sank roo doe noo" (5 rue Daunou), Harry's was originally just "The New York Bar." It opened Thanksgiving Day 1911 as the enterprise of a popular American jockey, Tod Sloan, and his partner, a man named Clancey, who had owned a bar in New York. Harry McElhone, the original maitre d', took over the bar in 1923 and added his name to the operation.

A patron from the twenties recalls the New York Bar as "a damn easy place to be mooched on by shabby sentimental drunks, get picked up by an Irish whore who claimed to be a duchess, and there was always a tout . . . who had a sure thing horse running that day if you'd put nine hundred francs on it for the both of you. The drinks were good at Harry's. [It] was a place where you could be wry and pungent, meet people you knew and people you wanted not to know. It had the smell and flavor of where you had come from."

RUE D'ANTIN

19 · Offices of the Consolidated Press Association and *Daily Herald*

William Bird used the office of his news service, the Consolidated Press Association, as the mailing address for his Three Mountains Press, which printed, among other important works, Hemingway's first book of narrative sketches, *in our time.* The actual printing press was located on the Ile Saint-Louis.

Also, while the *Transatlantic Review* was in its planning stages in late 1923, its editor and owner, Ford Madox Ford, temporarily used Bird's C.P.A. address and his own (Ford's) residence at 65 boulevard Arago for the journal's business address and editorial office, respectively.

George Slocombe, the popular, red-bearded English journalist who lived on rue Duhesme in Montmartre, ran the Paris office of the *London Daily Herald* out of different quarters at this same address.

3

MOSTLY LOST SITES: ITALIENS TO THE LOUVRE

RUE DU HELDER

1 · Hotel Haussmann (now gone)

Will Irwin operated the Paris office of the *Saturday Evening Post* here. Sent to cover the postwar peace talks, Irwin soon began to detach himself from the conservative *Post*. While the *Post* was backing Harding for President in 1920, Irwin wrote for and supported James M. Cox, the Democratic candidate. By the time Irwin returned to the United States in 1923, most of his writing was being carried by *Collier's*.

Room 48 in the hotel was used by Frank Harris, whose permanent residence had shifted from London to Nice. Despite the subsequent notoriety he received for his salacious memoirs, *My Life and Loves*, Harris was a respected and influential editor during the first decades of the twentieth century. He was also, of course, an entertaining, if lecherous, storyteller.

RUE DES ITALIENS

1–3 · Guaranty Trust (Bank and Offices)

Many expatriates used the Guaranty Trust as their mailing address when they traveled around Europe or simply sought to keep their residence private. Among those who at one time or another gave 3 rue des Italiens as their mailing address (number 1 was the bank itself) were Scott Fitzgerald, Ernest Hemingway, John Peale Bishop, and Gilbert Seldes. At the end of the decade the Guaranty Trust moved to 4 place de la Concorde, and still later it merged with the Morgan Bank on the place Vendôme.

RUE TAITBOUT

3 • Sam's (now gone)

This American restaurant was popular in the late twenties among homesick U.S. tourists and Right Bank businessmen. The customers' entrance was actually around the corner at 26 boulevard des Italiens. At Sam's they could get a real chocolate sundae at the soda fountain and, for breakfast, buckwheat cakes and maple syrup. Also on the menu was such standard American fare as pork and beans, corned-beef hash, and club sandwiches.

32 • American Chamber of Commerce (now gone)

Walter Berry, a member of the Morgan family, cousin of Harry Crosby, and friend of Edith Wharton's, served as president of the American Chamber of Commerce, a strictly Right Bank concern.

RUE LAFFITTE

6 • Ambroise Vollard's gallery (now gone)

Vollard operated his first gallery at 39–41 rue Laffitte from 1893 to 1895. During his most important years, 1895–1914, Vollard ran a gallery here at number 6, where he handled works from Picasso's Rose and Blue periods. Vollard was not enthusiastic about Picasso's Cubist pieces.

PASSAGE DE L'OPERA (NOW GONE)

No number • Café Certa

In *Le Paysan de Paris* (1926), Louis Aragon offers a rich and humorous depiction of the now-gone *passage*. Leading off 12 boulevard des Italiens, the *passage* had two thoroughfare galleries. The western one was called the "Baromètre" and the other "l'Horloge" or, sometimes, the "Thermomètre."

The Café Certa was in the western gallery of the *passage*. According to Aragon, the Certa "was the principal seat of the sessions of Dada, where that formidable association plotted some of its trivial and legendary events which caused its grandeur and decay."

In the Thermomètre was Du Petit Grillon, a bar-annex of the Certa's run by the same proprietor. When they couldn't find room in the Certa, the Dadaists congregated in the Petit Grillon, which had a tiny meeting room in back.

André Breton, Tristan Tzara, and other Dadaists deliberately chose the cafés in this *passage* for their Dada sessions precisely because they were midway between Montmartre and Montparnasse, the two traditional centers of art in Paris.

RUE CHABANAIS

12 · The Chabanais (now gone)

Called variously a *"maison de passe," "maison close,"* or *"maison de tolérance,"* the brothel was an entirely legitimate institution in Paris during the twenties. (Sometimes, the generic term for "night spot," *boîte de nuit,* was used to indicate such an establishment as well.)

One resident spoke rather candidly: "Running a cathouse in Paris is almost a family heritage, and respectable — as respectable as auto repairing or politics." Various laws following World War II effectively closed the houses and drove the workers into the streets. The Chabanais itself was known for its pleasantly spacious lobby, among its other, more feminine features, of course.

RUE DE BEAUJOLAIS

9 · Residence of Colette

The celebrated novelist Colette died here in 1954 at the age of eighty-one. She had previously lived in the same building in 1927–28. Most of her major work behind her, Colette remained an active writer during the twenties, attended Natalie Barney's salons, and befriended Josephine Baker, whom she greatly admired. Colette's own experiences as a dance-hall performer served as a basis for her 1912 novel, *L'Envers du Music-Hall.*

15 • Hotel Beaujolais (now gone)

The founder and principal editor of *The Little Review,* Margaret Anderson, came to Paris in May 1923, having turned the editorial chores over to Jane Heap. After her first residence on rue Vaneau, she took a room in the Beaujolais, which looked out upon the Royal Palace gardens. A bright, courageous, and lively woman, Anderson lived with her lover, Georgette Leblanc, in various Parisian hotels during the twenties. (This same hotel, incidentally, is where Sylvia Beach stayed when she first arrived in Paris in the spring of 1916.)

RUE JEAN-JACQUES-ROUSSEAU

33 • Editorial offices of the *Paris Times* (now gone)

No relation to the London or the *New York Times,* the *Paris Times* was an afternoon daily. Started up by the American millionaire Cortlandt Bishop, the *Times* began printing in the spring of 1924. Unlike the *Herald* and the *Daily Mail,* which had their own presses, the *Paris Times* jobbed out its printing to a commercial print shop across the street, between the *Herald*'s offices and its own. The *Times* folded shortly after the stock market crashed in 1929.

Of the four English-language newspapers (the *Herald,* the *Daily Mail,* the *Tribune,* and the *Times*), the *Times* had the smallest circulation, even though many of its writers — including Vincent Sheean, who had written for the *Tribune,* Martin Sommers, and Victor Weybright — were extremely talented. Most of the writers, according to Sheean, "lived in small hotels near by." The managing editor of the *Times* was the sternly demanding Gaston Archambault, who'd previously been with the Paris edition of the *New York Herald.*

RUE DU LOUVRE

38 · Paris edition of the *New York Herald* (now gone)

Usually referred to as, simply, the Paris *Herald*, this paper was started in 1887 by James Gordon Bennett. Besides the editorial offices here on the rue du Louvre, and a business and advertising office at 49 avenue de l'Opéra, Bennett worked out of two apartments on the Champs-Elysées, at numbers 120 and 104. The former he used to receive visitors and handle the mail; the latter was his private office. Bennett also issued orders from his residence on the avenue d'Iéna when he was in town. "None of the employees of any one office," one of his editors reported, "knew what the other office was doing, a system which Bennett felt protected him from intrigue."

Bennett died in May 1918 and in January 1920 the trustees of the Bennett estate sold the *New York Herald* and its Paris edition to Frank A. Munsey, the publisher of the *New York Sun*. In May 1924 Ogden Reid and his *New York Tribune* bought out Munsey. Reid appointed the talented Englishman Eric Hawkins managing editor of the Paris edition of the *Herald*, a post he held until 1960.

Reid also changed the name of the New York paper to the *Herald-Tribune*. Such a name change was not advantageous in Paris, however, since the *Chicago Tribune* was issuing a popular Paris edition at the time. So, in Paris the *Herald* did not become the *Herald-Tribune* until 1934, when the *Chicago Tribune* sold its Paris edition to the New York conglomerate. After operating as the *Paris Herald-Tribune* for a couple decades, the paper eventually changed hands again and became the *International Herald-Tribune*, the name by which it is known today.

Bennett's *Herald*, which had operated since 1889 at the corner of the rues du Louvre and Berger, grew so dramatically in the twenties that by 1930 the business required new quarters on the rue de Berri. In 1924 the circulation of the *Herald* was 12,000; in 1925 it was 15,000; in 1926 it grew to 22,000; and by 1929 it had reached a tops of 35,000. These figures are especially impressive considering the American residential population of Paris at the time. In 1926 the Paris police estimated the number of Americans in Paris at 25,000. In the late twenties, it was generally believed that there were 40,000

Americans in Paris, although the American Chamber of Commerce could turn up only 10,000. (There were over 35,000 British, 60,000 Russians, and 100,000 Italians residing in Paris at the time.)

The Right Bank *Herald* was more of a standard, steady newspaper than the livelier, rambunctious Paris *Tribune*, which catered to the Left Bank Bohemians. The *Herald* editors claimed to envy only one feature of the irreverent *Tribune:* the work of the *Trib*'s Waverley Lewis Root. Still, as Al Laney, the *Herald*'s night editor, noted, "The files of the *Tribune* for the period would give a much better picture of the Young Intellectual movement."

Joining the staff on the *Herald* in May 1928 was Martha Foley, the future short-story critic. City editor at the time was her husband-to-be, Whit Burnett. One of the most colorful and popular writers was Sparrow Robertson, whose "Sporting Gossip" column began around the time of the 1924 Paris Olympics and ran for the next two decades.

The paper's first society editor (until 1926) was May Birkhead, a Missouri seamstress. She was on board the *Carpathia* when it rescued survivors from the *Titanic* in 1912. Bennett found her name on the *Carpathia*'s passenger list and, taking a shot in the dark, radioed her at once. Birkhead was entirely unknown to Bennett. Some of the *Herald*'s staff knew of her slightly from a story on her sewing that the home (New York) edition had run a few months earlier. "Wireless every possible detail of sinking and rescue," Bennett's message commanded. And May Birkhead responded with such thorough reports and follow-ups that, when she arrived in France, Bennett hired her on the spot.

THE FOLIES-BERGERE AND SCATTERED RIGHT BANK SITES

RUE RICHER

32 • Folies-Bergère

The postwar fascination with glamorous nightclubs made the Folies-Bergère one of the best-known nightclubs in the world. It had also been famous before the war. Americans Lillian Russell, Nora Bayes, and Maude Adams starred here in the 1890s. Colette based her 1912 novel, *L'Envers du Music-Hall*, on her days as a dancer at the Folies-Bergère. Charlie Chaplin also played the Folies — as did Fernandel and Barbette, the female impersonator from Round Rock, Texas, who usually performed at the Cirque Médrano. In the 1926 spectacular, "La Folie du Jour," Josephine Baker introduced her outlandish banana costume here.

But many believed these shows were overrated. "Why do American visitors in Paris pursue . . . the French revues of the type to be found usually at the Folies-Bergères and the Casino de Paris?" Florence Gilliam asked in the *Tribune* (May 1924). "The French frankly preserve these institutions as an allurement for the foreigner. . . . The revues and [other entertainments] in New York far outrank the Parisian brand."

RUE DU CONSERVATOIRE

2 • Conservatoire National d'Art Dramatique

On 11 December 1923 in one of the large halls here in the National Conservatory, George Antheil and Olga Rudge gave a concert of works by Antheil and Ezra Pound. One critic observed that Rudge's "readiness to play [such experimental works] has been the inspiration of at least two composers who, but for her, would not have written violin music." Since the "composers" were the talented Antheil and the tone-deaf Pound, Rudge's "readiness" was probably not an unqualified good. A similar concert was held six months later in the Salle Pleyel, but the reviewer was considerably less sympathetic, observing that "more than once [he] thought the fiddlers were playing out of tune. . . ."

One of the semiprivate premieres of George Antheil's *Ballet Mécanique* was presented here by Benoist-Méchin at ten-thirty P.M. on a deliberately chosen Friday-the-13th in November 1925. In attendance were Syliva Beach and Adrienne Monnier, who'd heard parts of the composition before in the Salle Pleyel. Most of the others in the audience, however, were surprised and hostile. Nevertheless, this performance in the National Conservatory was undoubtedly tame by comparison with the official premiere at the Théâtre des Champs-Elysées the following June, when people were reported to have stomped loudly out of the hall shortly after the concert began.

CITE BERGERE

5 · Hôtel Mondial

Thomas Wolfe stayed here during the week of 20 May 1930, although he apparently spent the night of the twenty-fourth at the Hôtel Burgundy. Like the Westminster, where he and Mrs. Bernstein stayed in the late twenties, the Mondial was relatively close to his favorite places — Prunier's, the Taverne Royale, the Café Weber, and the Café de la Régence.

RUE DU SENTIER

36 · Office of the *Daily Mail* (now gone)

The well-known *Daily Mail* logo is still visible above the door here, although the operation has long been closed. In 1906, Alfred

Harmsworth, who would later become Lord Northcliffe, began printing a Continental Edition of his London newspaper, the *Daily Mail*, in Paris.

Around 1923 the operation moved to this address. Along with the *Herald*, the *Tribune*, and the *Times*, the *Daily Mail* was one of four English-language newspapers published in Paris. Although never a rival to the powerful *Herald*, the *Mail* probably outsold the *Tribune* and the *Times*.

BOULEVARD DE BONNE-NOUVELLE

34 · Hôtel Marguery

Whenever the master printer Maurice Darantière came to Paris from Dijon, he stayed at the Marguery. Darantière was the printer for Adrienne Monnier's publications (including her journal, *Les Cahiers des Amis des Livres*), under the aegis of her bookshop, La Maison des Amis des Livres.

When Monnier's friend Sylvia Beach needed an able and willing printer for James Joyce's controversial *Ulysses*, she quickly decided on Darantière, who'd been printing her stationery.

And, when Robert McAlmon initiated his Contact Editions in 1923, he jobbed most of the printing out to Darantière as well.

RUE SAINTE-APOLLINE

25 · Brothel (name unknown; now gone)

The building at 25 Sainte-Apolline was tall and narrow, with a cherry-pink light over the door. According to John Glassco, "a narrow dark corridor led directly into a large red-lighted and red-papered room filled with low tables and plush-covered benches. Drinks were being served [the evening Glassco went there] to mixed couples by an elderly waiter in the usual black alpaca waistcoat and floor-length white apron, and it took a few moments to realize that all the women were young and completely nude."

RUE DUPETIT-THOUARS

8 · The flat of Marie-Louise Lallemand

During the five weeks in 1917 when the Norton-Harjes Ambulance Corps lost track of him, E. E. Cummings met Marie-Louise, a prostitute, at the Oasis Restaurant on rue du Faubourg-Montmartre. Double-dating with his friend Slater Brown, Cummings spent much time with Marie-Louise. She even invited him here to her flat for dinner one evening, a practice unusual for a prostitute. Cummings spent that night in bed with Marie-Louise, but whether because of his sternly religious upbringing, his fear of disease, or his innate shyness, Cummings emerged in the morning still a virgin — and very much romantically in love.

RUE AMELOT

110 · Cirque d'Hiver-Bouglione

In the twenties the main entrance was around the corner at 6 rue de Crussol.

Most of the major boxing matches were held in this huge building just off the boulevard des Filles-du-Calvaire. An avid fight fan, Ernest Hemingway could often be found out here, along with Ezra Pound, William Carlos Williams, Robert McAlmon, Morley Callaghan, and anyone else who was touched by Hem's contagious enthusiasm.

The circus itself featured the Fratellinis, the famous clown brothers — François, Paul, and Albert. An admiring Eva Le Gallienne listed them along with Chaplin, Sarah Bernhardt, and Isadora Duncan as "the artists [she] had been privileged to watch in [her] life."

RUE PIERRE-LESCOT

16 · Au Père Tranquille

One of the many all-night restaurants in Les Halles, the Père Tranquille served the expatriates as an evening's final stop. In 1924, for instance, Burton Rascoe, Morris Bishop, and E. E. Cummings wrapped up a night of carousing with an early-morning visit to this restaurant, a setting that Cummings later used in his play, *Him*.

In 1927 a regular recommended the place "for onion soup." The Père Tranquille is, he said, "a quaint working man's cafe [only] go upstairs. The hucksters drink and eat downstairs." Simply by virtue of its being located on the east side of Pierre-Lescot was this restaurant spared the razing that leveled the rest of Les Halles. Today, the unflappable *père tranquille* faces a shopping center of tubular chrome, molded Plexiglas, and disco music.

BOULEVARD DIDEROT

12 · Gare de Lyon

In 1922 Hadley Hemingway, intending to surprise Ernest, had gathered up all of his manuscripts, including the carbons, and was preparing to take them to him in Switzerland. Unaccountably, the suitcase containing the material disappeared here at the Gare de Lyon. When the tearful Hadley arrived empty-handed and explained what happened, Ernest was livid. Years of work had been lost.

The loss, however, may have been a blessing in disguise, for Ernest had learned much about writing since he'd written these youthful pieces. By starting over, he could put into practice the techniques, ideas, and discipline that he'd acquired over the previous months working with writers like Ezra Pound, Gertrude Stein, and Lincoln Steffens. Later, Scott Fitzgerald told Hadley he wished someone would have lost his embarrassing early work.

PONT NEUF

At the place du Vert-Galant · The de Geeteres' barge

At the base of Ile de la Cité, near Pont Neuf, Frans and Mai de Geetere moored their barge, *Le Vert-Galant*, named for the square nearby. Harry and Caresse Crosby became the de Geeteres' friends and unofficial sponsors, using their quaint quarters for lavish parties and private assignations.

THE INNER LEFT BANK

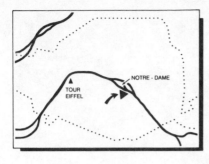

MAP 3

includes addresses from ...

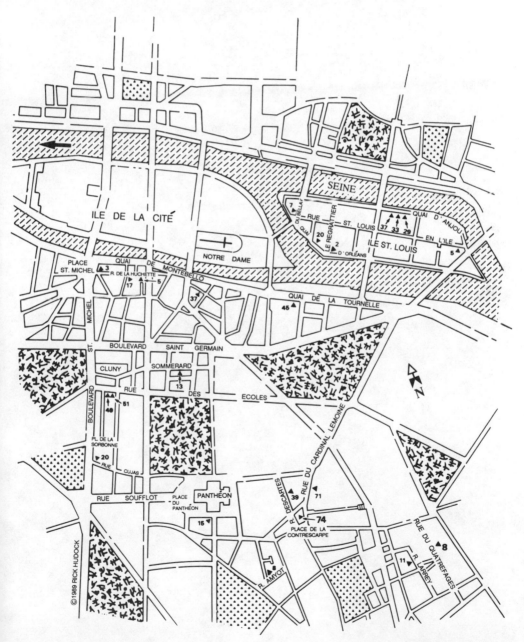

ILE SAINT-LOUIS

QUAI D'ANJOU

37 · Apartment of John Howard Lawson

A prominent Expressionist playwright in the twenties, John Howard Lawson wrote such plays as *Roger Bloomer* (1923) and *Processional* (1925). His work later in the decade (for example, *The International*, 1928) explores Marxist themes. When he moved to Los Angeles, he began writing films (his best known may be *Algiers*, which introduced Hedy Lamarr in 1938). Lawson's fame came in the forties, when, as a member of the Hollywood Ten, he testified angrily before the House Un-American Activities Committee and was eventually sentenced to one year in prison and fined $1,000 for having belonged to the Communist Party (he'd joined in 1934).

As in 1919, John Dos Passos spent the summer of 1921 in Paris, and once again he used the apartment of his friend John Howard Lawson. Having left New York in mid-March 1921, Dos Passos and E. E. Cummings steamed to Portugal. Touring Spain and hiking in the Pyrenees, where they met Lawson, Dos Passos and Cummings reached Paris in May. Cummings took a room at the Hôtel Marignan, and Dos moved into Jack Lawson's quarters here, where he finished his second major work, *Rosinante to the Road Again*.

33 · Le Rendezvous des Mariniers (now gone)

Operated as a small hotel and restaurant by Madame Lecomte, Le Rendezvous des Mariniers attracted many American expatriates in postwar Paris. It was a good place, according to Virgil Thomson, for "dining well at almost no cost."

John Dos Passos may have started it all in 1919 while he was studying and writing in Paris. His playwright friend Jack Lawson lived just across from the Ile Saint-Louis in those days, so Dos Passos, Lawson, and others came to Le Rendezvous almost daily — to eat, drink, and discuss Dos's work in progress ("Seven Times Round the Walls of Jericho," a lengthy novel that went unpublished).

Sherwood Anderson also patronized Madame Lecomte's Le Rendezvous during his first visit to Paris in spring of 1921. Harry and Caresse Crosby ate there frequently in 1923 and 1924, according to Harry's diaries. The hotel-restaurant had also been a "favorite haunt of Alan Seeger's before his Rendezvous with Death," Crosby notes, alluding to Seeger's famous poem and his World War I death.

With Bill Bird's Three Mountains Press, Robert McAlmon's Contact Editions, and Ford Madox Ford's *Transatlantic Review* all operating next door, the café was a handy meeting place for American editors, writers, and critics.

The English writer Richard Le Gallienne (father of the actress, Eva, and stepfather of the painter and model, Gwen) was another patron who sang the praises of the Rendezvous des Mariniers.

And, on one Thanksgiving in the mid-twenties, Elmer Rice, another writer of Expressionist drama (*The Adding Machine* in 1923 and *Street Scene* in 1929), asked Madame Lecomte if she'd prepare a "traditional American dinner" for some friends, provided they could find the proper ingredients. She agreed, and the dinner was a big success. Finding the mincemeat for the pies, Rice later recalled, proved the biggest challenge.

29 · Three Mountains Press

The facade of number 29 has been renovated since the days when William Bird's Three Mountains Press was located below street level here in a former wine vault. By October 1922, Bird had purchased and installed a huge seventeenth-century Belgian "Mathieu" printing press. The press itself and the forms took up all the floor space, except for a small kitchen area where Bird kept his inventory. With Ezra Pound advising him, Bird printed several important little volumes of expatriate prose and poetry. The name he selected for his publishing company alluded to the three mountains of Paris (Montmartre, Montparnasse, and Mont Sainte-Geneviève).

Having received a large gift of money from his father-in-law (Sir John Ellerman), Robert McAlmon decided to publish some works by his friends Mina Loy, Marsden Hartley, William Carlos Williams, and others. Once word got around that McAlmon was looking for manuscripts, his room at the Hôtel Foyot wasn't big enough to hold all the material he received. Bird agreed to let McAlmon share the office (and, importantly, the secretarial help) at number 29. So, McAlmon moved his Contact Publishing Company to 29 quai d'Anjou and resumed collecting manuscripts.

Even though McAlmon listed both Bird's Three Mountains Press and his own Contact Publishing Company on some of the Contact books, McAlmon used Bird's Mathieu press to print only a couple of volumes, including what may be McAlmon's best collection of his own stories, *Distinguished Air*. Most of the Contact Editions were run on linotype by Maurice Darantière, the Lyon printer whom Sylvia Beach had hired to print *Ulysses*. Perhaps McAlmon's greatest coup was *Three Stories and Ten Poems* (1923), Ernest Hemingway's first book.

In 1928, Bird sold the Mathieu to Nancy Cunard for £300, agreeing to arrange for its shipment to Réanville (fifty miles from Paris) and to help her find an appropriate printer. Cunard's Hours Press Editions were thus run on the same press as Bird's Three Mountains Editions and some of McAlmon's Contact Editions.

In addition to Bird and McAlmon, Ford Madox Ford also used the quarters at 29 quai d'Anjou. Even though it was decidedly cramped here, Ford needed a place to edit the *Transatlantic Review*, and Bird made room for him.

"At the rear," Bird recalled later, "accessible by a flimsy flight of stairs, was a sort of gallery running the whole width of the shop, say 15 feet, and perhaps 6 feet deep. There Ford, a hefty 6-footer, installed a desk, an editorial chair and a chair for callers, and there he edited the [*Transatlantic*] review." Ford's assistant, Marjorie Reid, was herself a tall woman. They both frequently bumped their heads on the gallery's five-foot ceiling.

Ford's journal carried its name in lowercase letters — "not from any desire to be 'arty,' " Bird recalled later. "I had bought at considerable expense a complete dress of Caslon Old Face in all sizes from 6 to 48-point, and the problem seemed to be to get the distinguishing word TRANSATLANTIC into the largest size possible." As it happened, the word would fit the journal's cover in 36-point type if its first 'T' weren't capitalized. If it were, the cover would require smaller and less impressive type. So, Ford opted for a lowercase *t* on the cover.

The journal was allowed to expire by the end of 1925, after financial exigencies compelled Ford to sell the controlling interest to Krebs Friend and his wealthy wife.

RUE SAINT-LOUIS-EN-L'ILE

5 · Residence of William Aspenwall Bradley

Although scarcely known today, William A. Bradley was nevertheless one of the most influential Americans in Paris during the twenties. In 1921 he married Jenny Serruys, a French literary figure who became popular for her salons. Bradley also lived at number 24 and number 18 quai de Béthune, on the southern rim of the island, before and after (respectively) his residence here. Earlier still, he had lived briefly at 54 rue Lhomond as well.

A translator and writer himself, Bradley was *the* literary agent in Paris at the time. At one time or other, he represented virtually all the major writers, including Gertrude Stein, John Dos Passos, Ezra Pound, Louis Bromfield, and Stephen Vincent Benét. (Only a few like Hemingway and Fitzgerald worked directly with Maxwell Perkins, an editor for Charles Scribner.) The Bradleys were among the first people Walter White (the black writer) and his wife, Gladys, looked up when they arrived in Paris in July 1927.

RUE LE REGRATTIER

2 · Nancy Cunard's flat

The heiress to the Cunard Line fortunes, Nancy epitomized the free spirit of the expatriate woman. Her father was English and her mother American, but Nancy was truly an international citizen.

Extraordinarily wealthy, generous, and daring, Cunard was the exemplary trendsetter: tall and thin, with bobbed hair, a writer of poetry, openly adventurous in matters sexual, and a collector of modern art. Nancy Cunard appeared in several novels, including Michael Arlen's *The Green Hat*, Aldous Huxley's *Antic Hay* and *Point Counterpoint*, and Louis Aragon's *Blanche ou l'Oubli*. Painted by John Banting, Eugene McCown, and Oskar Kokoschka, she was also the inspiration for Brancusi's most famous wood sculpture, *Jeune Fille Sophistiquée*.

The ground-floor flat on the corner of rue Le Regrattier and quai d'Orléans served as her residence from 1924 to 1927. Prior to this period, she lived at 12-bis place de la Sorbonne. Nancy's residences invariably reflected Nancy's personality. "In my apartment," she wrote, "there were then two Chiricos, two Tanguys, and a large Picabia gouache of a man with four pairs of eyes, a body spotted all over with vermillion dots and one arm sheathed in black. There were other contemporary paintings and drawings . . . but not in the direct line of vision. There was also a comfortable settee in plum-colored velvet."

QUAI D'ORLEANS

At the western edge of the island • The Crosbys' residence

Although the exact house number is not known, on 1 June 1923 Harry and Caresse Crosby moved into a "romantic balcony apartment" on this street, which curves around the southwest edge of the Ile Saint-Louis. Caresse noted that "the lacy towers of Notre Dame were framed between the curtains of our bedroom windows."

Their first few months as husband and wife in Paris had been spent in the large flat on Belles-Feuilles. Before finding this apartment, they spent four days at the Hôtel de la Gare d'Orsay — "over the trains," as Harry said. Accordingly, Caresse noted, it was while living at this apartment on the quai d'Orléans that they finally "began to live like newlyweds."

In her fanciful memoirs Caresse claims that at eight-fifteen weekday mornings, she'd slip into her bathing suit and row Harry down the Seine in their crimson bark, *The Red Arrow*, to the place de la Concorde. Once ashore, Harry supposedly walked to work at the Morgan Bank, while Caresse rowed back upstream, attracting considerable attention and flattering comment from onlookers.

At the end of the summer when their lease expired (7 September 1923), they moved to Princess Marthe Bibesco's flat in the rue du Faubourg-Saint-Honoré before settling "permanently" at their rue de Lille residence.

20 • Paris residence of Iris Tree

The niece of Max Beerbohm, Iris Tree was a British actress who dabbled in writing poetry. Most of the decade Tree lived in London, though she made frequent tours of the Continent and North America with stage companies.

RUE JEAN-DU-BELLAY

7 • Residence of Stuart and Moune Gilbert

After Oxford-educated Stuart Gilbert gave up his civil-service post as a judge in Burma in 1927, he and his French wife, Moune, moved to France. At first they lived outside Paris at Bécon-les-Bruyères. By the end of the decade they had moved to this apartment on the Ile Saint-Louis. Gilbert soon became a close and trusted friend of James Joyce, and his analytical study of *Ulysses* was the first to unlock many of the doors to the novel's hidden treasures.

THE EASTERN EDGE

QUAI DE LA TOURNELLE

45 • Apartment of John Howard Lawson

A close friend of John Dos Passos', Lawson lived here during the year that Dos was studying at the Sorbonne (1918–19). When Lawson left Paris in mid-April 1919, Dos Passos moved into his quarters at number 45.

RUE DE LA BUCHERIE

37 • (The present) Shakespeare and Company

George Whitman has salvaged bits of material and some of the spirit of Sylvia Beach's famous lending library and bookshop.

RUE DE LA HUCHETTE

5 • Hôtel du Caveau (de la Terreur)

In this dilapidated, dank building Elliot Paul said, "I found Paris — and France." A writer for the *Tribune*, Paul moved into a top-floor, two-room apartment in 1923 and kept the residence for eighteen years. Waverley Root recalls Paul's having another apartment at the time "on the Champ de Mars, an aristocratic address that was a far cry from the hotel on the rue de la Huchette." Root's recollection notwithstanding, Paul's book *The Last Time I Saw Paris* is a loving and thorough portrait of this two-block-long street. Noted in the twenties for its rotisseries, rue de la Huchette is today lined with gyros.

A stone spiral staircase led down from the hotel lobby to two cellars, one beneath the other. The lower showed evidence that it had once been a dungeon. On special occasions, the Caveau's manager might prepare a huge feast by roasting an entire pig or goat in the center of the vast lower cavern.

Except to see Paul or to attend a special dinner, few expatriates patronized the Caveau. Nevertheless, when Bravig Imbs left the Hôtel Regnard sometime in 1926, he moved in here. By 1929 Imbs had moved again — to 64 rue Madame. Living here too was Jules Frantz, who also worked for the Paris edition of the *Trib* (1925–34), serving as its news editor in the twenties and its managing editor in the thirties. The little-known poet Virgil Geddes took a room here in 1926, while he was serving as the financial editor of the *Tribune*.

17 · Le Panier Fleuri (now gone)

As the most celebrated of three brothels on this 300-yard-long street, the "Basket of Flowers" stood on the southeast corner of Huchette and rue Zacharie (now rue Xavier-Privas, honoring a celebrated street singer). The prostitutes housed at Le Panier grossed about 150 francs a day ($7.50), half of which went to Madame Mariette Lanier, whose profit from her girls alone totaled nearly 100,000 francs ($5,000) a year.

West of Le Panier Fleuri across rue Zacharie was a laundry that employed three young women. While an actual laundry, it also served as a *clandestin* — where men not wanting to be seen entering Le Panier Fleuri could make an arrangement with Madame Lanier to select one of the three laundresses and take her to a room upstairs, over the laundry.

North across rue de la Huchette at number 14 stood a Bureau de Police, a neighborhood beat station without so much as a squad car.

RUE DU SOMMERARD

13 · Hotel Marignan

In May 1921, E. E. Cummings checked into this hotel, where he lived until September, at a rate of $12 a month. Cummings had come to Europe with John Dos Passos, who stayed in Jack Lawson's room on the Ile Saint-Louis during this period.

This was Cummings's first extended visit to Paris since his release from the makeshift prison at La Ferté-Macé in December 1917. Slater Brown, his friend and fellow ambulance driver whose pacifist letters had gotten them arrested during the war, stayed with Cummings at the Marignan periodically. While living here, Cummings learned of Liveright's intention to publish *The Enormous Room*, his autobiographical novel about the Ferté-Macé ordeal.

RUE MONTAGNE-SAINTE-GENEVIEVE

Number unknown • First Paris apartment of John Dos Passos

When the Army Overseas Educational Commission accepted his application to study anthropology at the Sorbonne in March 1919, Dos Passos was released from active service. He took a room near the Panthéon on this narrow street and spent much time writing, attending Sorbonne lectures only occasionally. He remained here until mid-April when he moved into Jack Lawson's quai de la Tournelle flat.

BOULEVARD SAINT-MICHEL

3 • Café de la Gare (now enlarged as Café Saint-Séverin)

A favorite breakfast spot for many expatriates, including Samuel Putnam and Elliot Paul, who lived on rue de la Huchette nearby, this was probably the place Hemingway describes in *A Moveable Feast:* "It was a pleasant cafe, warm and clean and friendly, and I hung up my old waterproof on the coat rack to dry . . . and I took out a notebook from the pocket of the coat and a pencil and started to write. . . ."

SAINT-ANDRE-DES-ARTS

QUAI DES GRANDS-AUGUSTINS

23 (1 rue Gît-le-Coeur) · Gerald and Sara Murphy's residence

The Murphys leased two floors (one for their children and one for themselves) in this building, which dates back to the sixteenth-century reign of Francis I. Although these apartments were the Murphys' principal Paris residence, Gerald also kept a studio out on rue Froidevaux. Gerald and Sara's most famous address, of course, was the Villa America on the Riviera, near Cap d'Antibes, where they and hosts of guests spent the summers. For a while in the second half of the decade, Gerald's sister, Esther, lived here as well. Through her efforts her friends Scott and Zelda Fitzgerald met Gerald and Sara.

RUE GIT-LE-COEUR

1 · Residence of Gilbert Seldes and, later, Dorothy Wilde

Seldes, the managing editor of *The Dial* and friend of E. E. Cummings and John Dos Passos, stayed in an apartment here at the intersection with the quai des Grands-Augustins. Seldes referred to his residence as "Chez Murphy," because of its location in Gerald and Sara's apartment building.

By May 1930, Oscar Wilde's niece Dorothy (Dolly) had taken a room here at 1 rue Gît-le-Coeur, where she lived until January 1931. In March 1932, Sylvia Beach made an inquiry about some overdue library books that Dolly had not returned to Shakespeare and Company. According to a note in her records, Sylvia "was informed by concierge that she [Dolly] has moved without leaving address." Dolly reappeared in Paris and returned the books in 1934, giving Natalie Barney's residence (20 rue Jacob) as her address.

At the corner of Gît-le-Coeur and Saint-André-des-Arts

At three o'clock one morning in July 1923, the story (apocryphal?) goes, while heading for "the Calvados joint on rue Gît-le-Coeur"* with John Dos Passos and Gilbert Seldes, E. E. Cummings paused here to urinate on a wall. No sooner had Cummings begun than "a whole phalanx of gendarmes" appeared, placed him under arrest, and carted him off to precinct headquarters on the quai des Grands-Augustins. The police were indifferent to the shouts of protest by Dos Passos and Seldes, and both men were kept out of the building while Cummings was booked. The arresting officer named the charge: Cummings was *"un Américain qui pisse."* *"Quoi?"* the recording clerk asked. *"Encore un pisseur Américain?"*

Seldes and Dos Passos were finally able to confirm that Cummings was indeed an American, and the police released him, requiring that he reappear the next morning for arraignment. In the interim, Seldes secretly called the writer Paul Morand, who was Ministre des Affaires Etrangères, and got the charges dropped. When Cummings showed up at the station the next morning completely unaware of Seldes's action, he received merely a suspended sentence (*sursis*) and was promptly dismissed. Greatly relieved, Cummings hurried back to share his good news with his buddies Dos Passos and Seldes.

Meanwhile, knowing that Cummings was to be released, Seldes and Dos Passos had spent the morning secretly rounding up friends and preparing posters and placards. Coming from the police station,

---

* Most likely, the "Calvados joint" the trio was heading for was the Bol de Cidre, which lay beyond a heavy door down a narrow passage off Gît-le-Coeur. It was run by a muscular Norman who wore a traditional long white apron. Inside were barrels of cider and a small back room whose walls were autographed by famous customers like Verlaine and Wilde. Down in the cellar was a brace of arches that dated back to 1145, four centuries before Francis I had converted the building into his private stables. The cider was drunk from flat bowls and frequently spiked with Calvados — a strong version of applejack made in Normandy.

Cummings met the band of friends, who were marching loudly toward the police station in mock protest carrying signs that read "Reprieve Le Pisseur Américain." Until he learned later that the demonstration was all a joke, Cummings was profoundly moved by what he took to be a sincere display of loyal support and friendship.

RUE SAINT-ANDRE-DES-ARTS

42 · Hôtel de la Havane (now gone)

Upon his return from a brief bicycling tour in Italy in October 1921, E. E. Cummings took a room in this hotel. Trying to live frugally, Cummings estimated his expenses at $85 a month, even though he ate frequently at his favorite restaurant, La Reine Blanche, on boulevard Saint-Germain, across from the Cluny. "I eat snails almost daily," he wrote his mother, "oysters biweekly, mussels weekly, mermaids once a month."

When he came to Paris in 1924 to divorce Elaine (Thayer) after seven months of marriage, Cummings took a room again at the Havane to wait out the required one-month residency. By Christmas, he'd returned to the States — a bachelor once again.

46 · Residence of E. E. Cummings

Cummings was living in a single room at this address when the *"pisseur"* incident (above) occurred in 1923.

RUE DE L'ANCIENNE-COMEDIE

3 · Residence of Waverley Root

The view from his sixth-floor apartment here made this Root's favorite residence during his Paris years. From his glass-walled studio, the *Tribune*'s celebrated writer could look out across the rooftops to the stone tower of Saint-Germain-des-Prés and beyond to the Eiffel Tower.

When he came to Paris in May 1927, Root lived the first month at a *pension de famille* (boarding house) on the corner of rues Saint-Jacques and Soufflot. With most of his co-workers on the *Tribune* at the Hôtel de Lisbonne, Root took an apartment a half block away on rue Monsieur-le-Prince for a short period.

By the end of the summer of 1927, Root — and a temporary roommate, a Mexican painter named José Pavon — had rented this apartment for $16 a month. "Once settled in my new home," Root noted, "I led a life of unbroken enchantment. . . . I arose [late in the morning], pulled up a flap that hung hinged under the great studio window for a table, and had my breakfast of fluffy croissants, or brioches yellow with egg, café au lait, a piece of cheese, and often . . . a glass of white wine. . . , enjoying with ineffable pleasure the view spread out below of my most precious possession, Paris." Root's success at the *Tribune* was rapid — within a year he was promoted into the *Trib*'s Foreign News Service — and by 1930 he was back in the newsroom as news editor, number two in the paper's hierarchy.

RUE CHRISTINE

5 • Post-1930s apartment of Gertrude Stein and Alice B. Toklas
When the owner of 27 rue de Fleurus gave the building to his son as a wedding gift in 1938, Gertrude and Alice packed up their belongings, including 130 canvases, and moved to this apartment, two blocks from the Seine.

RUE GUENEGAUD

15 • Nancy Cunard's Hours Press
After buying Bill Bird's huge Belgian printing press in 1928 and moving it fifty miles to Réanville, Nancy Cunard brought it back to Paris in the winter of 1929–30. With the profits she had made in eight months of operation in Réanville, Cunard was able to cover a nine-year lease on this small shop.

Although the master printer Maurice Lévy declined to accompany her back to Paris, Nancy was able to get along without him, since her "enchanting aide and companion," the black American musician Henry Crowder, had acquired considerable skill as a typesetter and printer.

The Hours Press office itself was decorated with African sculpture, paintings by Miró and others, and ceremonial masks. A handsome Boule writing desk, once owned by Nancy's father (of the Cunard ship lines), sat in the main office. Not surprisingly, the Hours Editions were elegant and valuable volumes.

QUAI DE CONTI

13 • Romaine Brooks's studio

Before she moved to her studio in Passy in the mid-twenties, the American-born, European-educated heiress and painter Romaine (Goddard) Brooks had a small apartment here. Having married John Brooks around the turn of the century and left him a year later, Romaine had an extended affair with pianist Renata Borgatti. In the twenties Brooks became a lifelong friend and lover of Natalie Barney's.

Unlike the spacious, open studio that she later designed for herself in Passy, Brooks's studio here reminded more than one visitor of a funeral parlor, despite the gleaming parquet floors and a nice balance of light and shade.

It was to this apartment on the quai de Conti that she invited Gertrude Stein to read her (Stein's) works. Eventually, Brooks proposed that Stein sit for a portrait. Claiming that her hair was too long, Stein cut it off drastically, which so horrified Brooks that the project was abandoned — the very effect, most likely, that Stein had sought.

FROM NATALIE BARNEY'S TO THE HOTEL JACOB

RUE JACOB

20 • Natalie Barney's apartments

After moving into this 300-year-old house in 1909, Natalie Barney lived here for the next fifty years. In the garden courtyard she built a small Greek "Temple à l'Amitié" on which she staged various dances, concerts (including a string quartet by George Antheil), and readings. Prior to World War I, Mata Hari is reported to have danced in the garden naked. Another rumor holds that during World War II, when the Nazis cleaned out an unused well in Barney's courtyard, they found that it opened into an underground cave with a passage leading under the Seine to the Louvre.

Besides writing some poetry and prose herself, Barney appears in Radclyffe Hall's lesbian novel, *The Well of Loneliness*, as Valerie Seymour and in other avant-garde works. On Friday afternoons from five to eight, Barney held her salons, which rivaled Gertrude Stein's for the importance of their guests. Whereas Gertrude Stein promoted cubism and emphatically identified with modernism, Barney held to the fashions of La Belle Epoque.

A devout patron of the arts, Barney claimed the friendship of Marcel Proust, Colette, Rainer Maria Rilke, André Gide, Djuna Barnes, Edna St. Vincent Millay, and Max Jacob. Given the coolness between Gertrude Stein and Ezra Pound, it's not surprising that T. S. Eliot, James Joyce, and other friends of Ezra's tended to take their conversation at Barney's. The grander afternoons might produce as many as 200 guests.

Barney's salons were perhaps most famous for their unabashed lesbian activity. Although her relationship with Romaine Brooks was open and undisguised, Barney also had several very close male friends. Nevertheless, visitors speak of women dancing sensuously together at the salons and pairing off to disappear for brief periods. Such sexual freedom made Paris attractive to many expatriates.

15 · Temporary residence of John Dos Passos

In May 1928, John Dos Passos left the United States for a tour of Russia. En route, he spent some time sightseeing in Copenhagen, London, and Paris, where he was shocked at the number of tourists. Paris had changed considerably since his early days in the city with his friends E. E. Cummings and Jack Lawson. Dos's letter to Hemingway (1 June 1928) refers to Paris as "a rotten dump after Copenhagen."

There is no indication where, exactly, Dos Passos stayed during his 1928 visit to Paris. However, Zelda Fitzgerald lists 15 rue Jacob for him in the same ink and handwriting that places Ford Madox Ford on the rue Notre-Dame-des-Champs — in a flat that Ford occupied only from mid-February to August 1928. In any case, Dos didn't stay in Paris long, for in June he was off to the Riviera to spend most of the summer with the Murphys before heading into Russia.

11 · Residence of Gwen Le Gallienne

The daughter of Richard Le Gallienne's third wife (Irma), Gwen was thus the stepsister (not the half-sister) of the famous actress, writer, and translator, Eva Le Gallienne. In the twenties, Gwen earned some acclaim for her painting but her reputation rested largely on her nonconformity — sexual and social — which was distinguished even among the Montparnasse Bohemians. According to an anonymous reporter (*Tribune*, 16 September 1930), Gwen "is incapable of insincerity. In speech, she is direct and frank, and she never talks unless she has something to say." Still, the reporter notes, "[Gwen's] temperament rests on chaos, [and] she . . . is the most chaotic looking" of all the Le Galliennes.

RUE CARDINALE

2 · The Black Sun Press

Harry and Caresse Crosby discovered this shop of master printer Roger Lescaret in 1927 and set up their Black Sun Press immediately. Lescaret's shop may have been tiny and thick with flies, but his work was impeccable. The editions printed by this craftsman were tastefully supervised by the Crosbys, and the volumes are remarkable for the quality of their paper and inks, their design, and their authors — including D. H. Lawrence and James Joyce.

RUE DE SEINE

57 · Hôtel du Maroc

At the corner of the rue de Seine and the rue Jacob stood the Maroc, where Thornton Wilder was staying in June 1921 — according to Sylvia Beach's records. Wilder himself says that upon arriving in Paris on 6 June 1921, he took a room in an unnamed hotel — located on the rue des Saints-Pères, not the rue de Seine. In any case, he notes that he soon tired of the bedbugs in the hotel, which probably was the Maroc, and moved to a pension on the rue Saint-Jacques.

51 · Galerie Carmine (now gone)

During June and July 1926, Grant Wood exhibited some forty-seven paintings here. Although his work received favorable attention in Paris and generated some sales, no notice of his paintings reached America, and Wood returned to Iowa greatly depressed. He had produced nothing, he felt, "that the French Impressionists didn't do a hundred times better." It wasn't until four years later that Wood began the kind of painting that would make him famous. *American Gothic*, for example, was completed in 1930. Perhaps the highlight of this visit was his appearance in a ballet costume at the Quatz' Arts Ball — the second he'd attended.

41 · Galerie Van Leer (now gone)

In November 1929, Man Ray exhibited twenty-nine works here. By then Ray was internationally famous. His photographs could be found in the big magazines as well as in the little reviews. Moreover, his reputation as an experimental filmmaker was also growing.

31 · Raymond Duncan's "Akadémia" (now gone)

Ostensibly attempting to continue a Greek tradition, Duncan offered lectures here on philosophy and antiquity and gave instruction in such time-honored crafts as rug weaving, printing, and sandal making. On his good days Raymond even wore a garland of leaves. At least as much a performer as his sister Isadora, Raymond was probably more egocentric.

RUE JACQUES-CALLOT

3 · Galerie de la Jeune Peinture (now Galerie Landrot)

In the late twenties Madame Liszkowska's tiny gallery exhibited works by Joseph Stella, Hilaire Hiler, Gwen Le Gallienne, Stella Bowen, Ann Neagoe, and others.

16 · Galerie Surréaliste (now Galerie Jean-Pierre Dutel)

Opening on 26 March 1926, this avant-garde gallery premiered with a one-man show of Man Ray's photographs, sculptures, and paintings. The invitations instructed the guests to arrive at midnight.

RUE VISCONTI

14 · Residence of Raymond Duncan

Raymond Duncan listed this as his residence in 1920, before setting up a commune in Neuilly. Although he taught in his own "Akadémia" and affected a Bohemian nonchalance in his sandals, flowing golden locks, and sweeping robe, Duncan owned and operated two lucrative fabric shops on the posh boulevard Saint-Germain and rue du Faubourg-Saint-Honoré.

RUE DES BEAUX-ARTS

13 · Hôtel Alsace (now L'Hôtel)

(The Alsace is the hotel where Oscar Wilde died in 1900. One of Wilde's visitors called it a "shabby, cheap, and unsanitary place with no drainage," but the manager was kind and sympathetic.)

Thomas Wolfe made several trips to Paris in the twenties. On his first visits, before he had the financial and emotional support of Aline Bernstein, Wolfe stayed here in the modest Alsace. According to Eugene Gant's "Paris Diary" in *Of Time and the River*, Gant (the novel's main character) had a room on the fifth floor of the Alsace from late November 1924 to early February 1925 — dates that correspond to Wolfe's own stay in Paris.

Wolfe may have stayed here in late November and early December 1926 as well. During his 1928 visit, however, he no doubt stayed in Mrs. Bernstein's Right Bank hotel, the Westminster. In 1930, after his success with *Look Homeward, Angel* and his attempted break with Mrs. Bernstein, Wolfe used a different Right Bank hotel, the Mondial.

Number unknown · Hôtel d'Assas

(John Joseph) Sherry Mangan, Harvard graduate, poet, gourmet, and classical scholar, sailed to Paris with his friend Virgil Thomson in the winter of 1925 and took a room in the Assas.

In February 1927, Mangan brought out the first number of his experimental magazine, *larus the celestial visitor*. The magazine folded in 1928 after seven numbers, and Mangan sold his subscription list to Richard Johns for his journal, *Pagany*.

RUE BONAPARTE

11 bis · The Restaurant des Beaux-Arts

A gourmand who admitted to verging at times on gluttony, journalist A. J. Liebling liked this little restaurant across from the famous art school. During his year in Paris, 1926–27, Liebling noted that he could eat a very nice meal here for as little as 6 francs, at a time when there were 26 francs to the dollar. A half-bottle of *vin ordinaire*, for example, cost a franc and a *plat du jour* of, say, *contre-filet* of beef, 5. In all, 6 francs, or 23¢.

13 · Galerie Pierre

After hosting a one-man show by Joan Miró (12–27 June 1925), the Pierre sponsored the first group exhibition of the Surrealists from the fourteenth to the twenty-fifth of November 1925. The exhibition included works by Hans Arp, Giorgio de Chirico, Max Ernst, Paul Klee, André Masson, Miró, Man Ray, and Pierre Roy. In addition, the show contained some pieces by Pablo Picasso, the only celebrity in the lot. André Breton and Robert Desnos wrote the catalogue.

14 · Ecole Nationale Supérieure des Beaux Arts

The annual Quatz'Arts (Four Arts) Ball sponsored by the Beaux Arts students was invariably orgiastic. Virtually any woman who was daring enough was freely allowed in, but men had to prove some connection with the Ecole. Harry and Caresse Crosby, for instance, claimed to be "patrons" of a particular atelier. Any man who failed to convince the doormen of his legitimacy was sent packing — sometimes with a splotch of green paint on his back to discourage him from trying again that night. Tickets were sometimes sold at very dear prices.

For the 1926 ball — the one to which Caresse Crosby rode topless on the back of a baby elephant — the Spanish filmmaker Luis Buñuel had obtained a set of tickets. He and his friends, however, were still denied admission. As they stood outside, pleading with the muscular doormen, "a naked woman [arrived, carried] on the shoulders of a student dressed as an Arab Sheik." The student's head, the amazed Buñuel noticed, "served as her fig leaf." Although the women in Buñuel's group were invited to enter, the men were dismissed. The tickets he'd bought were phonies.

24 • Hôtel de Paris (now gone; not to be confused with the expensive hotel of the same name that opened in 1929 on the boulevard de la Madeleine)

Henry Miller and his wife, June, spent a couple months here in the spring of 1928, before heading off to bicycle through southern France.

30 • Le Pré aux Clercs (main entrance now at 31 rue Jacob)

A block from the Hôtel Jacob, this café was Hadley Hemingway's favorite while she and Ernest lived at the Jacob during December and early January of 1921–22. Ernest referred to this restaurant as "our regular eating place [where] two can get a high grade dinner . . . with wine, à la carte for 12 francs" — less than six bits.

36 • Hôtel Napoleon Bonaparte (also went by the name of Hôtel Saint-Germain-des-Prés, by which it is known today; not to be confused with the Napoleon Bonaparte currently at number 61)

When Janet Flanner and Solita Solano arrived in Paris in September 1922, they stayed briefly in a pension on the rue de Quatrefages. Soon thereafter, they moved into this hotel, where they lived for the next nineteen years. The hotel was only "two rooms wide," but it was just a block or so north of the Deux Magots and the Flore, two popular cafés, and a few blocks south of the Ecole des Beaux Arts.

Flanner's father had left her a small income, so she could afford the $1 per day that her fifth-floor room cost. Flanner's room was number 15; Solano's, number 16. In 1932, after Solita had published three novels and Janet had begun her Paris column (as "Genêt") for *The New Yorker*, the women rented number 13 for their "overflow."

In 1924 Jean Cocteau rented room number 6, where he held small, intimate gatherings and smoked opium to relieve his grief over the death of his friend Raymond Radiguet.

After Cocteau moved out, Kathryn Hulme, the American novelist, moved into number 6, where she wrote much of her first book (*We*

Lived as Children) with editorial advice from her fellow residents Solano and Flanner. Like Katherine Mansfield, both Hulme and Solano fell under the influence of the Russian mystic Georgei Ivanovitch Gurdjieff.

Margaret Anderson and Georgette Leblanc stayed in various places during the decade, including hotels on the rues de Beaujolais, de l'Université, and de Grenelle and — toward the end of the decade — in an apartment on the rue Casimir-Périer. In 1928, Solita Solano obtained a room in this hotel, the Bonaparte, for Anderson and paid for it. She wanted the former editor of *The Little Review* to have a quiet place to finish *My Thirty Years' War*, the first volume of Anderson's autobiography.

Another resident of the Napoleon Bonaparte was George Davis, a midwestern writer whose first novel, *The Opening of a Door*, was highly acclaimed but whose second novel never got past its third chapter.

One night, unable to pay his hotel bill and with nothing further written to mortgage for an advance, Davis slipped into Raymond Duncan's fabric shop on the boulevard Saint-Germain for a night's sleep. There, he found Kay Boyle, who had secretly gone to the shop to escape the madness of the Duncan commune for an evening. Davis wrapped himself up in one of the tunics on sale and slept with Boyle on the floor. Eventually, Davis became an influential editor, at first for *Vanity Fair* and then for *Harper's Bazaar*.

Yet another resident of this hotel was Emily Holmes Coleman, who went to Paris in 1926 and subsequently became the society editor of the Paris edition of the *Chicago Tribune*. Apparently, she had initially sought employment more menial, since a note next to Coleman's name in Sylvia Beach's address book indicates that Coleman was seeking work as a typist or secretary.

Waverley Root tells of Coleman's dismissal from the *Tribune* by Jack Hummel, its de facto publisher (denied that title by Colonel McCormick, who kept it for himself). Locked out, the frail society editor was pleading with the night watchman, when Hummel arrived — drunk and belligerent. He tried to bully her, and she slapped him. His equilibrium shaky, Hummel crashed to the ground and broke his glasses.

Coleman sued for her back pay, plus severance; Hummel countered with charges of assault. According to Root, "the judge stared unbelievingly at the cracked glasses, the burly Hummel, and the slender Emily. 'I cannot believe that madame could have done any grievous harm to monsieur,' he remarked. Then he awarded her the full amount she sought."

42(?) • La Quatrième République

The exact number of this restaurant is not known, although the location is described by Janet Flanner as being "just down from the place [Saint-Germain-des-Prés]." In the twenties a restaurateur named Thoyer operated a business here at number 42, which makes it the most likely spot for the "Fourth Republic." Another but less likely location is further down, at number 23, where a man named Cerisier was registered as operating a café. In the late twenties the editorial office of a political journal called *La Quatrième République* was at 28 rue Bonaparte, but it probably had no connection with the restaurant of the same name.

Janet Flanner and Solita Solano liked this tiny restaurant with the odd name. President Poincaré's *Third* Republic was still governing France, but the restaurateur felt that the way things were going, the Fourth was surely near at hand. To save himself the trouble of having to make a new sign, he named his place La Quatrième République. The decor was as avant-garde as the clientele (composer Virgil Thomson and newspaperman Vincent Sheean also ate here), and the food was "civilized, countrified, appetizing, and inexpensive." The shrewish waitress was named Yvonne, which explains Flanner's pun that ordinary meals cost "thirty cents, plus a ten-cent tip for *Yvonne the Terrible.*"

Number unknown • Apartment of Elmer Rice and his family

Rice stayed in Europe two and a half years, living most of that time in an apartment on the rue Bonaparte. Later, the author of *The Adding Machine* and *Street Scene* would write a satiric play, *The Left Bank*, about the disenchanted expatriates he saw in Montparnasse. A family man, Rice was no "Bohemian," although he did occasionally venture out to the expatriates' cafés and bistros. Sherwood Anderson visited Rice frequently at the apartment in late 1926 and early 1927.

RUE JACOB

44 · Hôtel Jacob (In 1921 it was registered as the Hôtel Jacob; in 1925, as the Hôtel Jacob-et-d'Angleterre; today, as the Hôtel d'Angleterre)

In what was once the British Embassy, the popular Hôtel Jacob served after World War I as temporary headquarters for many newly arrived Americans. For instance, when Djuna Barnes came to Paris in 1920 as an aspiring writer, she stayed here for several weeks before traveling to Berlin.

Lewis Galantière, a Chicagoan who worked in Paris, often acted as advance man, handling the reservations for the Americans. During the visit of Sherwood and Tennessee Anderson and Paul Rosenfeld in the spring of 1921, Galantière booked rooms for them at the Jacob.

Just after the Andersons left, Harold Loeb arrived, and he noted that "the rooms were dingy, but Djuna Barnes was staying there . . . , and Man Ray was expected any day." With Loeb were Frances Midner and the Kreymborgs, Alfred and Dorothy. Alfred was coeditor with Loeb of their artistic little magazine, *Broom.*

Kathleen (Kitty) Cannell, a friend of the Kreymborgs and later Loeb's lover, had made the arrangements for them. She was in Paris awaiting a divorce from her husband, the poet Skipworth Cannell. When Kreymborg signed in, he saw the names of Anderson and Rosenfeld in the guest book, and he spotted Barnes in the lobby. With so many old friends in town (he didn't know that the Anderson party had already left), Alfred felt like he was back in Greenwich Village.

When newlyweds Ernest and Hadley Hemingway arrived in December 1921, Galantière also booked them into the Jacob, where they lived for a couple weeks until they found an affordable apartment on rue du Cardinal-Lemoine.

This influx of expatriates continued through the decade. Virgil Thomson stayed there briefly in 1927, and when Hart Crane arrived in Paris in January 1929, he also took a room at the Jacob. Around 1930, after Sisley Huddleston left his boulevard Raspail apartment, but prior to his move to Saint-Pierre-d'Antels, Huddleston also took a room here.

The Jacob served as the Paris address for *The Little Review*. After starting the journal in Chicago in 1914, Margaret Anderson moved it to New York and then, in 1924, to London, where Jane Heap took over the editorial chores. The final number appeared in May 1929, listing 44 rue Jacob as the French editorial office.

Whenever they were in Paris, Anderson, Heap, and Georgette Leblanc (Maeterlinck's former lover) usually divided their time between this hotel and Janet Flanner's hotel, the Bonaparte. But by 1930–31, the year Georgette came down with a serious case of pneumonia, they had settled into the Jacob.

RUE DES SAINTS-PERES

29 • Michaud's (now Brasserie l'Escorailles)

This restaurant at the corner of rue Jacob was a favorite with the expatriates, especially while they were living at the hotels nearby.

According to Harold Loeb, Michaud's served simple and unpretentious food: "haricots verts, petits pois, new potatoes, and fraises des bois with a freshness and delicacy unknown in the United States."

This is the place, too, where Hemingway and Fitzgerald supposedly went to the men's toilet to discuss the "matter of measurements," at least as it's recounted in *A Moveable Feast*.

RUE DE L'UNIVERSITE

9 • James Joyce's hotel (now Hôtel Lenox)

Probably acting upon the recommendation of T. S. Eliot, who stayed here when he was studying at the Sorbonne in 1910, Ezra Pound booked rooms in this hotel for James Joyce in 1920.

Presumably bound for London, the Joyces stopped off for what was intended to be a visit of a week or two. In all, they ended up using this hotel three different times and spending the next twenty years in Paris.

The Joyce family — James, Nora, Giorgio, and Lucia — lived here from July eighth until the fifteenth, 1920, at which time they moved to a flat on the rue de l'Assomption. When Joyce gave up that flat in November, he and his family returned to this private hotel, which he liked because it reminded him of Dublin. This time they stayed here only during November 1920. Then, they moved to an "expensive flat" on boulevard Raspail. During the summer and fall of the following year, the Joyces occupied the rue du Cardinal-Lemoine apartment of the critic Valéry Larbaud.

On 1 October 1921, after leaving Larbaud's apartment, the Joyces returned for a third time to this hotel at 9 rue de l'Université. Although he should have known what he was getting into, Joyce was by then accustomed to more lavish quarters, such as those he'd had on Raspail and Cardinal-Lemoine, and he referred to this hotel as a "damned brothel." Nevertheless, Joyce and his family remained here for the next three and a half years, until they moved to 2 square de Robiac in June 1925.

Waldo Frank, the American novelist, editor, and cultural critic who called himself a "philosophical, social revolutionary," kept a residence here for most of the decade, having first checked into Cayre's Hotel when he arrived in Paris shortly after the Armistice.

THE CROSBYS' ENVIRONS

QUAI VOLTAIRE

17 · Virgil Thomson's residence

A trusted friend of many expatriates, including Gertrude Stein and George Antheil, Thomson moved into an apartment here on 1 November 1927, having previously resided in a rue de Berne hotel. Actually, number 17 consists of two L-shaped buildings. Thomson's fifth-floor, high-ceilinged flat was in the second — the one with its back to the Hôtel du Quai Voltaire at number 19.

Bravig Imbs observes that Thomson had several splendid paintings in the apartment, noting also "a great expanse of yellow curtained glass [beneath which] was a little door, which when opened, showed just a glimpse of the great grey Louvre . . . like a picture." The day after moving in, Thomson began working on the score for his opera, *Four Saints in Three Acts*, the libretto of which was written by Gertrude Stein. Considering it his permanent residence, Thomson kept this apartment until World War II.

Along with Aaron Copland and others, Thomson studied under the acclaimed musician and teacher Nadia Boulanger, renowned for her work with Les Six. One of the leading American composers of the twentieth century, Virgil Thomson was a major contributor to the "All-American Concert" held in the Salle Gaveau in 1926.

During 1927–28 Thomson was "editor in France" of Sherry Mangan's little review, *larus, the celestial visitor*, for which he acquired pieces by Gertrude Stein, Mary Butts, Robert McAlmon, Bernard Faÿ, and others. When *larus* folded in 1928, Thomson became the European editor of its replacement, Richard Johns's *Pagany*.

19 · Hôtel du Quai Voltaire

According to a plaque, some of the residents of this hotel were Charles Baudelaire, Richard Wagner, and Oscar Wilde. In 1920, American writer Willa Cather stayed here during her two-month visit to Paris, the setting for her Pulitzer Prize—winning novel, *One of Ours* (1922).

Another resident in the twenties was the critic Clive Bell, a member of London's Bloomsbury group and the husband of Vanessa Stephen, Virginia Woolf's sister. The Bells' son Julian, who didn't share his father's Francophilia, lived for a while on boulevard Port-Royal.

Dolly (Dorothy) Wilde, Oscar's niece, lived in the quai Voltaire from March to June 1925.

In December 1925, Irma Le Gallienne, Richard's third wife, moved into this hotel, where she lived until 1927.

RUE DE BEAUNE

9 · Hôtel Elysée (now gone)

Coming to Paris late in June 1920, Ezra Pound took a room in this hotel to prepare for the arrival of James Joyce from Trieste (by way of Venice, Milan, and Dijon). Joyce's arrival in Paris would be an event of considerable importance, but Bill Bird felt that Pound's move to Paris was even more significant. *"Le premier événement d'importance pour la littérature américaine des années 20 fut l'émigration d'Ezra Pound de Londres à Paris,"* Bird wrote.

Having set the stage by circulating the news of Joyce's July (1920) arrival, and having reserved rooms for the Joyces in a hotel on rue de l'Université, Pound introduced Joyce to various friends and returned to London to prepare for his own move to Paris.

When T. S. Eliot and Wyndham Lewis visited Paris in mid-August 1920, they brought a box of old shoes that Ezra had intended as a gift for Joyce. Eliot and Lewis stayed in this hotel and invited Joyce over, ostensibly to pick up Pound's package. After a rather lively literary discussion, Eliot invited the Irish novelist to join them for dinner. Joyce turned to his son, who'd accompanied his father to the Elysée, and instructed him in Italian to run back and tell Nora that James wouldn't be home for dinner. Giorgio, however, did not consider himself his father's errand boy. He and his father exchanged a few heated words in Italian, and then Joyce, Lewis, and Eliot headed off to dinner, leaving Giorgio behind.

RUE DE LILLE

19 · Harry and Caresse Crosby's "permanent" Paris residence

Having left the rue Boulard *pavillon* in the early autumn of 1925, the Crosbys spent a few weeks in the Hôtel Goya (on rue du Faubourg-Saint-Honoré) looking for suitable permanent quarters. Here on the rue de Lille they found an elegant but unostentatious townhouse that afforded them three floors (one wing) of spacious rooms with high ceilings.

Harry and Caresse added a sunken marble bathtub, an open fireplace, a "Sicilian" dining room, and a formal drawing room. Harry's library spanned the length of the third floor. A block from the Seine and just down from the rue Allent, this 300-year-old building was near the home of Harry's influential cousin, Walter Berry.

Harry and Caresse moved in on 27 October 1925. According to Caresse's (often unreliable) memoirs, they had first leased a flat at number 55 for a considerable sum, but while she and Harry were walking away, having closed the deal, they passed this townhouse here at number 19. It was vacant. The magnificent doors opening onto the impressive cobbled courtyard persuaded them to race back to number 55 and beg the manager to let them out of the lease they'd just signed. He did — for the price of six months' rent.

In these apartments Harry and Caresse held their famous dinners for art students on the evenings of the Quatz'Arts Ball. So raucous were these affairs that the Crosbys first removed their paintings and the Chinese porcelains from the library and turned the bookcases to the wall.

In July 1928, the Crosbys made arrangements with Armand, Comte de la Rochefoucauld, for a twenty-year lease of an old mill on his estate near Ermenonville (about sixty kilometers north of Paris). That summer after remodeling the mill, the Crosbys moved in, and Caresse kept the mill after Harry's suicide in 1929.

RUE DE VERNEUIL

6 • Apartment of Eugene and Maria Jolas

In addition to serving as a rewrite man for the Paris edition of the *Chicago Tribune*, Eugene Jolas also produced a regular column, "Rambles Through Literary Paris," which began in 1924 and ran for nearly a year. Leaving this apartment sometime around 1926, Gene and Maria, his wife, moved to rue Valentin-Haüy, where Gene and Elliot Paul began planning *transition* as a journal to replace *This Quarter*, whose editor, Ernest Walsh, had died.

11 • Residence of George Stevens

Twenty-year-old George Stevens, the cinematographer and, later, director, lived in France from July 1924 through June of the following year. Stevens first stayed at the Chez Madame Falaise in Gargenville at Seine-et-Oise, but he later moved to this address in Paris. According to the books he checked out of Sylvia Beach's library, Stevens was particularly interested in the plays of Eugene O'Neill.

24 • Apartment of Janet Scudder

After leaving 70-bis rue Notre-Dame-des-Champs, Scudder moved to this address. She traveled frequently between New York and Paris, studying sculpture in the former and selling it in the latter. Her prewar friend Gertrude Stein called Scudder "the doughboy" because "there were only two perfectly solemn things on earth, the doughboy and Janet Scudder."

In 1924, Scudder helped Stein set up the memorial fund to support Mildred Aldrich, whose pension had run out and who, in desperation, was about to sell off her priceless library.

29(?) • Hôtel du Pavillon

Sylvia Beach's records indicate that John Rodker — the writer, literary agent, and publisher — resided in this hotel from May to September, probably in 1922, when he was working at the Librairie Six on bringing out a second edition of James Joyce's *Ulysses*.

Number unknown • Laurence Vail's apartment

Peggy Guggenheim notes that in 1921 she followed Laurence Vail from her room at the Hôtel Plaza-Athénée to his apartment on Verneuil and casually surrendered her virginity to him. They were married within the year and, until their children were born, traveled extensively and lived in some of Europe's finest hotels.

RUE DE L'UNIVERSITE

50 • Hôtel de l'Intendance (now gone)

After staying briefly at the Hôtel des Saints-Pères in early 1921, Edna St. Vincent Millay moved here to this hotel, where she lived from May through July while "working like the devil" on various poems.

Then, after traveling for nearly a year, Edna returned to Paris in April 1922, at which time she and her mother had arranged to meet. At first, the Millay women booked into the Intendance, but it proved too costly, so shortly thereafter they moved to the Hôtel Venetia on the boulevard Montparnasse.

RUE DU BAC

34 • Paul Scott Mowrer's apartment

A highly regarded foreign correspondent for the *Chicago Daily News*, Mowrer spent the twenties and early thirties in Paris, before returning to Chicago to assume the management of the paper. While living in Paris, Mowrer married Hadley Hemingway in 1933, some six years after her divorce from Ernest. It was a long and happy marriage.

44 • Residence of Jo Davidson, Berenice Abbott, and the Mac-Leishes

The "Residential Directory" of the 1921 *Franco-American Yearbook* twice lists this as Jo Davidson's address. In a third section of the directory, however, the American sculptor's "residential" address is given as 14 avenue du Maine, a street where several sculptors and painters had studios and workshops.

In fact, after Davidson came to Paris at the time of the Armistice in November 1917, he and Lincoln Steffens roomed together at the Chatham Hôtel, until Davidson found a suitable studio-residence on the avenue du Maine.

Then, when his wife, Yvonne, joined Davidson in Paris in the spring of 1920, they took this apartment here at 44 rue du Bac, although Jo retained the rooms at the avenue du Maine address for a workshop studio. The new apartment was "beautifully furnished," Davidson notes. "The artistic discomfort of the avenue du Maine was replaced by comfortable bourgeois surroundings."

That spring Jo and Yvonne decided to send for their children, who joined them in the summer of 1920. Shortly thereafter — probably in the autumn of 1920 — they all moved into a house on the rue Masseran.

In 1926, with loans from Peggy Guggenheim, Robert McAlmon, and Bryher, Berenice Abbott set up her own photographic studio in this building, "up the second stairway to the left." While serving as Man Ray's assistant, Abbott was herself growing in demand as a photographer. By this time Abbott was paying Ray more for the rental of his equipment, which she used to take photographs during her off-hours, than the $50 a month in wages she's said to have received as Ray's full-time assistant.

The split between master and apprentice came the day Peggy Guggenheim arrived at Ray's shop and asked for a portrait session with Abbott. In May 1927, the *Tribune* spoke of Abbott as "one of the outstanding creators of camera portraits in Paris" and praised her for "the simplicity of her studies." Abbott kept this one-room studio at number 44 until January 1928, when she moved to rue Servandoni.

Another resident here was the novelist and journalist John Gunther, who in the late twenties was put in charge of the Paris office of the *Chicago Daily News*.

Apparently the poet Archibald MacLeish and his wife, the soprano Ada, lived at this address on two different occasions, once in 1925 and again in 1928.

The records of Sylvia Beach's lending library at Shakespeare and Company first mention 44 rue du Bac as the MacLeishes' address on

16 November 1925. In a letter to John Peale Bishop on 3 February 1926, Archibald MacLeish writes, "Back [in Paris] three months & seven lines of bum verse to show for it." The February reference to "three months" would suggest that Archie and Ada spent the winter of 1925–26 here, before heading to the Riviera the following summer.

Archie and Ada and their children returned to Paris — to the Pierpont Morgan Hamilton house on what is now the avenue Foch — in September 1926.

At some point, perhaps as early as 1925, the MacLeishes bought the flat at 44 rue du Bac, since in a letter to Harry Crosby, dated August 1927 (when Archie and Ada were in the States), MacLeish writes, "Utterly no news here except that they had rats at 44 rue du Bac. . . ." There was apparently some reason for MacLeish's being informed about the conditions here. Otherwise, why should MacLeish refer to the condition of an apartment he and Ada had left two and a half years before?

The MacLeishes were back at 44 rue du Bac for a brief spell in 1928. Archie wrote Harry Crosby from this address, this time to say that he was "back to work as an interior decorator . . . and then we sold the goddamn apartment." The MacLeishes spent their last couple of months in Paris in a brand-new apartment building on the rue Guynemer, near Ernest and Pauline Hemingway and the Fitzgeralds.

BOULEVARD RASPAIL

4 • Cayré's Hôtel (so listed then; now, the Cayré-Copatel)

When the cultural critic Waldo Frank, a founder and editor of *The Seven Arts*, came to Paris after the Armistice, he first took a room here before moving to a residential hotel at 9 rue de l'Université.

During her trip to Paris in 1924 and again in 1928, the American popular novelist Kathryn Hulme stayed at Cayré's Hôtel, which was especially popular with American women traveling alone. Because she was in Paris, Hulme missed the New York lectures of the man whose unusual notions drastically changed her life: Georgei Gurdjieff. When she returned to Paris in 1930, Hulme lived in the same hotel as Janet Flanner and Solita Solano, another Gurdjieff enthusiast.

5 · James Joyce's apartment

Joyce rented a flat here from the beginning of December 1920 to June 1921 for a mere £300. "Is it not extraordinary," he noted, "the way I enter a city barefoot and end up in a luxurious flat?" Robert McAlmon traced Joyce to this address and, carrying a letter of introduction from Harriet Weaver (Joyce's principal patron), introduced himself to the Irish writer. The meeting was especially fortuitous for the Joyce family, since McAlmon had recently married into money and was therefore able to contribute a monthly allowance of about $150 to the Joyces during this period.

FROM
SAINT-GERMAIN
TO THE
LUXEMBOURG

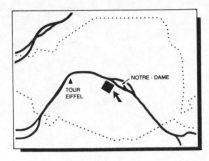

MAP 4

includes addresses from ...

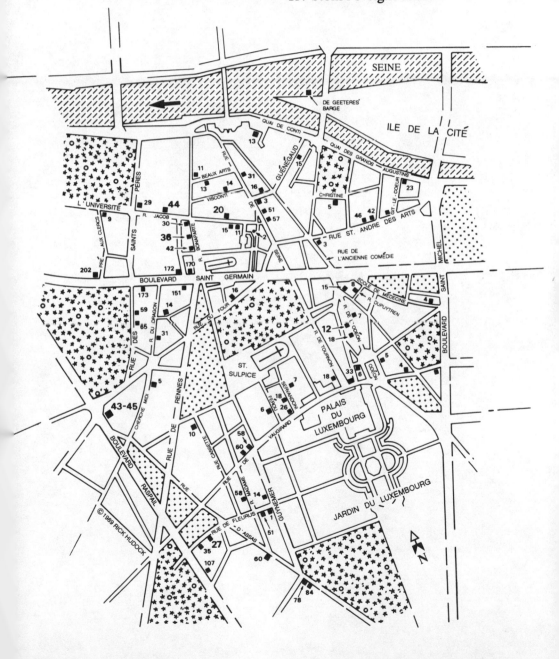

SAINT-GERMAIN AND SOUTH

BOULEVARD SAINT-GERMAIN

218 · Galerie Artiste et Artisan

In July 1928, Kay Boyle and Sharon, her daughter by Ernest Walsh, took up residence in Raymond Duncan's Neuilly commune. When Boyle moved out six months later, Sharon would have been held hostage, had not Boyle — aided by Robert McAlmon, the Dayang Muda, and the Crosbys, Harry and Caresse — virtually kidnapped Sharon from Duncan's assistant, Ayah.

While at the commune, Boyle paid for her keep by working as a clerk in Duncan's fabric shops — one of which was on the Right Bank, on the rue du Faubourg-Saint-Honoré. The other was here, on the Left Bank. Boyle's duties were menial, and the shops were not exactly what their names implied. The "handmade" sandals for sale had been obtained as prefab parts and assembled, and "the tunics and robes we sold," Boyle recalled, "had not been woven on hand looms in Neuilly, as Raymond declared. . . ." Unlike his two sisters, Elizabeth and the famous Isadora, Raymond Duncan was not above a hustle or two.

202 · Apartment of Guillaume Apollinaire

According to Stein's *Autobiography of Alice B. Toklas* and Hemingway's *A Moveable Feast,* the poet and art critic Guillaume Apollinaire died here on Armistice Day (11 November 1918). People in the streets, ecstatic over the Armistice, were supposedly shouting "A bas Guillaume," in reference to the German Kaiser ("Guillaume" being the French version of "Wilhelm"). Guillaume Apollinaire, the story goes, believed the shouting referred to him, and thus he died thinking the people of Paris were calling for his death. It makes a poignant story, but in truth Apollinaire fell into a coma and died of the Spanish flu on 9 November 1918 — two days before the Armistice.

173 · Apartment of Djuna Barnes

When Djuna Barnes came to Paris early in the decade, she took a room at 2 rue Perronet. After returning from Berlin in 1922, she moved into an apartment here, where she was later joined by Thelma Wood, the Missouri artist who had been living in an apartment on the rue Delambre. Wood would become the model for Robin Vote in Barnes's *Nightwood* and the "T. W." to whom Barnes dedicated her first novel, *Ryder*.

The few years the two women lived here included bouts of jealousy, periods of excessive drinking, and a couple nervous breakdowns — as well as spells of profound mutual affection and admiration. By the middle twenties, Barnes had made enough money from her writing to be able to buy an apartment on the rue Saint-Romain, where she and Wood lived until they parted in December 1931.

151 · Brasserie Lipp

Across from the Café de Flore and the Deux Magots, Lipp's had a comparatively small patio and large interior, which minimized its use by café-sitters but increased its appeal to serious diners. Moreover, Lipp's served late-evening meals, so "by midnight," according to one patron, "[Lipp's] would be full of Left Bank Americans." In *A Moveable Feast*, Hemingway describes Lipp's splendid beer, potato salad, and *cervelas* — "a sausage like a heavy, wide frankfurter split in two and covered with a special mustard sauce."

170 · Café aux Deux Magots

The Deux Magots has long been popular with Americans. When philosopher George Santayana visited Paris before the war, for example, he frequented the Deux Magots regularly with his friend philosophy professor Charles Augustus Strong, who lived at 9 avenue de l'Observatoire.

In 1926, William Shirer, the journalist, and Grant Wood, the American painter, spent many hours in the Deux Magots recollecting their days back in Cedar Rapids, Iowa.

In the late twenties Janet Flanner learned that Ernest Hemingway's father, like her own, was a suicide — "a piece of personal duplicate history that he and I discovered one day at a quiet back table in the Deux Magots cafe, which he always favored for serious talk, such as his reading aloud in a rumbling whisper the first poetry he had written after the war."

At the Deux Magots in January 1929, Eugene Jolas introduced Hart Crane to Harry Crosby, the latter to commit suicide within the year and Crane three years later.

The Deux Magots was also popular with the Surrealists, who — according to Janet Flanner — "had their own club table facing the door of the Deux Magots, from which vantage point a seated Surrealist could conveniently insult any newcomer."

172 · Café de Flore

Next door, the Flore passed in and out of fashion — unlike the Deux Magots, which retained a constant popularity. Prior to the twenties, for example, the critic and poet Guillaume Apollinaire held his "Tuesdays" at the Flore, afternoons of conversation and, at times, heated discussion. At one of these sessions, André Breton met Philippe Soupault, both of whom would later figure in the Dada and Surrealist movements.

Virgil Thomson notes that the Flore was "a dreary place till bought by a progressive managment and done over to look less nineteenth-century. Offering toast, ham and eggs, and surprisingly good coffee, it came to be frequented by many of the better-off late risers."

RUE DES SAINTS-PERES

59 · Hôtel du Pas-de-Calais

In July 1921, while his wife, Dorothy Shakespear, was staying with family and friends in England, Ezra Pound took a room in the Hôtel du Pas-de-Calais. The Pounds were waiting to move into the *studio-pavillon* Ezra had just leased on the rue Notre-Dame-des-Champs.

Scofield Thayer, who came to Paris that month on his way to Vienna, went to see Pound at the Pas-de-Calais. "When one arrives at his hotel on the street of the Holy Fathers," Thayer said, "one usually learns from the young lady that Mr. Pound is *au bain*. But the young lady consents to going upstairs to see Mr. Pound and to inquire if Mr. Pound will see guests. Mr. Pound receives beaming and incisive [wearing] a pointed yellow beard and elliptical pince-nez and an open Byronic collar and an omelette-yellow bathrobe. . . ."

65 · Hôtel des Saints-Pères

The Saints-Pères was popular with Americans even before the twenties. In 1908, for instance, Alice Toklas and Harriet Levy took a room here, where Etta and Dr. Claribel Cone — the Baltimore sisters — were staying. And, before heading home in 1917, E. E. Cummings spent three days here after his release from the La Ferté Macé prison. On 20 January 1921 the poet Edna St. Vincent Millay stayed here before moving to the Hôtel de l'Intendance a couple months later.

RUE DE GRENELLE

15 · Hôtel de Bérulle

In 1924, the year of André Breton's *First Surrealist Manifesto*, Louis Aragon and others established La Central — a Central Bureau for Surrealist Research — here. The building manager (*concierge*) was, conveniently, the father of the Surrealist painter Pierre Naville.

22 · Margaret Anderson's residence

Although the Hôtel Beaujolais was Margaret Anderson's very first (1923) Paris residence, this address is the earliest one that Sylvia Beach lists. Anderson was widely admired for the courage and taste she exhibited in managing her important journal, *The Little Review*. From here, Anderson apparently moved to the rue de l'Université.

BOULEVARD RASPAIL

43–45 · Hôtel Lutetia

Still an impressive hotel, the Lutetia was described by Harold Loeb in the twenties as "a large, modern, not-too-expensive hotel with push-button elevators." Until Loeb found an apartment on rue Monttessuy when his little magazine, *Broom*, folded, he usually stayed at the Lutetia during his visits to Paris. Loeb, of course, was Hemingway's model for Robert Cohn in *The Sun Also Rises*.

Although Robert McAlmon lived in various hotels during his many years in Paris — usually preferring the Foyot — he occasionally stayed at the Lutetia. While living here in January 1924, he reserved a room for the William Carlos Williamses, who were about to arrive in Paris from the States. McAlmon and James Joyce, to whom McAlmon was giving a monthly allowance of $150, occasionally ate lunch together at the Lutetia Brasserie.

After their marriage in the early twenties, Laurence Vail and Peggy Guggenheim stayed at the Lutetia whenever they were in Paris. With the birth of their son, Sinbad, they took more spacious quarters on the boulevard Saint-Germain.

From 1925 to early 1927, the Lutetia was the main Paris residence of Isadora Duncan. Low on funds, Duncan was persuaded to live *en pension* in 1926, an economical plan that provided meals as well as lodging. But Isadora didn't like to eat alone, so she'd invariably invite friends or, for that matter, strangers to eat with her. This practice, obviously, was costing the hotel money, and so during the winter of 1926–27, an executive from the Lutetia brought up the matter and inadvertently offended the dancer. Consequently, when Isadora returned to Paris from Nice that spring, she adamantly refused to return to the Lutetia and moved instead to the new Studio-Apartment Hotel, which had just opened.

Nathanael West came to Paris in October 1926 and took a room at the Lutetia before seeking out cheaper lodgings on the rue de la Grande-Chaumière. Max Eastman, social critic and editor of *The Masses* and *The Liberator*, also stayed at the Lutetia on his trips to Paris.

RUE DU CHERCHE-MIDI

5 · Galerie Sacre du Printemps (now gone)

On 8 June 1926 the first exhibition of Berenice Abbott's photography opened here. Her portraits of Joyce, Beach, Cocteau, Barnes, and others were simple and straightforward, in contrast to the self-consciously experimental photography of Man Ray, for whom Abbott apprenticed. Alexander Calder and other painters and sculptors also showed works here in the mid and late twenties.

RUE DU DRAGON

31 · Académie Julian

One of the oldest and most traditional academies of art in Paris, the Julian provided separate studios for male and female artists during *croquis* classes involving nude models. Most academies did not operate like the *écoles* (schools), exactly. The academies were more or less institutionalized workshops where students could work and receive periodic instruction and criticism from an established artist or two. Thus, when a student didn't particularly wish to hear what the resident artists might have to say about his work, he simply didn't show up on, say, Saturday mornings when "rounds" were made.

Numerous young American painters attended the Julian in the twenties, including Niles Spencer, Leo Stein, Stuart Davis, and Julien Levy. In 1921 Morrill Cody left the *Tribune* to study at the Julian. During her year in Paris (1925), Howard University professor Gwendolyn Bennett — already an established poet — studied at the Julian (and also at the Colarossi and the Panthéon).

Learning of the academy on his first visit in the summer of 1920, Grant Wood enrolled during the autumn of his fourteen-month European stay in 1923–24. At the time, he was living in a studio room off Raspail and, as a rural Iowa youth, was much taken by the extravagance and license of Paris. He attended the annual Quatz' Arts Ball that year wearing (only) a draped fishnet. After a trip to Italy, Wood returned to Iowa in 1924 without having had a single exhibition. He returned two years later, however, for his first show, which took place in a prestigious gallery on the rue de Seine.

RUE BERNARD-PALISSY

14 • Residence of Morrill Cody

Cody, who ghost-wrote *This Must Be the Place* for Jimmy the Barman, was very much a part of Montparnasse life. In 1921–22 Cody lived in Madame Pons's student hotel here at number 14.

In 1923 Cody returned to Paris with his wife, Frances, and took a job on the *Tribune* for $15 a week. They made their residence at 25 rue d'Ulm. Decades later, Cody worked for the American government in Paris.

RUE BONAPARTE

61 • Hotel Napoleon Bonaparte (not to be confused with the hotel of the same name at number 36)

In February 1930, Henry Miller rented a fifth-floor garret in the tiny Bonaparte for less than $20 per month. Hard times were about to hit Miller. By December, when he was "rescued from starvation" by Richard Galen Osborn, Miller wasn't able to afford even this modest residence.

RUE DU FOUR

16 • Edmund Wilson's pension

Wilson, the critic and novelist, came to Paris in the summer of 1921 partly to see Paris but mostly to see his old flame, Edna St. Vincent Millay. After staying a few days in the Hôtel Mont-Thabor on the Right Bank, Wilson moved to this pension during the first week of July 1921. Having encountered the poet a couple of times by then, Wilson resigned himself to the impossibility of their ever getting back together. Millay had found a new lover, Wilson wrote John Peale

Bishop, his former classmate and friend. "She looks well," he added, stiffening his upper lip, "and has a new distinction of dress, but she can no longer intoxicate me with her beauty, or throw bombs into my soul. . . ." The poignancy of Wilson's expression and the power of his metaphor would suggest otherwise. In any case, by mid-August, Wilson had left Paris for England and, soon thereafter, the U.S.A.

THE ODEON AND EAST

RUE DUPUYTREN

8 · Shakespeare and Company (1919–21)

Sylvia Beach opened her first lending library, bookstore, and mail repository here on 17 November 1919. On a cast-iron hook over the shop door she hung a portrait of Shakespeare, painted by Adrienne Monnier's friend Charles Winzer.

Beach's early sales were mostly of British rather than American books, and her first customers were mostly Monnier's French friends. In the beginning, Sylvia's greatest service was to carry racks full of English and American little reviews for "the bunnies." (Since *abonné* is French for "subscriber," Sylvia's sister Holly and others called the patrons "bunnies.") A year and a half later Sylvia moved her shop to rue de l'Odéon.

CARREFOUR DE L'ODEON

15 · Residence of Florence Gilliam and Arthur Moss

In 1922 Florence Gilliam and her husband, Arthur Moss, moved here from their apartment on the rue Campagne-Première, where they'd been editing *Gargoyle*, one of the first of the little magazines of the twenties. According to Gilliam, "it became obvious that the role of our apartment as a sort of annex to Montparnasse took up too much of our time." After changing their residence, Gilliam and Moss continued to edit *Gargoyle* for a few more months until it folded.

Gilliam and Moss's suite of rooms here on the carrefour de l'Odéon was above a ground-floor restaurant called "The Little Brown Jug," which was understandably popular among Americans. The restaurant was run by a Frenchwoman, whose American husband managed the apartments. Previously, he'd been associated with the American Red Cross and, accordingly, he had many friends in Paris.

RUE DE L'ODEON

12 · Shakespeare and Company (after 1921)

Sylvia Beach moved her bookstore and lending library to this location on 27 July 1921, making 12 rue de l'Odéon probably the most famous expatriate address in Paris. Madame Tisserand was the concierge, and Sylvia's primary assistant in the shop was Mlle. Myrsine Moschos, who lived in the Twentieth Arrondissement at 6 rue Henri-Dubouillon.

After 1922, Beach's *carte de la maison* rightfully carried the word "publisher," since she supervised and helped finance the publication of Joyce's *Ulysses* when all others avoided the risk. (Margaret Anderson and Jane Heap had been found guilty of violating American obscenity laws when they ran parts of the novel in *The Little Review*.)

Sylvia's decision to move Shakespeare and Company from the rue Dupuytren to the rue de l'Odéon was prompted by James Joyce's wealthy American patron, John Quinn, who'd come to Paris to meet the woman who was to publish *Ulysses*. Quinn thought that Sylvia's place on Dupuytren looked like a hovel. Meanwhile, Adrienne Monnier had noticed that an antique dealer at number 12 — across from her own bookstore at number 7 — wanted out of a lease. Sylvia eagerly took over the lease and moved her personal things to a room in Adrienne's apartment at number 18, just up from the new location. Nestled among a shoemaker's shop, a corset maker, a music store, and a manufacturer of nose spray, Shakespeare and Company was now directly across from Adrienne's La Maison des Amis des Livres.

For a while Sylvia sublet the mezzanine rooms above her shop to George Antheil, the eccentric young composer who'd arrived in Paris on 13 June 1923 with Böske (sometimes spelled "Boski"; real name, Elizabeth Markus), whom he would marry in Budapest in November 1925. At first the Antheils lived in the smallest of the rooms, but soon they moved into the adjoining rooms as well. When Böske wasn't there to let him in, Antheil puckishly entered the second-floor apartment by climbing up the awning and window ledges outside Shakespeare and Company. Antheil kept a composing room around the corner in the Hôtel de Tournon on the rue de Tournon, just opposite the Garde Républicaine.

Beach's contribution to expatriate life is immeasurable. Not only did she carry — and thus promote — the expatriates' books and little reviews, she also lent money on occasion, provided free mailing services, sponsored readings, and in general served as hostess, message bearer, and confidante.

In 1923, the poet Archibald MacLeish described the sensation of walking up this short street: "Turning up from St. Germain, one kept Shakespeare and Company to starboard and Adrienne Monnier's Amis des Livres to port, and felt, as one rose with the tide toward the theatre, that one had passed the gates of dream. . . . It was enough for a confused young lawyer in a grand and vivid time to look from one side to the other and say to himself . . . Gide was here on Thursday and on Monday Joyce was there."

Like most of the other American writers, Ernest Hemingway visited Shakespeare and Company regularly. Indeed, Sylvia Beach was one of the few persons with whom he seems never to have had a serious falling-out.

During World War II, prior to the French liberation of Paris from the Nazis, Hemingway commandeered a troop of American soldiers and took them to 12 rue de l'Odéon. Adrienne Monnier published an account of this incident in 1945, shortly after it occurred — setting the date as "Saturday the 26th, the day of the assassination attempt on General de Gaulle."

Noting the gunfire in the street and her own fear as she and Sylvia hid in their fifth-floor apartment, Adrienne described Sylvia's shock and joy when she heard a man's voice calling, " 'Sylvia! Hemingway is here!' " The two women raced down the stairs to greet Hemingway, who seemed, in Monnier's words, "more of a giant than ever, bareheaded, in shirt-sleeves." Grabbing the bird-sized Sylvia by the waist, Ernest hoisted her high in the air. Having arrived in "four little cars (not jeeps)," Ernest and his sixteen men had already cleared the rooftops of snipers. The previous night they'd stormed the Ritz, and, according to Monnier, they "naturally . . . installed themselves in the best rooms." After seeing that Sylvia was safe and that Adrienne was in no danger of being thought a collaborator, Hemingway and his men departed.

7 · La Maison des Amis des Livres

Adrienne Monnier's bookstore (The House of the Friends of Books) opened on 15 November 1915 and almost immediately became popular with French writers, critics, and other intellectuals. "I am not interested only in famous personages," Monnier wrote. "The great joy is to discover. And then, you know, famous people, they were not born so."

18 · Adrienne Monnier's apartment

After 1920 Sylvia Beach lived with Adrienne in her fifth-floor apartment just a few buildings south (toward the Odéon) of Shakespeare and Company.

PLACE DE L'ODEON

1 · Café Voltaire (now gone)

Situated opposite the Odéon, this celebrated café was frequented by Gauguin, Verlaine, Rimbaud, Whistler, Rodin, and Mallarmé prior to the expatriate years. In 1891 a going-away banquet was held here for Paul Gauguin before he left for Tahiti. In the twenties the Voltaire was still popular with French artists and intellectuals, but not so much with the non-French Bohemians.

6 · Hôtel de l'Odéon, a.k.a. Hôtel Regnard (now Michelet-Odéon)

Although abroad he preferred Berlin, the American artist Marsden Hartley occasionally passed through Paris. When he did he stayed at this hotel, according to Sylvia Beach's records. Hartley was articulate, intelligent, and well liked. Born in 1877, he served as a kind of elder rebel for some of the younger expatriates.

Louis Bromfield also stayed here during the twenties, though his principal Paris residences were in Passy. Later in the decade the Bromfields moved permanently to Senlis, some thirty-five miles north of the city.

During Sherwood Anderson's second visit to Paris (1926), he took a room in this hotel, which was then called the Hôtel Regnard. Others who stayed briefly in the Regnard were Bravig Imbs and, prior to their rue de Verneuil years, Eugene and Marie Jolas.

In April 1928, the composer Roger Sessions and his wife stayed in this hotel before moving to an apartment at 166 boulevard Montparnasse. A highly respected musician, Sessions had received one of the first Guggenheims in 1926. Like his friend Aaron Copland and others, Sessions had come to Paris to study under Nadia Boulanger.

In the fall and early winter of 1929, just before their return to the United States in December, poet Allen Tate and his wife, writer Caroline Gordon, lived in this hotel, having left Ford Madox Ford's rue de Vaugirard apartment.

RUE CORNEILLE

5 · Hôtel Corneille

Although the poet Hart Crane first checked into the Hôtel Jacob when he arrived in Paris in January 1929, he used the Hôtel Corneille as his primary Paris residence until he returned to the States six months later. Crane rarely stayed anywhere very long. During these six months, he traveled extensively, spent many days and nights with the Crosbys at Le Moulin in the French countryside, and even did some time in La Santé prison.

(Maurice Saillet, who was Adrienne Monnier's assistant at her bookstore/library, La Maison des Amis des Livres, notes that Sherwood Anderson stayed at the Corneille during his 1921 trip to Paris. Several others, however, who mention Anderson in their memoirs and journals list him only at the Hôtel Jacob during the 1921 visit.)

RUE DE L'ECOLE-DE-MEDECINE

4 · Hôtel Saint-Pierre

When the League of Nations sponsored the formation of the International Society of Intellectual Cooperation in 1925, Luis Buñuel discovered that a friend of his was to be the representative from Spain. Eager to see Paris, the future filmmaker applied for a position on the Spanish staff and was soon off, instructed simply to prepare himself by learning the city and perfecting his French.

Upon arriving, Buñuel took a room in the only hotel he'd heard of, the Ronceray in the passage Jouffroy. This hotel had been where his parents honeymooned and, incidentally, where Luis had been conceived. A week later, he moved into the Saint-Pierre, where he witnessed a way of life that deeply moved him. The Greek restaurant across the street, the champagne that a French friend had recommended for Buñuel's mild case of the flu, the unmarried couples kissing in the hallways and openly living together, the Chinese cabaret next door — all this caused Buñuel to observe that "the abyss between Spain and France widened with every passing day."

After leaving the pricey Hôtel Théâtre des Champs-Elysées, journalist and travel writer A. J. Liebling moved into this cheaper hotel in November 1926. He lived here for nearly a year at 450 francs ($20) a month.

Attending the Sorbonne, Liebling assiduously avoided the Left Bank expatriates, although during his first weeks in Paris he did frequent the Café du Dôme. Liebling exercised at the American Baptist Center's gymnasium on the rue Denfert-Rochereau instead of the American Artists' Club on Raspail, where Hemingway, Bob Coates, and Morley Callaghan sparred. Liebling notes that "during my residence in the Hotel Saint Pierre [1926–27] I never heard of Gertrude Stein, and although I read *Ulysses*, I would as soon have thought of looking the author up as of calling on the President of the Republic."

RUE DES ECOLES

49 • Balzar Brasserie

A favorite after-work spot for *Tribune* copy writers on the night shift, the Balzar closed at three A.M. Having put the paper to bed, Elliot Paul, William Shirer, Eugene Jolas, and James Thurber would merrily cross the river to the Latin Quarter and head toward this Alsatian brasserie for a plate of *choucroute formidable* and a few glasses of what Shirer called "the best beer in Paris."

51 • Apartment of Max Eastman

Max Eastman usually checked into the Hôtel Lutetia when he visited Paris during the twenties, but in 1920 he stayed at this residence. Eastman was the founder of the Socialist weekly *The Masses*, and in 1912 he took over as editor. The journal was suppressed by the U.S. government in 1918, so Eastman and others replaced it three months later with *The Liberator*.

PLACE DE LA SORBONNE

1 • Hôtel Select

Katherine Mansfield lived here for three weeks in October 1922 before moving to Georgei Gurdjieff's commune near Fontaine-bleau, where she died in January 1923.

3-bis • Residences of Mary Reynolds and Luis Buñuel

Before moving to her more famous rue Hallé residence, where she opened her home to the Surrealists, Mary Louise Reynolds lived here, just off the boul' Mich'. Through her own artistic interests, her relationship with painter Marcel Duchamp, and her friendship with the Surrealists, Reynolds became the unofficial historian of Surrealism, and her priceless collection of material pertaining to the movement is now housed at the Chicago Art Institute.

Luis Buñuel, who was to become one of the world's most important filmmakers, moved to number 3-bis in 1926. He kept this residence for a couple years until he returned to Spain for a brief visit. When he came back to Paris in 1929, Salvador Dali tagged along to help Buñuel make his first film, the Dadaesque *Un Chien Andalou.*

Besides being exposed to French filmmaking in Paris, Buñuel also discovered a group of Spanish expatriates — some of whom were old friends — who met regularly at the Rotonde for discussions under the guidance of Don Miguel de Unamuno.

Buñuel was shocked by the incidents of anti-Semitism he witnessed in Paris, something rare in Spain at the time, and he experienced racial prejudice firsthand. Right-wing organizations like the Camelots du Roi and Jeunesses Patriotiques periodically raided the *métèques* (foreigners of mixed race). A dark-skinned Spaniard himself, Buñuel endured his share of fistfights with these racist hooligans, who would suddenly arrive in trucks, leap out, and, wielding yellow truncheons, begin beating the *métèques* who they claimed were "cluttering up" the sidewalks of Montparnasse.

RUE CUJAS

20 · Gypsy's Bar (now gone)

Robert McAlmon refers to this place as "the Gypsy Bar," rather than *Gypsy's* Bar. In fact, there was a joint called the Gypsy Bar, but it was an entirely different kind of operation (sleazier) from Gypsy's Bar. McAlmon's descriptions, that is, indicate that he could be talking only about this establishment.

Gypsy's was "a large ball-hall," McAlmon says, "generally empty, but students and their mistresses collected there some nights, and a three-piece orchestra played American jazz very badly."

James Joyce liked this bar, and he and McAlmon went there often, usually to discuss literary or financial matters. Occasionally, they were joined by the French critic Valéry Larbaud (whose rue du Cardinal-Lemoine apartment Joyce used while finishing *Ulysses*) and other literary figures.

When the British critic, poet, and novelist Wyndham Lewis came to Paris, he also patronized Gypsy's. It's reported that Lewis particularly enjoyed the company of some of the bar girls, who tended to be less brassy than those in other clubs.

McAlmon notes that "one night Djuna Barnes and I were at the

Gypsy Bar [*sic*] when Sinclair Lewis barged in. He evidently had written a story about Hobohemia in which he feared Djuna would believe he had used her as one of the characters." Sinclair Lewis left without acknowledging either Barnes or McAlmon.

The journalist A. J. Liebling favored Gypsy's during his Sorbonne year, 1926–27. Here he met Angèle, a rather plain and stocky young Frenchwoman whose company he preferred to that of the British or American expatriates. Her friendly companionship, Liebling said, saved him "a debt the size of a small Latin American republic's in analyst's fees."

VAUGIRARD AND NORTH

RUE DE VAUGIRARD

1-bis and 3 • Trianon Palace Hôtel (as listed in twenties telephone books; today in operation as Trianon Hôtel at 1-bis)

Although not exactly plush, this hotel was somewhat more elegant than the Lisbonne across the way. When philosopher George Santayana visited Paris during the twenties, he usually stayed with his friend Professor Charles A. Strong at 9 avenue de l'Observatoire. At times, however, Santayana needed to get away from the Strong family, and he checked into the Trianon. (Prior to 1914, Santayana used a hotel near the place de la République.)

4 • Hôtel de Lisbonne (now Hôtel du Luxembourg)

According to William Shirer, a plaque once noted that Baudelaire and Verlaine had lived in this hotel, which at one time had buttresses jutting out onto the sidewalk. Apparently the plaque was not around long, for Waverley Root does not recall seeing it during his frequent visits to the hotel in the summer of 1927 and thereafter. Jacques Hillairet (*Dictionnaire Historique des Rues de Paris*) makes no mention of Baudelaire or Verlaine's ever having lived here.

In the winter of 1925–26, William Shirer moved from his pension on boulevard de Port-Royal to this hotel. Many of his colleagues from the Paris *Tribune* lived here, including sports editor Herol Egan and reporter-rewrite man Albert Wilson. The Lisbonne so impressed Ned

(Edgar) Calmer, Shirer's fellow *Tribune* reporter, that he set his 1961 novel, *All the Summer Days*, in this hotel.

At 250 francs ($10) a month, Shirer's room was spacious and well-lighted with tall, floor-to-ceiling windows. The room was nicely furnished with a large writing table, a bidet (which served Shirer as a bathtub), a wash basin, and a large double bed. The major inconvenience was the "Turkish" toilet, a set of raised footprints on either side of an open four-inch crater.

30 · Hôtel Savoy (now gone; area completely reconstructed)

Arriving in Paris on 16 June 1921, Aaron Copland checked into the Savoy for a week before enrolling in Walter Damrosch's American Conservatory of Music in Fontainebleau. Copland was the first student of the new conservatory, where Nadia Boulanger had been hired to teach.

Glenway Wescott, who by 1929 would achieve acclaim as a novelist and short-story writer, stayed in this hotel directly across from the Luxembourg Gardens during his February–March 1925 visit to Paris. Wescott was traveling with his friend Monroe Wheeler, who in 1920 had printed Wescott's first book, a collection of poems. Later, Wescott and Wheeler left the Savoy and moved to 218 boulevard Raspail.

32 · Ford Madox Ford's apartment (now gone; area reconstructed)

After leaving his Notre-Dame-des-Champs studio for the summer of 1928, Ford returned to Paris in October and took a seventh-floor apartment here in this "beautiful old house that the Senate in its madness is now [1933] pulling down." When Ford left Paris for six months in 1929, he turned over the apartment rent-free to writer Caroline Gordon, who'd once been his secretary, and her poet-husband, Allen Tate.

Ford notes that he took this apartment because "after I left Eton, I went to the Sorbonne [and became the friend of the professor who] lived in this particular flat." Passing by one day in 1928, Ford noticed that his old professor's apartment was vacant and, prompted by sentiment, he leased it and moved in. Ford, however, didn't attend

Eton nor, formally at least, the Sorbonne. Stella Bowen was now gone, and Ford's wife during the Vaugirard years was Janice Biala, a Polish-born painter.

A previous resident of number 32 was Dorothy Wilde, Oscar's wild niece. Although Dolly usually kept her tracks covered, she seems to have been in residence here sometime after her brief tenure at the Métropolitain Hôtel in May 1927. By April 1929, Dolly had moved to the Hôtel Montalembert (3 rue Montalembert), and yet again within the year to 1 rue Gît-le-Coeur.

58 • Apartment of Scott and Zelda Fitzgerald

Having arrived in France on 27 April 1928, by the second of May, Scott and Zelda had leased and moved into this large apartment, which has an elegant and spacious courtyard. Here, they were near the Paris residences of the Murphys on the quai des Grands-Augustins and the Hemingways on rue Férou, two blocks away. During this period, Zelda began her ballet lessons with Madame Egorova. Returning to America in October 1928, Scott and Zelda were back in Paris the following April, when they moved into an apartment on the rue Palatine.

Another resident at 58 Vaugirard was Canon Killian A. Stimpson, the inspiration and overseer of the American Students' and Artists' Club on boulevard Raspail.

60 • Post-1929 residence of Richard Le Gallienne

A journalist, poet, and editor, Le Gallienne was, in the words of his daughter, Eva, "a true lover of beautiful words . . . truly representative of the nineties." Eva's mother, Julie, was Richard's second wife. Around 1903 Julie and the four-year-old Eva left Richard and fled to Paris, moving into an apartment here at 60 Vaugirard. Later, mother and daughter moved to 1 rue de Fleurus.

In 1931 came a remarkable coincidence. Having become a celebrated actress, writer, and translator by then, Eva visited Paris and decided to look up her father, whom she hadn't known very well. She found him living at 60 rue de Vaugirard, the very building to which she and her mother had fled in 1903, when Eva was four years old.

Gwen Le Gallienne, an expatriate painter and something of a celebrity herself, was not related to Richard or Eva by blood. Gwen was the daughter by a previous marriage of Richard's third wife, Irma, and was thus Richard's stepdaughter.

89 • Residence of Richard and Irma Le Gallienne

There were so many Le Gallienne residences, not to mention Richard's rue Servandoni writing studio, that it's an irresistible challenge to keep track of them all. It shakes down this way:

1903: Leaving Richard in London, Julie (Richard's second wife) and Eva (his daughter) split for Paris, where they find an apartment at 60 rue de Vaugirard.

1925: A Mrs. Richard Le Gallienne is registered at the Hôtel du Quai Voltaire. This is most likely Irma, Richard's third wife and Gwen's mother.

1927: A Mr. and Mrs. Le Gallienne — probably Richard and Irma — are living here, at 89 rue de Vaugirard.

1929: Richard has moved to 60 rue de Vaugirard, where Eva is startled to find him (see above). Meanwhile, Irma Le Gallienne — Gwen's mother — has taken an apartment of her own at 29 quai de Bourbon. A short while later, Irma will move to yet another residence, 35 rue de Fleurus.

Throughout most of these moves, Richard has been writing a regular newspaper column in a garret-studio at 7 rue Servandoni.

RUE CASSETTE

10 • Grand Hôtel de Bretagne (now Hôtel de l'Abbaye)

When Malcolm and Peggy Cowley made their weekly visits to Paris from Giverny, some fifty miles south, they usually stayed at this secluded hotel. A writer, critic, inspiration, boon companion, and biographer of the age, Cowley spent much time in Paris, and his memoirs of those days — including *Exile's Return* and *A Second Flowering* — are treasures.

PLACE SAINT-SULPICE

7 · Chez Rieder (residence of Jean Prévost)

Jean Prévost helped his friend Adrienne Monnier edit her journal, *Navire d'Argent*. Between 1924 and 1928, Prévost had written three works, including one on sports (*Plaisirs des sports*, 1925) and a biography of Montaigne, one of Prévost's idols. A rugged young Norman, Prévost boxed with Hemingway during the summer of 1925 and through the following spring. Prévost was living here in 1927. Later, he moved to the avenue de Versailles in Passy.

RUE FEROU

6 · Residence of Ernest and Pauline Hemingway

After his divorce from Hadley in 1927, Ernest Hemingway married Pauline Pfeiffer, and the newlyweds were directed to this apartment near Saint-Sulpice by Archibald MacLeish. Since Ernest had abandoned journalism and had assigned the royalties from *The Sun Also Rises* to Hadley, he had virtually no income. So, after some strong hints from Pauline, her uncle offered to cover their initial rent.

These were unusually posh quarters for Ernest. Unlike the sawmill apartment or the flat above the *bal musette*, this house had a lovely garden courtyard that circled off the tiny, cobbled rue Férou. The apartments themselves included a large master bedroom, a splendid dining room with a superb kitchen, two bathrooms, a small study, a salon, and a spare room. With Pauline, Papa was in the chips.

Pauline's sister, Virginia ("Jinny"), used number 6 briefly as her own residence in 1927. Jinny may have stayed here during Ernest and Pauline's three-week honeymoon following their May 10 wedding. Or, Jinny may have lived here in July and August 1927 while Ernest and Pauline took in the bullfights in Spain. When Ernest and Pauline returned, Jinny moved to the Hôtel de Fleurus and, in 1930, on to the Hôtel Foyot.

Pauline persuaded Ernest to keep this apartment when they left Paris in 1928. After Patrick's birth, the Hemingways were back in Paris and living at 6 rue Férou when *A Farewell to Arms* was released in September 1929. By November, the novel led all bestsellers in America.

In January 1930, Ernest and Pauline were preparing to move to Key West, not suspecting that they wouldn't return to Paris for nearly four years. In parting, Ernest called Paris "a fine place to be quite young in." This was thus Ernest's last home in Paris. In the 1930s, he turned his attention to Florida, Cuba, Africa, the Civil War in Spain, and above all to his own image as "Papa."

RUE SERVANDONI

26 • William Faulkner's pension (now occupied by the Grand Hôtel des Principautés Unies)

William Faulkner sailed out of New Orleans on 7 July 1925 for Genoa, Italy. From there, he traveled by train to Paris and arrived August 13. After a two-hour search, he found a room in a hotel "near the Luxembourg gardens." He boasted that he was spending only 30 francs ($1.50) a day for full (three-meal) board and lodging. On August 18, he changed quarters, moving into a room on the top floor of this pension-hotel, his residence until he left for home on 9 December 1925. His expenses at this pension, he wrote, came to 20 francs ($1.00) per day, 11 (55¢) of which were for the room.

Faulkner spent most of his time exploring Paris and enjoying the Luxembourg Gardens, where he wrote and watched the children with their sailboats. On September 6, he wrote his mother that "I have come to think of the Luxembourg as my garden now. I sit and write there. . . ."

While in Europe Faulkner also toured the World War I battlefields and spent ten days hiking in England. When he returned to Paris from England on October 16, he found in his mail Boni and Liveright's official acceptance of his novel *Soldier's Pay*.

Later, Faulkner recalled that the letter of acceptance also contained a check for $200, which no one would cash. So, he took it to the British Consul, where he identified himself by displaying his British dogtags. (Faulkner had joined the RAF-Canada during World War I.) It did the trick, apparently, for the British Consul cashed the check with no hesitation.

During his four months in Paris, Faulkner visited Shakespeare and Company, but he didn't meet Sylvia Beach — or any other expatriates, for that matter. This would have been the tail end of Fitzgerald's "summer of a thousand parties and no work." A friend of Faulkner's recalls their seeing Ezra Pound, but Faulkner himself mentions only catching glimpses of James Joyce. Faulkner confessed that he made a habit of hanging out at a place de l'Odéon café (probably the Café Voltaire) that Joyce frequented — just to see the author of *Ulysses*. Like Hemingway, Faulkner was probably persuaded to visit Paris by Sherwood Anderson, whom he had known in New Orleans.

18 • Berenice Abbott's studio

Her reputation, if not her business, was growing dramatically by January 1928 when photographer Berenice Abbott moved from the rue du Bac into this slightly smaller studio. She unwittingly found herself in competition with Man Ray, with whom she had apprenticed. Their relationship worsened when they both showed works in the First Salon of Independent Photographers in April 1928.

"I was not in any way competing with Man Ray," Abbott recalls, "but the papers made out I was. . . ." And, heaven forbid, one reviewer blasted Ray while praising Abbott, who tried to play down the importance of the show by noting that "it was, in fact, a small show, simply hung down the staircase in a theater." Indeed, it was the Théâtre des Champs-Elysées, perhaps the most important in Paris. Abbott continued her work here in this studio until she returned to New York in 1929.

7 • The garret-studio of Richard Le Gallienne

Although he lived elsewhere, Le Gallienne wrote his weekly *New York Sun* column, "From a Paris Garret," in a tiny room seven flights above the street.

Le Gallienne once noted that he could look out his window and see number 12 on the courtyard entrance opposite. Discovering that Servandoni had once been called Fossoyeurs (gravediggers), he made the further discovery that number 12 once housed Monsieur d'Artagnan, whom Dumas had fictionalized in *The Three Musketeers*. In fact, as Le Gallienne found out, all of the actual Musketeers had lived in the area: Athos on rue Férou, Aramis on Vaugirard, and Porthos on Vieux-Colombier. Moreover, the house of the Captain-General of the Musketeers stood on the corner of Tournon and Vaugirard — in the very building occupied in the twenties by the popular Hôtel Foyot.

RUE PALATINE

6 • Residence of F. Scott and Zelda Fitzgerald

After Scott and Zelda Fitzgerald sailed to Europe in March 1929, they traveled from Genoa and arrived in Paris on April 1. Their residence during this visit is difficult to pin down because Fitzgerald was using the Guaranty Trust as his mailing address. According to one biographer, Scott and Zelda spent a few days in a rue du Bac hotel before moving to a flat on the rue de Mézières. A second biographer has them in "a large apartment in the rue Palatine," which is confirmed by Sylvia Beach who lists them here, at 6 rue Palatine. Thus, this was probably the model for Lincoln and Marion Peters's rue Palatine apartment in Fitzgerald's most famous story, "Babylon Revisited." In late June 1929, Scott and Zelda left for a summer in Cannes.

RUE SAINT-SULPICE

22 • Hôtel Riberia

Robert and Maeve Sage lived here from 30 September to the end of December 1927, when Robert was named assistant editor of *transition* and Maeve served as its secretary.

In addition to this residence, the Sages lived in several other places during the decade. From December 1925 to February 1926, they lived at 23 rue de Tournon. During this period Robert first began working as a reporter and book reviewer for the *Trib*. The Sages also lived at 20 rue Monsieur-le-Prince, 4 rue de Quatrefages, 16 ave. de Tourville, 11 rue Clauzel, and 43 ave. Paul-Doumer.

Among Sylvia Beach's undated materials is a scrap of paper listing "Mrs. ~~Robert~~ [*sic*] Maeve Sage" at the Hôtel du Dragon (36 rue du

Dragon). Besides dissociating Maeve from Robert, the note also mentions that Maeve is looking for work as a typist.

RUE DE TOURNON

33 · Hôtel Foyot (now the square Francis-Poulenc, an empty lot)

With a south entrance at 22-bis Vaugirard, the Hôtel Foyot and its celebrated restaurant figured frequently in the lives of the expatriates. The rooms at the Foyot were not too expensive, but the hotel's restaurant was fairly dear. The cuisine, however, drew raves from virtually everyone. Nina Hamnett put the matter directly: "Foyot's had probably the best food in Paris." Since the restaurant closed in 1938, we'll never know. Some of its tasty legacy lives on, however, in the exquisite "Sauce Foyot," an enriched Béarnaise sauce. (Blend a teaspoon of liquified *glace de viande* into a cup of Béarnaise.)

In 1922, Robert McAlmon shared his room at the Foyot for a while with Louis Aragon, until — as the story goes — McAlmon couldn't tolerate the chaotic young Dadaist any longer. While residing at the Foyot in 1923, McAlmon started the Contact Publishing Company. When the word got out, McAlmon received so many unsolicited manuscripts that he had to set up an editorial office in Bill Bird's Three Mountains Press shop on the Ile Saint-Louis.

In the spring of 1924, the poet H. D. (Hilda Doolittle) and Bryher — McAlmon's wife and H. D.'s lover — decided to visit Paris. Sylvia Beach reserved rooms for the two women at the Foyot so they would be near her bookstore. At the time, McAlmon himself was returning from the south of France. Keeping conveniently out of the way, McAlmon took a room at the Hôtel Unic, where he was joined by William Carlos and Florence ("Flossie") Williams.

In the autumn of 1924, after McAlmon had returned to the Foyot, he was persuaded to take Adrienne Monnier and Sylvia Beach to the Quatz'Arts Ball. By the time his companions got him back to the hotel after the ball, McAlmon was completely naked. Such was life at the Foyot.

The Czech-born, Austrian-educated poet Rainer Maria Rilke first went to Paris in 1902, having been commissioned to write a monograph on Rodin. Thereafter, he returned to Paris as frequently as possible. After a particularly long absence caused by the war, Rilke returned to Paris in late October 1920. "Just think, Lou," he wrote his oldest friend, *"I was there!* Six days . . . !"

Rilke had to leave, however, for reasons of his ill health and poor financial condition. When he returned in early January 1925, he began a visit that proved to be much more satisfying for him. Staying at the Foyot, Rilke was widely received by fellow writers, various intellectuals, friends, patrons, readers, and former (and current) lovers. Rilke left Paris on 18 August 1925. Fifteen months later he was dead.

When George Moore, the esteemed English writer (and intimate of the Cunards), came to Paris in the twenties, he tended to stay at either the Foyot or the Continental. The Foyot was also the residence from time to time of such expatriates as:

- Mary Butts, poet and novelist
- Tommy Earp, the English essayist who kept a permanent room here
- T. S. Eliot, the American poet who became a British citizen
- John Barrymore, the actor
- Virginia ("Jinny") Pfeiffer, the sister of Ernest Hemingway's second wife, Pauline
- French novelist Raymond Radiguet, Cocteau's protégé
- Dorothy Parker, the American writer and wit, who, according to McAlmon's recollection, stopped over in Paris a couple times on her way to the Murphys' summer home on the Riviera

18 • Trois et As (exact address unknown, but 18 fits all other descriptions of the bar and the site)

Connected with a small hotel, the Trois et As was opened by Madame Camille in 1927, and soon Jimmy Charters began tending bar there. The Trois et As (Trey and Ace) was his "most interesting" bar — or, "perhaps it was the most exciting, for something was always happening there."

Located some distance from the Dingo, Dôme, and Select, the Trois et As was not as packed or as frenzied as the Montparnasse hangouts. Its clients were mostly nontourist "regulars" and serious drinkers. Laurence Vail recalls (incorrectly, since the dates don't match up) that it was here that "Hemingway narrated his first bull and fish stories to the blond elf of Vassar — Edna Millay." At one time Nancy Cunard spoke to Jimmy the Barman about buying the Trois et As and running it as a semiprivate enterprise. Their plans went nowhere.

GERTRUDE STEIN'S NEIGHBORHOOD

RUE GUYNEMER

14 • Final Paris residence of Archibald and Ada MacLeish

After moving out of their rue du Bac apartment, which they'd renovated and sold, Archibald and Ada MacLeish and their children moved here in March 1928. March and April were supposedly their last two months in Paris. Curiously, however, Sylvia Beach's library records list Archibald at this address as late as November 1929.

Apparently Ernest and Pauline Hemingway had found this apartment for the MacLeishes. The brand-new building was located directly across from the Luxembourg Gardens and a little over two blocks from Ernest and Pauline's rue Férou residence. If the Hemingways did indeed find the flat for them, it was appropriate, for the previous year Archie and Ada had found the rue Férou quarters for the newlywed Hemingways.

RUE MADAME

58 • Residence of Michael and Sarah Stein (now the Reformed Church of France)

Prior to the twenties Michael, the eldest of the three Stein children, lived here, three and a half blocks from his sister and brother, Gertrude and Leo, who lived at 27 rue de Fleurus. Sarah, Michael's wife, claimed she — not Leo or Gertrude — was the true discoverer of Matisse's genius. She may have been right.

64 · 1929 residence of Bravig Imbs

In 1926, Bravig Imbs talked his way onto the staff of the Paris edition of the *Chicago Tribune* by claiming he'd been on the *Tribune* staff in Chicago. He also claimed that he was fluent in French. Both claims were patently false. When Imbs's lies were found out, he was fired. He was soon rehired, however, and assigned to the advertising department and to the proofroom.

Imbs had first taken a room in the Hôtel Regnard. Then, he moved into the Hôtel du Caveau, where another *Tribune* writer, Elliot Paul, was living. In 1928, when Imbs was traveling in Latvia, he met a young girl, Valeska, whom he brought back to Paris and married. Imbs and Valeska took an apartment here at 64 rue Madame. Later, they moved to Boulogne-sur-Seine outside Paris. And sometime before his death in an auto accident after World War II, Imbs had a residence at 131 rue de la Tour, near the Bois de Boulogne.

RUE DE FLEURUS

1 · Residence of Julie and Eva Le Gallienne

From the age of four, Eva Le Gallienne spent many of her childhood years in Paris, most of them at this address. Her mother, Julie, loved the theatre and no doubt sparked young Eva's interest by frequently taking her to the Comédie Française and the Odéon, as well as to the Parisian circuses (Médrano and d'Hiver).

5 · Hôtel de Fleurus (now gone)

Dorothy (Dolly) Wilde, Oscar Wilde's niece, gave this hotel as her address in 1920. Although it's not known how long Dolly lived in the Fleurus, she next showed up in the Hôtel du Quai Voltaire in 1925.

In 1928–29, during Allen Tate's Guggenheim year, the poet and his wife, Caroline Gordon — who was awarded a Guggenheim herself four years later — rented a suite of rooms at the Fleurus. Later, Tate and Gordon lived for six months at Ford Madox Ford's rue de Vaugirard apartment a few blocks away before moving to the Hôtel de l'Odéon.

27 · Residence of Gertrude and Leo Stein and Alice B. Toklas

In *Everybody's Autobiography* Gertrude Stein describes her arrival at number 27 in 1903: "Well anyway he [her brother Leo] was painting, he had taken the pavillion and atelier on the rue de Fleurus although he was not painting there, he was painting at the school and drawing from the model at the afternoon drawing class as a matter of fact and he never did paint at the rue de Fleurus atelier. I joined him and I sat down in there and pretty soon I was writing, and then he took a studio elsewhere and we lived together there until 1914."

Before World War I, Gertrude and Leo held "open" Saturday evening salons where nearly anyone who wished could show up to discuss art and literature, to look at the Steins' collection of Cubist and other Post-Impressionist paintings, and perhaps to meet some of the writers or painters under discussion. Following the war and after Leo had moved out, Gertrude and Alice continued the salons pretty much at irregular intervals, sometimes issuing invitations.

Most of the Americans who visited her had either obtained invitations or made appointments. Some, like Hemingway, carried letters of introduction; some, like Hart Crane, effectively invited themselves by means of a courteous letter or a reference to a mutual friend; others, like Scott Fitzgerald, were taken there by someone who had a more-or-less standing invitation. In any case, visiting 27 rue de Fleurus was a veritable pilgrimage made by nearly every American writer, composer, or painter who came to Paris in the twenties.

In 1921 Sylvia Beach brought Sherwood Anderson to meet Gertrude. Then, Kate Buss brought Alfred Kreymborg. A couple months later (summer 1921), Ezra Pound brought Scofield Thayer, when the editor of *The Dial* passed through Paris on his way to Vienna. In 1923 Mina Loy took Robert McAlmon to call on Gertrude and Alice. Jane Heap brought T. S. Eliot and his patron, Lady Rothemere, in November 1924. Ernest Hemingway brought F. Scott Fitzgerald in the summer of 1925. Thus passed the parade.

35 · Hadley Hemingway's apartment

Three doors down from Gertrude Stein's residence, Hadley Hemingway took an apartment in 1926, after she and Ernest had separated. Their son, Bumby, stayed with his mother, although

Ernest came by periodically to take him for walks. Later, Hadley moved to an apartment on the boulevard Auguste-Blanqui in the Thirteenth Arrondissement.

In 1929, the third Mrs. Richard Le Gallienne, Irma, rented an apartment in this building.

Number unknown • Residence of Elmer Rice

When the playwright Elmer Rice and his family came to Paris in 1925, they lived on rue de Fleurus "practically next door to Gertrude Stein," though they didn't know it at the time. The Rices later moved to the rue Bonaparte.

BOULEVARD RASPAIL

107 • United States Students' and Artists' Club

A kind of social hall, the American Students' Club — as it was popularly known — opened around 1920 at 261 blvd. Raspail. Then, under an expanded name, it moved here to number 107, where it was in operation by 1924.

The U.S. Students' and Artists' Club provided a place for Americans and others to congregate. One could play cards or table tennis here, attend French classes in the evenings, or spar with a boxing partner. It also contained a small dance hall, which gave young women a safe place to meet respectable escorts. Or so, at least, their parents believed.

Canon Killian Stimpson was called "The Angel of the Students' and Artists' Club" by its patrons, one of whom noted that Canon Stimpson helped feed "many a starving would-be artist."

RUE D'ASSAS

60 • Anaïs Nin's first pension (completely new building now)

Shortly after their marriage, Anaïs Nin and Hugh Parker Guiler decided to leave the United States and move to Paris. Having been born in Neuilly, Anaïs had been carted from country to country as a child. The move posed no problem for Guiler either, since he worked for the National City Bank, which had an office in Paris. They arrived in Paris shortly before Christmas 1924 and took a room in an unnamed Left Bank hotel, which was filled with Americans. On 3 January 1925 they rented a small room (number 27) in this pension and stayed a month before moving to the avenue Hoche.

78 • Apartment of Jean Schlumberger

The French novelist and one of the founders of the *Nouvelle Revue Française*, Schlumberger had moved into this apartment by May 1928 — and he was still living here in 1954. Along with André Gide and others, Schlumberger was a loyal friend and longtime supporter of Adrienne Monnier and Sylvia Beach.

84 • George Biddle's studio (84 no longer exists)

Philadelphia painter George Biddle, who had studied at the Julian Academy in 1911, returned to Paris in 1922 to stay for a few years. Biddle tells of a spring evening in 1923 when he was at the Dôme with Moïse Kisling, Jules Pascin, and others. A critic who disapproved of Kisling's work approached the group and "delivered a short and angry harangue and hurled [a] missile . . . at Kisling's head. It was horse manure."

"During the winter of 1924," Biddle further recalls, "I gave a party in my studio at 84 rue d'Assas. Chagall was there," he notes, mentioning several other artists, including Fernand Léger. Also there was an old friend, Louis Ritman, who'd brought Chaim Soutine as his guest. Soutine, people noticed, was unusually surly and obnoxious. And, suddenly, the normally friendly Léger left in a snit. That was when Biddle discovered "Soutine was furious because Léger had been invited," and Léger had huffed off when he spotted Soutine at the party. Artists storm and sulk. Critics sling manure.

In 1930, Louise Bryant moved into an apartment here, while back in Philadelphia her husband, William Bullitt, was secretly pursuing a divorce. During 1923–25, the Bullitts had been close friends of Biddle's, which is no doubt how Louise learned of a vacancy in this building.

90 • Residence of Marjorie Reid

As Ford Madox Ford's assistant at the *Transatlantic Review*, Marjorie Reid wrote occasional book reviews and bits of filler. In her assessment of Hemingway's first little volume of sketches, *in our time*, Reid insightfully notes that each of the pieces is "much longer than the measure of its lines." In a filler piece on "Paris Fashions," Reid observes sarcastically that Robert McAlmon "has just arrived with a hibred [*sic*] hat . . . designed along the lines of the cap of [M]ercury and carried out in brown felt."

Sylvia Beach has other addresses as well for Reid: 80 rue Lauriston, for the date of December 17 (no year given); and 41 rue Monsieur-le-Prince, with the marginal note "after January 20" but again without specifying the year.

100-bis • Residence of sculptor Ossip Zadkine (now a museum)

Zadkine, born in Russia in 1909, moved to Paris when he was nineteen. He lived here from 1928 until his death in 1967.

RUE JOSEPH-BARA

3 • Residence of Moïse Kisling

Born in Krakow (Poland), Kisling moved to Paris in 1910, when he was nineteen years old. After living on the rue des Beaux-Arts, Kisling moved to Montmartre — to the Bateau Lavoir, made famous by Picasso. In 1913, as his skill as a painter and sculptor was beginning to win acclaim, Kisling rented a working studio in Montparnasse, here at 3 Joseph-Bara, and a short while later he moved his residence here as well. Although he spent much time in the south of France during the twenties, Kisling kept this apartment. (His first son was born in Paris in 1922.) After his self-exile during World War II, Kisling returned to Paris and found his apartment plundered.

14

PLACE DE LA CONTRESCARPE AND THE OUTER FIFTH ARRONDISSEMENT

PLACE DU PANTHEON

15-bis • Residence of Robert W. Service

Robert W. Service considered himself a versifier, reserving the title "poet" for a man like his Paris friend James Stephens, the Irish writer: "So, we pounded along, [with careers] parallel to each other, a poet [Stephens] and a rhymster [Service]." By the end of the war, however, Service's verses were far more famous than Stephens's poetry. The Canadian rhymster's first book of Yukon ballads, which contained his extraordinarily popular pieces "The Shooting of Dan McGrew" and "The Cremation of Sam McGee," was published in 1907 and had gone through thirty-six printings within a decade.

Service married a Frenchwoman in Paris in 1913, and after the war in 1919, they moved to this "magnificent residence on the Place du Panthéon. . . . There were two floors, the upper one had a huge studio giving on a terrace that overlooked the roof of the Panthéon." Robert and Germaine Service kept the apartment until they left Paris in 1929. Service once reflected that all together "for fifteen years Paris was to be my only love."

6 • Residence of the Dudley sisters

Caroline, Katherine, and Dorothy Dudley were living here in 1925 when Caroline brought the first black stage show ("La Revue Nègre") to Paris. The sisters, John Dos Passos notes, created a style of living based on their familiarity with French novels and Impressionist paintings. "Life," Dos wrote, "must be a déjeuner sur l'herbe [for the sisters]. . . . They carried this special style into their conversation and their cookery and their whole way of living."

RUE DESCARTES

39 • Hemingway's early writing room

In 1922, Hemingway rented a room on the top floor of this former hotel to write in, claiming that it was the same room in which the poet Paul Verlaine had died in 1896.

RUE DU CARDINAL-LEMOINE

71 • The apartment of Valéry Larbaud

Since he was to be out of town from June to October 1921, the French literary critic Valéry Larbaud turned over his third-floor flat to James Joyce, who was finishing *Ulysses* at the time. To get to Larbaud's back apartment one passed through a massive iron gate and traveled down a long gravel driveway. The key to the huge gate was enormous — "about a foot long," according to Robert McAlmon, who frequently found himself escorting the tipsy Joyce home. Three months after Joyce moved out, the Hemingways moved into their apartment up the street.

74 • The first apartment of Ernest and Hadley Hemingway

Shortly after their arrival in Paris, Ernest and Hadley — who had been married four months — moved from the Hôtel Jacob into a tiny, fourth-floor apartment here on 9 January 1922. Directly across from their building stood a handy Bois-Charbon-Vin shop. Around the corner on the place de la Contrescarpe was the Café des Amateurs, which Ernest called "the cesspool of the rue Mouffetard." In other words, this was your basic Tough Working-Class Neighborhood, "Apache" territory. Nevertheless, in a letter to a friend from his ambulance-driving days, Hemingway boasted that the apartment was in "the best part of the Latin Quarter."

The stairway of number 74 was damp and dark, with a rancid-smelling toilet closet (*pissoir*) for men on each landing. The Hemingways had no running water, and their bed was a mattress on the floor. After living here a year and a half, Ernest and Hadley left in August 1923 to return to Toronto so their baby would have a North American birth and, hence, citizenship.

Next to 74 • A *bal musette* (at one time in the twenties called "Bal du Printemps"; became a disco, an art kino, etc.)

The designation *"bal musette"* refers to bars with a dance floor and some kind of music. This *bal musette*, which angled back from number 74 in the general direction of the place de la Contrescarpe, sat directly beneath Ernest and Hadley's windows. Besides being mentioned in *A Moveable Feast*, it's probably the prototype of the *bal* where Jake Barnes meets Lady Brett at the opening of Hemingway's *The Sun Also Rises*. Ford Madox Ford liked to rent the *bal* for his parties, which had grown too large and unmanageable for his boulevard Arago cottage. The music here was provided by its accordion-playing owner, who dangled a half-smoked cigarette from his lower lip as he sat in a sort of pulpit above the dance floor. Less dancing went on here, according to reports, than shuffling and jostling and groping.

RUE AMYOT

8-bis • The Hébuterne family residence

In January 1920, after learning of the death of her lover, the painter Amedeo Modigliani, Jeanne Hébuterne went to see the body of the man for whom she had modeled for over two years. It was a particularly grim occasion, for not only was Jeanne nearly nine months pregnant with Modi's child, but also Moïse Kisling's death mask had pulled bits of skin from the dead artist's face. Despondent and hysterical, Jeanne raced back here to her family's apartments.

Knowing her to be distraught, Jeanne's father assigned her brothers to keep watch on her. On the top floor of the building, above the fourth-floor living quarters, a small, balconied bedroom fronted the quiet, narrow street. When her brother dozed off, Jeanne threw herself over the thigh-high iron railing — backward, so as not to see the street below. Her death was immediate, although Jeanne's mother was first told that Jeanne had only been injured.

The family, having been embarrassed by Jeanne's unconventional conduct in life and now by her suicide, insisted that her body be removed from the family residence. The corpse was initially taken to 8 rue de la Grande-Chaumière, where during happier times Jeanne and Modi had lived together. Eventually, the family consented to her body's being placed beside Modi's in the Père Lachaise cemetery.

RUE LARREY

11 · Marcel Duchamp's studio

Duchamp first received acclaim in the United States at the 1913 Armory Show in New York, where his controversial *Nude Descending a Staircase* (1912) was exhibited. One of the promoters of Dada, in 1919 Duchamp exhibited a reproduction of the Mona Lisa on which were drawn a fake mustache and beard. He'd titled it with the letters LHOOQ, which when pronounced in French, form an obscene pun: *"Elle a chaud au cul"* ("She's got a hot ass".)

After 1923, Duchamp kept a small, one-room studio at this address, while he lived at the Hôtel Istria, where Man Ray and Kiki were then residing.

On 8 June 1927 Duchamp married the daughter of a well-known French automobile tycoon. Duchamp must have been playing some kind of absurd Dada joke, for he and his wife hardly knew each other. They lived together only a week, and the marriage itself lasted no more than a few months. The fact is, after 1923 Duchamp spent most of his time with Mary Reynolds, an American widow who had settled in Paris in 1920.

RUE DE QUATREFAGES

8 · Pension of Janet Flanner and Solita Solano

When they first arrived in Paris in 1922, Flanner and Solano took rooms here. Neighborhood noise, however, made the residence unsuitable for these two women who were determined to make it as writers. Not only were they bothered by "a diligent piano student down the hall" (Solano's words), but also they had to cope with the noise caused by the construction of the Arab mosque a quarter of a block south. So, Flanner and Solano soon moved to a tiny hotel on the rue Bonaparte, where they lived — as successful writers — for the next nineteen years.

RUE GEOFFROY-SAINT-HILAIRE

51 • The 1930 residence of Ludmilla Bloch-Savitsky

Principally an essayist, Ludmilla Bloch-Savitsky brought out a translation of James Joyce's *Portrait of the Artist as a Young Man* in March 1924. Savitsky and her husband provided the Joyces a rent-free apartment on the rue de l'Assomption shortly after they arrived in Paris in 1920. Savitsky had also lived at 22 rue de Boulainvilliers — around the corner from the Assomption flat.

RUE BERTHOLLET

3 • Residence of Harold J. Salemson

Salemson was the editor of a little bilingual journal, *Tambour*, which appeared irregularly in 1929 and 1930. An opponent of *transition*, which he thought to be full of psychoanalytical babble, Salemson was derided for his "lurid and distorted" (according to Robert Sage) pieces on Americans in Paris.

RUE D'ULM

45 • Ecole Normale Supérieure

In 1928, Samuel Beckett received a two-year appointment to teach at the Ecole Normale Supérieure. Such a position traditionally included meals and living quarters. The rooms normally reserved for the *lecteur* in English, however, were still occupied by Beckett's predecessor, Thomas McGreevy. Hearing of the difficulty, James Joyce interceded for the young Irish teacher and McGreevy graciously moved his things into smaller quarters upstairs. Shortly thereafter, as Beckett's own writing career was about to take off, Joyce's daughter,

Lucia, fell madly and unilaterally in love with Beckett, who by then was serving as Joyce's unpaid secretary and gofer.

RUE SAINT-JACQUES

269 • Thornton Wilder's pension (now the Franco-Vietnam Institute)

After a few days residing in what was probably the Hôtel du Maroc in June 1921, Thornton Wilder moved to this somewhat remote pension, where he remained the rest of the summer. Since he'd not yet published any of the plays or novels that would eventually make him famous, Wilder used a letter of introduction from Stephen Vincent Benét to meet his fellow expatriates.

When he came back to Paris late in 1926, Wilder stayed briefly in a room above the Closerie des Lilas before returning to his old lodgings here on the rue Saint-Jacques. At this pension he wrote much of his prize-winning novel, *The Bridge at San Luis Rey*, which was published shortly after his return to New York at the end of January 1927.

RUE DU VAL-DE-GRACE

8 • Man Ray's residence and studio

By 1929 Ray had become a major celebrity, and his photographs were in great demand. He needed more space — and, no doubt, he needed as well to get away from the throngs of American tourists around the Dôme and the Jockey. So, Ray leased one section of this out-of-the-way new building for his atelier and another suite of rooms for his residence.

Everyone, it seems, wanted a portrait by Ray, even though he seldom did such work. He was more interested in the nonconventional possibilities of photography. So, he continued to experiment with his Rayographs, his Dada material, and his innovative motion pictures.

6 • Residence of Hilaire Hiler

This multitalented man, whose real name (Hiler Harzberg) was known by very few, was the friend of nearly everyone. Robert

McAlmon described Hiler this way: "He looks rather like a handsome frog: dark and sorrowful . . . , wearing often a lugubrious expression which instantly suggests comedy and clowning. . . . He sings and plays the piano. . . . He knows Yiddish recitations, and his burlesques of every type of dance would ensure him a success . . . on the stage in any country. . . .

"Hiler is not only a serious painter but a good one," McAlmon continued. And, "after writing a scholarly book on the history of raiment [Hiler had a vast library on costume and attire], he . . . was soon doing research for a book on the medium of paint."

In the twenties Hiler was also in demand as a decorator — since he'd been so successful in transforming the Jockey Club and the College Inn.

RUE HENRI-BARBUSSE (WAS RUE DENFERT-ROCHEREAU)

16 · Ford Madox Ford's flat

Stella Bowen still with him, Ford left the cottage on the boulevard Arago and bought a flat here, where he and Stella were in residence by 1 January 1925. Working steadily on his novels by then, Ford found that he could not write in Paris, so he maintained a small studio at Guermantes-près-Lagny, a tiny village of eight small residences.

When he gave up this Henri-Barbusse flat in 1926, Ford began traveling in earnest. In February 1928, after he and Stella had separated, Ford returned to Paris and rented a studio on the rue Notre-Dame-des-Champs.

BOULEVARD SAINT-MICHEL

85 · Home of Lewis and Dorothy Galantière

Lewis and Dorothy were popular figures among the various expatriates. Around 1924 they lived on the Ile Saint-Louis "in the shadow of Notre Dame cathedral," according to their old friend Burton Rascoe, the literary critic and editor. They also lived for a while at 5-bis rue Joseph-Bara. By 1926 or 1927, however, they were in residence here, at 85 boulevard Saint-Michel, where they remained for the rest of the decade.

When Ernest and Hadley Hemingway arrived in Paris in December 1921, they found an invitation to dine at Michaud's with the Galantières, fellow Chicagoans to whom Sherwood Anderson had written introducing Ernest and Hadley. A week or so later, Lewis helped Hem find a flat on the rue du Cardinal-Lemoine. Thus the Galantières were Ernest and Hadley's first friends in the city.

86 · Residence of Archibald and Ada MacLeish

MacLeish's *Letters* indicate that in September 1923, Archie, Ada, and their children had settled in a rue Las-Cases apartment and were preparing to enroll their six-year-old son, Kenny, in the Ecole Alsacienne on the rue d'Assas. There is no mention of any subsequent move in the letters, until the MacLeishes take up residence in Granville on the Normandy coast in June 1924. However, in his "Autobiographical Notes," MacLeish says that they spent their first winter and the following spring here, at 86 boulevard Saint-Michel in "a flat . . . four floors up, stairs only and no heat. . . ."

It's reasonable to conclude that the MacLeishes moved from their Las-Cases apartment to this address, which would have put them only two blocks away from Kenny's school. Moreover, they — particularly Ada — regarded the Las-Cases apartment as being dirty and very small. And, finally, Archibald's letter of 12 November 1923 speaks of enjoying the Luxembourg Gardens, which would have been a considerable distance from the Las-Cases residence but virtually adjacent to the boulevard Saint-Michel address.

Confirming these conclusions is Sylvia Beach's handwritten library card, which lists the MacLeishes as living on the boulevard Saint-Michel on 11 October 1923. Sylvia's scribble, alas, puts them at *85*, not 86.

Wherever they were living during these first months, the Mac-Leishes enjoyed considerable success — especially Ada, whose singing was praised and, better yet, *promoted* by Nadia Boulanger, the famous teacher of Copland, Thomson, and Les Six. In February 1924, Ada was invited to give a concert of Copland material in the Salle Pleyel.

Nevertheless, the MacLeishes left Paris that summer and moved to Normandy. They were lured back to the city in the autumn of 1926 when Pierpont Morgan Hamilton invited them to use his mansion in Passy.

145 · Chez Emile (now gone)

This café, next to the Bal Bullier, was one of Ezra Pound's favorites. Emile himself was a picturesque Alsatian who wore white twill clothes and a tall chef's hat. In the early twenties Pound, Ford Madox Ford, Pierre Loving, and Sisley Huddleston frequently got together in Emile's upper room where they heatedly discussed art, literature, and Ezra's odd (and perhaps not yet entirely odious) theories about international politics and economics.

MONTPARNASSE: THE HEART

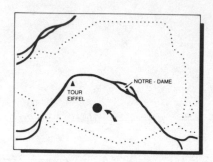

MAP 5

includes addresses from ...

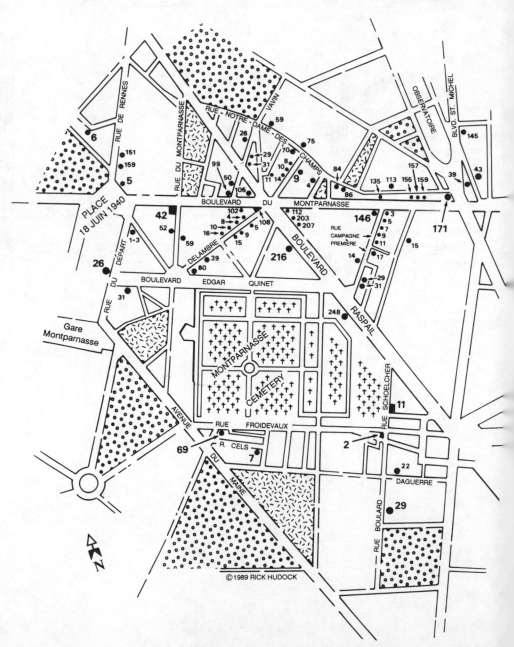

©1989 RICK HUDOCK

15

THE PRIMARY CHAMBER

RUE VAVIN

50 · Hôtel de Blois

For his 1921 book, *Civilization in the United States*, Harold Stearns compiled the opinions of some of America's foremost intellectuals. This collection of cultural criticism established Stearns's reputation as a spokesman for the American expatriates, since he himself emigrated that July — immediately after submitting his manuscript to his publisher.

Meeting Sinclair Lewis in England, Stearns accompanied the novelist to Paris in August 1921. When Lewis returned to England three days later, Stearns moved to Montparnasse, reportedly to a hotel on the rue Delambre. He's listed here on Vavin, however, in Zelda Fitzgerald's address book (ca. 1926–27) and in other contemporary recollections. Sylvia Beach has an early address for him on the rue Jules-Chaplain as well.

In 1925, Stearns was serving as the Paris representative of the publisher Horace Liveright and writing for various newspapers, frequently as a racing tout. His "Peter Pickem" column for the Paris edition of the *Chicago Tribune* from 1925 to 1930 was exceptionally popular.

The café life of Paris seemed to feed Stearns's cynicism and to destroy his reputation, not to mention his health. Hemingway's portrait of him as Harvey Stone in *The Sun Also Rises* is apparently fairly accurate, if somewhat extreme. Most observers agree that despite the best efforts of his long string of mistresses, including the attractive, gracious, and wealthy American divorcée Josephine Bennett, Stearns became an unproductive, bitter man in Paris. Apparently Stearns himself knew what was happening to him. Looking back upon his Paris years, which concluded when he left in the summer of 1929, Stearns said, "It was a useless, silly life . . . and I have missed it every day since."

En route to the south of France in 1922, Ford Madox Ford stopped over in Paris from mid-November to mid-December and stayed here, at the Hôtel de Blois on rue Vavin. In September 1923, Ford came back to Paris, this time moving in with his brother on the boulevard Arago.

Another occasional resident of the Hôtel de Blois was the self-proclaimed diabolist, Aleister Crowley, who sometimes referred to himself as "The Beast 666." Crowley, whose real name was Edward Alexander Crowley, spent considerable time at his temple in Cefalu in Sicily, where he reputedly practiced black magic.

Crowley once suggested to Man Ray that Ray require his customers to have their astrological charts done by Crowley so Ray could photograph them "properly." In return, Crowley would tell those who came to him for chart readings that they had to be photographed by Ray first. Ray, no fool, chose not to align himself with Crowley.

Some expatriates found Crowley difficult. One night, for example, Crowley was teased into taking a celebrated Montparnasse model to dinner to "find out what she's really like." The next morning Crowley grumbled that it was "rather like waving a flag in space" — which may say more about Crowley's anatomy than the model's.

Most likely Crowley exaggerated his diabolical nature for effect. Stories about him made hot newscopy. In February 1922, for instance, the *London Sunday Express* reported an incident that presumably took place at Cefalu. The story carried this disclaimer: "The facts are too unutterably filthy to be detailed in a newspaper, for they have to do with sexual orgies that touch the lowest depths of depravity." Now, if that don't fetch 'em, as the King told Huck, I don't know Arkansaw.

Crowley, it must be admitted, deliberately contributed to this image in his 1922 book, *The Diary of a Drug Fiend.* Most people who didn't know Crowley assumed this highly imaginative work of fiction to be literal fact.

Crowley's eccentricities amused many of the expatriates, however, and several of them, notably Mary Butts, visited him at Cefalu. Among those his diabolism did not amuse were the French police. On 17 April 1929, they gave the fifty-four-year-old Crowley forty-eight hours to leave the country for holding a black mass. "It did not help his case," the *Tribune* reported, "that he is alleged to have been a spy for Germany in the United States during the war." In any case, his biography makes a sad, eerie tale.

BOULEVARD DU MONTPARNASSE

Near the intersection with the boulevard Raspail, at the Vavin Métro station, are four cafés: the Dôme, Rotonde, Select, and Coupole. Veritable expatriate "institutions," the cafés served as assembly points for parties; de facto bulletin boards, where one could learn of cheap hotels; literary agencies, where editors could search for contributors; and, often, informal banks, where one might obtain a loan for a few days "until the mail boat arrived."

Each of the four cafés had its own identity and clientele. One expatriate observed that "it is easier to change one's mind than to change one's café." Americans, for example, seemed to prefer the Dôme over the Rotonde. An explanation, perhaps apocryphal, holds that one morning in 1922 the Rotonde's owner spotted a young American woman — hatless and smoking! — on the *terrasse*. When he insisted that she sit at a table inside, where her "looseness" wouldn't be so conspicuous, she stormed across the street to the more tolerant Café du Dôme, effectively taking the English and American trade with her.

99 • Le Select

The Select opened in 1925, before which an old furniture shop had been located at number 99. Part of the attraction of the Select, no doubt, was the fact that it was open all night. Monsieur Select wore "long melancholy moustaches like Flaubert," and he tended to stay at the tiny stove behind the bar cooking Welsh rarebits. The volatile Madame Select was an imposing figure, with sternly arched eyebrows, high color, and heavy bosom. She wore little fingerless gloves to keep her hands warm without restricting her facility for counting coins.

Madame Select was the one who ordered Hart Crane's arrest in July 1929, for brawling — or refusing to pay his bill (accounts differ). By 1929 Americans had become less popular than they were immediately after the war, as was indicated by the Paris cops' brutal treatment of Crane. After beating him severely and dragging him facedown over the cobblestones of boulevard du Montparnasse, they dumped Crane in La Santé slammer.

102 • La Coupole (recently remodeled)

Located just down from the Dôme, in what had once been an old coal and wood yard, this large café opened on 20 December 1927, with Josephine Baker and other celebrities in attendance. Street gossip holds that this date was chosen deliberately because "*le vingt dissipe la tristesse.*" ("The twentieth drives away sorrow" — *vingt* is pronounced like *vin*, "wine," making the pun.) Aiming to attract tourists, the good-natured barman and part owner, Gaston, arranged for tour buses to include the Coupole in their itineraries. "Without his [Gaston's] handsome presence, his quiet generosity to artists, his beguiling smile, and his white-lipped fury for any kind of violence," Kay Boyle noted, "the Coupole would have been a quite undistinguished place."

Besides its facade of neon lights, the Coupole boasted two magnificent pillars, one designed by Moïse Kisling and the other by Fernand Léger. The café soon caught on with the Americans. When Robert McAlmon prepared to leave Paris in 1929, he didn't get a chance to say goodbye to Kay Boyle. Knowing that sooner or later she'd appear at the Coupole, he left her a farewell note there, telling her among other things where she could pick up his trusty, "fairly new" Remington portable typewriter. The Coupole, like the other cafés, was more than a place to have a drink.

105 • Café de la Rotonde

Describing what this café was like between its founding in 1911 and World War I, one early patron noted: "The Rotonde was then a small zinc bar, a long narrow room with a terrace, where we drank our grog *Américain* in the coldest weather, warming ourselves at great porcelain stoves. [We] were its first artist patrons. . . . " In 1924, the Rotonde expanded by annexing what had been the Café du Parnasse at number 103. At the height of its operation, the Rotonde was a café, grill room, gallery, dance hall, card room, and *boîte de nuit* — all rolled into one.

Directly across from the Dôme, the Rotonde was a favorite hangout for expatriate Mensheviks and Bolsheviks, before, during, and after the 1917 revolution. To cultivate its appeal, the proprietors kept racks of Eastern European newspapers for its customers. Eventually, the Rotonde became the center for those caught up in the "Baltic fad," eager for Greek liqueur, Turkish coffee, and colorful Serbian costume.

Hemingway hated the Rotonde, claiming that "on entering you get the same feeling as when entering the bird house of the zoo." His contempt showed during his very first months, in a piece he wrote for a Toronto paper: "The scum of Greenwich Village, New York, has been skimmed off and deposited in large ladlesful on that section of Paris adjacent to the Café Rotonde. New scum, of course, has risen to take the place of the old, but the oldest scum, the thickest scum and the scummiest scum has come across the ocean, somehow, and . . . has made the Rotonde the leading Latin Quarter show place for tourists in search of atmosphere."

The Rotonde had at least one attractive feature: an upstairs banquet room. One Christmas Nancy Cunard threw a dinner party for George Moore, seating him "at the top of a long, narrow table of twelve . . . in the room upstairs at the Rotonde." Everyone except Brancusi (and, of course, Moore himself) was quite young, Cunard notes proudly: the nieces of Max Beerbohm and Oscar Wilde, Tristan Tzara, Eugene McCown, Iris Tree, Clotilde Vail.

In 1921 the back room, "where [all-night poker games] used to be played," according to Malcolm Cowley, "was then furnished, or upholstered, with four dispirited prostitutes who never seemed to have any clients. . . ."

The manager of the Rotonde was widely suspected of being a *mouchard* — a stool pigeon. According to rumor, he had turned in several of the Marxist revolutionaries who frequented the Rotonde. On Bastille Day (July 14) 1923, a group of American and French writers and artists barged into the café, and in the heat of the "invasion," Malcolm Cowley slugged the proprietor. Collared by a celebrating and somewhat inebriated policeman, Cowley was immediately surrounded by dozens of his compatriots — all of whom emphatically testified to Cowley's innocence. Thereafter, Cowley was something of a local hero for punching the *mouchard*.

108 · Café du Dôme

Located on the southwest corner of the Montparnasse-Raspail intersection, the Dôme is the oldest and most famous of the Montparnasse cafés. Prior to the end of World War I it was a rundown joint, small and ugly. A corner *bistro*, principally for working men in 1922, the Dôme had only modest space inside with a rough green billiard table — and no terrace tables.

During the years before the Great War, the Dôme was frequented on occasion by Lenin, Trotsky, and other revolutionaries. Later, the Marxists took their custom to the Rotonde, when the Americans and British co-opted the Dôme. The modernization of the Dôme in 1923 quadrupled its size by adding rows and rows of tables inside and out. It became *the* place for an expatriate writer or artist to be — and to be seen.

Although Ernest and Hadley Hemingway frequented the Dôme during their first months in Paris, Hemingway soon was berating the Americans who flocked there. "They are nearly all loafers expending the energy that an artist puts into his creative work in talking about what they are going to do . . . ," he wrote in a piece for the *Toronto Star Weekly*.

During the summer and fall of 1923, Sinclair Lewis visited these cafés and encountered considerable hostility, some of it no doubt deserved. One evening, for example, when Lewis was quite drunk, he announced loudly to the patrons of the Dôme that he could construct characters better than Flaubert. When he added that he was a better stylist than Flaubert too, someone shouted, "Sit down, you're just a best seller!" Used to respect, if not downright adulation, Lewis was devastated. When he came back to Paris in 1924, he avoided "the pro-Joyce crowd at the Dôme." And, in his 1925 *American Mercury* article, "Self-Conscious America," Lewis sneered at "the geniuses and their disciples who frequent the Cafe du Dôme at Montparnasse." Inexplicably, in his Nobel Prize acceptance speech on 12 December

1930, Lewis praised the writing being done by the expatriates in Paris.

RUE DELAMBRE

4 · At the Sign of the Black Manikin (Edward Titus's bookshop)

Separated from — but nonetheless on mutually agreeable terms with — his wealthy wife, Helena Rubinstein (of cosmetics fame), Edward Titus ran a small, elegant bookstore in his residence here. Established in 1924, his operation was less a shop than a rare-book library and gallery. Titus also collected Americana, including a letter by George Washington commissioning some false-teeth repair, a first edition of Whitman's *Leaves of Grass*, and an account of one of John Paul Jones's exploits, with marginal annotations by the admiral himself.

In 1926, Titus began the Black Manikin series of books pressed by the Crete printery, up the street at 24 rue Delambre. Among the important and experimental works issued by the Black Manikin Press were D. H. Lawrence's *Lady Chatterly's Lover* (1928), Djuna Barnes's satiric *Ladies Almanack by a Lady of Fashion* (1928), and Samuel Putnam's English translation of *Kiki's Memoirs* (1930). The press closed in 1932.

In 1929 Titus took up the editorship of Ethel Moorhead's little magazine, *This Quarter*, after its inspiration and original editor, Ernest Walsh, had died. More conservative than either Walsh or Moorhead, Titus put out a cautious magazine that soon lost its fire, its uniqueness, and its audience.

5 · Studio of Tsugouharu Foujita

The first major Japanese painter in Montparnasse, Foujita was beloved by the Montparnos, especially the Dadaists. He came to Paris in 1913 to study at the Ecole des Beaux Arts and quickly established himself as an important painter. After marrying Fernande Barrey, Foujita moved into her residence here on the rue Delambre. (Later, he married the young model Youki.)

Near-sighted and by nature quiet, Foujita appeared somber and serious, but his high-pitched laugh — when he could not hold it in — bubbled contagiously. When Kiki, the celebrated Montparnasse model, first went to pose for Foujita, she entered number 5 naked beneath a coat, "wanting to provoke, without any hindthought, the giggly laughter of this son of a Samurai." (Foujita was actually the son of a major in the Japanese army.) Dropping the coat, Kiki got the laugh she was after by explaining to the surprised painter that she came this way "to avoid the awkwardness of undressing in front of someone with whom she'd never made love." Kiki's sessions posing nude in the courtyard at number 5 understandably caused some consternation among the neighbors. Not much, though.

8 · Apartment of Samuel Putnam and his wife

Living "for one hectic season [1930] practically above Lou Wilson's Dingo bar," Putnam served as associate editor of *This Quarter* with Titus for a while, before launching a little magazine of his own in 1931 (*New Review*). Thomas Wolfe visited the Putnams here, and they threw "at least one typically Montparnasse vodka party" for playwright Elmer Rice in this apartment.

9 · Studio-Apartment Hôtel

Across from the Dingo Bar, this apartment complex contained forty split-level suites with a studio and bath on one level and, a flight above, a bedroom and overlooking balcony. Built in 1926, this hotel stood where Pizzuti's popular Italian restaurant had been. The official rates were about $5 a day, although under certain conditions apartments could be had for $100 per month.

When Isadora Duncan returned from Nice in early 1927, she'd resolved never to return to the Hôtel Lutetia, whose management had offended her. So, she took a lease on one of the suites in the new Studio-Apartment Hôtel.

Isadora's life was unraveling. Sergei Esenin, the young "peasant poet" she'd married in Moscow in 1922, had hanged himself in 1925 (in the very room, supposedly, where they'd honeymooned), and Isadora was virtually broke. Her most recent concert at the Mogador Théâtre was a financial disaster.

The brilliant Russian pianist Victor Seroff, her companion at this time, was her primary consolation — he and her undying popularity. Tourists and sightseers flocked to her hotel, and Isadora received them graciously. She used what few funds she could raise to entertain friends and well-wishers.

Isadora died tragically in Nice when her scarf caught on the wheel of a Bugatti racing car and broke her neck. Her body was brought to Paris for the funeral on 19 September 1927 — the very day of an enormous American Legion parade down the Champs-Elysées. Isadora's funeral cortege had to detour around the huge parade, and the English-language newspapers ignored the funeral, concentrating instead on the Legionnaires.

A typical headline that day read: "Few Attend Isadora Duncan's Rites as Compatriots Parade." In fact, however, the newspapermen didn't know. Over 5,000 mourners were at the burial in Père Lachaise, standing in the chilly September drizzle. "We published not a line of the moving ceremony at Père Lachaise," Al Laney, an editor of the *Herald*, lamented later, "but there were fifteen columns about the Legion parade."

The painter Augustus John also lived at 9 rue Delambre — specifically in apartment number 38. In the early twenties, John had used Mrs. Mary Rumsey's apartment on the rue Boissière. In 1928 Sisley Huddleston wrote that Augustus John "is perhaps the handsomest man I know, with great flashing eyes, long-lashed, soft yellowish hair falling loosely over his ears, and soft yellowish beard and moustache. His voice is splendid — ranging from a soft singing cadence to a deep imperious boom."

9-bis • Parnasse Bar (now a cinema)

Jimmy Charters, who tended bar at the Parnasse for a while, says that the manager's "idea of making a successful bar was to fill it up with girls who would attract the men." Directly opposite the Dingo, the Parnasse "stayed open all night, and most of its clients, who were largely French, came after the other places closed."

His English and American patrons followed Jimmy to whichever bar he happened to be working. Soon after his move to the Parnasse, for instance, one patron observed that "it was a madhouse in which one could rarely find a seat, and never a table, during drinking hours. When Jimmy took over and brought the Americans and British with him, the receipts jumped from five hundred francs to three thousand francs (roughly from $25 to $150) a day."

10 · Dingo Bar (now L'Auberge du Centre)

Lou Wilson and his Dutch wife, Jopie, bought this celebrated hangout in 1924. It was a small place, with only six tiny tables and a few stools along a short bar. Jimmy Charters tended bar here also, making it a friendly place attractive to an English-speaking clientele. Jopie was especially solicitous of women like Zelda Fitzgerald and Duff Twysden, who were having emotional problems, and Jimmy the barman was a good audience for the men. "We let some of the clients run up bills," he recalls. "I'm told the unpaid bills over a nine-year period in the Dingo totaled half a million francs."

According to Hemingway's recollections in *A Moveable Feast*, he first met Fitzgerald in the Dingo. "He [Scott] had come into the Dingo bar in the rue Delambre where I was sitting with some completely worthless characters [and] introduced himself. . . ." Typifying Hemingway's cattiness, his memoirs claim that he "much preferred" Fitzgerald's companion — Dunc Chaplin, "the famous pitcher" — to Scott himself. (Duncan Chaplin, it might be noted, was "famous" primarily in Hemingway's mind, for no one of that name ever reached the big leagues. Besides, as Matthew Bruccoli notes in *Scott and Ernest*, Dunc Chaplin "was not even in Europe in 1925.")

15 · Hôtel des Ecoles (now [another] Hôtel Lenox)

When Arthur Moss and his wife, Florence Gilliam, came to Paris in February 1921, they settled in this hotel for a few months before moving to rue Campagne-Première, where they first put together their little magazine, *Gargoyle*.

Man Ray's first studio and photographic darkroom were in this tiny hotel. Gertrude Stein, who visited him one day, notes, "I have never seen any space, not even a ship's cabin, with so many things in it. . . . He had a bed, he had three large cameras, he had several kinds of lighting, he had a window screen, and in a little closet he did all his developing." That "little closet," before Ray converted it, had been his toilet.

When Ray first arrived in Paris in July 1921, he took over Tristan Tzara's hotel room in Passy. Subsequently, he stayed in Yvonne Chastel's garret in Montmartre. In the winter of 1921, when Ray had to find other quarters, he moved here to the Hôtel des Ecoles, where he took up experimental photography. While living at the Ecoles, Ray exhibited his first Dada items at the Librairie Six and photographed Gertrude Stein, James Joyce, Jean Cocteau, and Georges Braque, among others.

When Tristan Tzara returned to Paris in January 1922, he rented a room in the same hotel as his friend Man Ray. A short time later, the model Kiki moved in with Ray. Since Ray's photographic equipment and supplies were requiring ever more space, Ray rented a studio on the rue Campagne-Première.

Another resident of the Ecoles was Manuel Komroff, the author of *The Grace of Lambs* and former editor at Boni and Liveright. Arriving in Paris in 1926, Komroff spent his first months working on his anticlerical short novel, *The Voice of Fire*, which was published by Edward Titus's Black Manikin Press. When Komroff returned to the States, he gained considerable fame as the author of a historical novel (*Coronet*) and considerable influence as the editor of the Modern Library Series.

For a short while in the autumn of 1930, Henry and June Miller also stayed in this hotel. The winter of Miller's destitution, when he would be rescued from virtual starvation by Richard Galen Osborn, was rapidly approaching.

16 · Apartment of Thelma Wood

A sculptor and silverpoint artist from Missouri, Thelma Wood was living here in February 1922 before she moved into the boulevard Saint-Germain apartment of her friend and lover, Djuna Barnes.

39 · Namur-Hôtel

Mina Loy, the English poet and artist (she took U.S. citizenship in 1946), lived here in 1922. Also in residence at the time was Robert McAlmon, whom Loy had known in Greenwich Village. It was Loy who introduced McAlmon to Gertrude Stein.

SQUARE DELAMBRE

1 · Residence of Margaret Anderson

This address was the one Anderson used when she registered at Adrienne Monnier's bookshop/library. Anderson lived in several different apartments and hotels during the decade, after she'd turned her journal (*The Little Review*) over to Jane Heap and come to Paris.

16

THE SECONDARY CHAMBER

BOULEVARD RASPAIL

218 · Brief residence of Glenway Wescott and Monroe Wheeler

When the two former classmates from the University of Chicago came to Paris in February, 1925, they first stayed at the Savoy Hôtel on the rue de Vaugirard. Soon they took rooms here, however, where they remained until they left Paris around the end of April.

216 · Titus/Rubinstein Studios

In an attempt to save their marriage, Edward Titus and Helena Rubinstein proposed to build several studio apartments here in the late twenties. They envisioned themselves living alongside dozens of artists. They also planned a "little American theatre." The studios were never finished, but a few controversial plays were performed in the theatre, which the police promptly closed. The marriage also failed.

207 · Hôtel du Carlton-Palace

Aaron Copland stayed in this hotel during the winter of 1921–22, after his summer of study at Walter Damrosch's new American Conservatory of Music at Fontainebleau. Copland signed on as a private pupil of Nadia Boulanger's, under whom he'd studied at the Conservatory that summer. Two other Americans, Virgil Thomson and Melville Smith, were also privately studying under

Boulanger, who officially taught organ playing and counterpoint at the Ecole Normale de Musique.

203 • Residence of Leo Stein

A gifted art scholar, critic, and collector, Leo Stein preferred the work of Henri Matisse to that of Gertrude's lion, Pablo Picasso. Having moved out of the rue de Fleurus residence in 1914, when he turned the apartments over to his sister and Alice Toklas, Leo was living here in August 1923. By the following July, Leo had moved to 42 avenue du Parc-de-Montsouris, where he lived for the next decade.

RUE VAVIN

31 • Chez Les Vikings (now a cabaret)

This café was very popular among the British, American, and (of course) Scandinavian expatriates and tourists. In 1928, after it had been in operation for little more than a year and a half, the owners expanded into number 29 next door, where they opened the Viking Hotel and Restaurant to complement the café business.

29 • Residence of Ken Sato

Although the best-known Japanese expatriate in the neighborhood was the painter Foujita, the writer Ken Sato lived here in the heart of Montparnasse until he moved to the Hôtel Square on the rue Boulard, out beyond the Montparnasse Cemetery. Five hundred and ten privately printed copies of Sato's English translation of *Quaint Tales of Samurais* by Saikaku Ibara were issued in Paris in 1926.

26 • College Inn

After his success with Le Palermo, a nightclub in Pigalle, Jed Kiley opened the College Inn here in Montparnasse. Hilaire Hiler designed and decorated the club in a style that can only be called "American Collegiate."

Kiley's partner in this enterprise was Jimmy Cossitt, an ex–Michigan football player. A famous athlete, Cossitt not only drew the crowds but also was an imposing bouncer who could control them.

Having previously worked for the *Paris Herald*, Kiley continued to write occasionally during this period, and he served as a co-editor of the *Boulevardier* (1927–28).

BOULEVARD DU MONTPARNASSE

112 • Hôtel Raspail

When Samuel Putnam, his wife, Riva, and their eight-month-old son arrived in Paris in 1927, they stayed here, directly across from the Dôme, before beginning their extensive European travels.

RUE JULES-CHAPLAIN

11-bis • Residence of Harold Stearns and Robin Kinkead

Harold lived here sometime around 1922, perhaps before taking up residence at the Hôtel de Blois on the rue Vavin.

Travel writer and journalist Robin Kinkead first visited Paris in 1923, when he was seventeen. He returned for a longer visit in 1926 and took a fifth-floor flat here in the midst of the Montparnasse action.

RUE DE LA GRANDE-CHAUMIERE

8 • Studio-Residence of Amedeo Modigliani and Jeanne Hébuterne

In this building where Paul Gauguin had his studio in the previous century, Amedeo Modigliani and his mistress and model, Jeanne Hébuterne, worked and lived in two long workshop rooms. After Jeanne's suicide in 1920, her body was removed from the family residence and brought to this atelier.

In June or July 1920, following the deaths of Modigliani and Jeanne Hébuterne, the English artist and model Nina Hamnett moved into the studio. Tending to associate with Continental rather than British or American expatriates, Hamnett lived here for several years with her Polish artist-lover and studied at the Académie Colarossi next door.

In December 1920, Stephen Vincent Benét moved here to number 8, where he first began formulating his ideas for "John Brown's Body," the poem that would earn him the Pulitzer Prize nearly a decade later. By the summer of 1921, Benét had returned to America, but he was back in Paris in 1926 with a Guggenheim grant and living out near the Etoile.

9 · Hôtel Libéria

One resident during the late twenties noted that "the Libéria is one of those small, comparatively cheap hotels which scarcely change, which have no pretensions to stylishness, but which still attract the generations of Montparnassians."

Nathanael West lived in Paris from late October 1926 to early January 1927. He first took a room in the Hôtel Lutetia, but it proved far too expensive for his modest budget, so he moved to the Libéria. For a brief time West also lived at 54 rue des Saints-Pères, the address he used when he applied for a subscription card at Adrienne Monnier's Maison des Amis des Livres. The only friendship West apparently developed during this period, while he was working sporadically on his first novel (*The Dream Life of Balso Snell*), was with Hilaire Hiler, the designer and manager of the Jockey Club.

10 · Académie Colarossi

Though not as highly regarded as the Grande-Chaumière, the Colarossi was second only to the Julian in popularity as an academy for aspiring painters. Prior to World War I, Robert W. Service — the Canadian author of "The Shooting of Dan McGrew" — studied painting here. "This *Vie de Bohème* phase," he later recalled, "must have lasted a year, during which I learned to loaf on the terrace of the Dôme Café, waggle a smudgy thumb as I talked of modelling, make surreptitious sketches of my fellow wine-bibbers, and pile up my own stack of saucers."

14 · L'Ecole Grande-Chaumière

The Grande-Chaumière was especially popular with expatriate artists. Jimmy Charters, the famous bartender, notes that "some [of the expatriates] really felt the necessity of making a stab at painting. This usually consisted in attending one of the *croquis* classes in the rue de la Grande-Chaumière two or three times a week. . . ."

William Gordon Huff, a California sculptor who spent his mornings in sculpture classes and afternoons in *croquis* classes at the Grande-Chaumière in 1924–25, describes the afternoons as exercises in discipline. A student had five minutes to sketch a model in charcoal before a new pose was struck for another sketch. These *croquis* exercises continued for an hour or two, after which the students took a ten-minute break. Then, the students drew from a pose lasting a couple of hours, less some break time for the model.

The morning sculpture sessions were taken more seriously. To enroll, one had to pay a fixed fee that covered the entire term. Consequently, the sculpture students were regarded as being more serious and dedicated than the *croquis* students. To work at an afternoon *croquis* session, one simply bought a metal token and presented it to the attendant at the door of the studio. *Croquis* students, that is, could attend or not as they wished, since they paid for only the sessions they attended.

Berenice Abbott studied here under sculptor Antoine Bourdelle when she first arrived in Paris in April 1921. Once she began her apprentice work with Man Ray, however, Abbott shifted to photography. By 1925, she had established herself as an eminently successful portrait photographer.

Others who attended the Grande-Chaumière to study under such instructors as Bourdelle, fellow sculptor Alberto Giacometti, or the painter Fernand Léger were

- Abraham Rattner, an often overlooked American painter, who was in residence during 1923–24
- Caresse Crosby, who claimed to have studied painting and sculpture periodically from 1923 to 1925 under Bourdelle
- Alexander Calder, who began work at l'Ecole virtually the moment he arrived in Paris in 1926

Anaïs Nin attended classes at the Grande-Chaumière for a couple weeks in March 1926. She improved her sketching skills so much that she sometimes worried "that the love of lines might take the place of my love of words." Nin considered enrolling again in August 1927, referring to the school as La Grande Poussière ("The Great Dustiness"), but apparently decided against it.

In 1927, sculptor Isamu Noguchi received a Guggenheim, which enabled him to study in Paris. He divided his time between the Grande-Chaumière and the Académie Colarossi. During his year in Paris, Noguchi did his only painting, for he was back working as a sculptor in New York by 1929.

RUE DE CHEVREUSE

4 • The American University Women's Club (Reid Hall)

Lodging here was available by the week to club members — anyone who belonged to the American Association of University Women and paid the $10 yearly dues. In the twenties, the Club averaged 450 members per year. Sixty-six "permanent guests" stayed here, and a dormitory of four or five beds was kept for unexpected arrivals. The buildings and its gardens were on loan from Elizabeth Mills (Mrs. Whitelaw) Reid, for whom the building was later named.

Crystal Ross, who was working on her doctorate at the University of Strasbourg, stayed here when she came to Paris in April 1924 to see her friend John Dos Passos. Ross accompanied the Hemingway party to Pamplona in July 1924, along with Dos Passos, Bill and Sally Bird, Chink Smith, Donald Ogden Stewart, and Robert McAlmon. Crystal and Dos were engaged over the summer, but apparently things didn't progress beyond a chaste betrothal.

17

THE AORTA

RUE NOTRE-DAME-DES-CHAMPS

59 • Brief residence of Robert McAlmon

Robert McAlmon stayed in a hotel here at least once during his various Parisian peregrinations in the twenties. Since he frequently used Sylvia Beach's Shakespeare and Company as his mailing address, poor Sylvia had to keep constant track of McAlmon's whereabouts. An impossible task, of course.

70 • Ralph Cheever Dunning's "Bird Cage"

A poet who produced only two slim volumes of purple verse in his life, Cheever Dunning lived in a tiny room on the ground floor here from 1905 until his death in 1930. Dunning's room was so small that Wambly Bald, columnist for the *Tribune*, called it "virtually a wooden box." The room contained one chair, a cot, a small potbellied stove, and a makeshift bookcase. Dunning's friends, few though they were, called it Dunning's "Bird Cage."

Dunning's poetry was lavishly praised by Ezra Pound, but it was roundly condemned by nearly everyone else, especially Ernest Walsh, editor of the important little journal *This Quarter*. Dunning's few poems were published in two collections by Edward Titus's Black Manikin Press: *Rococo* (1926) and *Windfalls* (1929).

Dunning was one of the oddest ducks to inhabit Montparnasse, which is saying something. Although he frequented cafés like the Dôme, he stayed psychologically remote while café-sitting by reading and periodically sipping a glass of hot milk.

It's been claimed that he uttered only a few sentences in all his twenty-five years in Paris. And, during the last few years of his life, when his friends took him food he frequently refused it. Some contemporary observers have suggested that his diet of milk and cheese was prompted by a heavy opium habit.

Robert McAlmon tells of the time Ezra Pound — who lived in the same courtyard complex for over three years — urged McAlmon to find some opium for Dunning, who was suffering from withdrawal agonies. McAlmon, who knew Paris perhaps as well as any American, was having little success when he spotted Hemingway in the Closerie des Lilas. Sidling up to Hem, McAlmon whispered Dunning's dilemma. "Hell," boomed Hemingway, "Ezra's told you too!" Dunning's problem, apparently, was no secret.

Eventually, McAlmon got Dunning placed in a sanatorium, where he stayed for two months. The treatment, though, didn't take, and Dunning had to undergo several more "cures" before his death in 1930.

Ford Madox Ford called the enigmatic Dunning "the living Buddha of Montparnasse," and Hemingway described him as the man who died because "he forgot to eat." Dunning's brother and Ezra Pound were his principal benefactors and caretakers.

70-bis • Ezra and Dorothy (Shakespear) Pound's residence

The iron gate at number 70-bis opens onto a small pathway, leading back to a *pavillon* (annex) in which the Pounds resided from the summer of 1921 until the winter of 1924. A flamboyant poet, rigorous editor, and generous critic, Pound commanded attention and respect wherever he went. Later, his sympathy with fascism and his unconscionable anti-Semitism would show itself. Dorothy Shakespear, Ezra's wife, was more reserved, unassuming, and gracious. She also was tolerant of his infidelities. (Olga Rudge had a daughter, Mary, by Pound in 1925.)

According to the 1921 *Franco-American Yearbook*, number 70-bis was occupied by two Americans, E. Blanchard Colliver and Bion Barnett (Chairman of the Board, Barnett National Bank, Jacksonville, Florida), until the Pounds moved in. Since the rent here came to only $30 a month, Ezra was able to renovate and decorate the apartment, making it into a small museum and gallery. Still, Ernest Hemingway noted that Pound's studio "was as poor as Gertrude Stein's was rich."

In this studio in February 1924, Ford Madox Ford met Hemingway and the suggestion was made that Hemingway help edit the *Transatlantic Review*. Ernest's handling of the review may well have contributed to its demise. He started a controversy in his very first number by insulting T. S. Eliot; he insisted on serializing Gertrude Stein's opaque and seemingly endless *Making of Americans*; and, when the journal was about to fold for lack of funds, he arranged for Krebs Friend — an old buddy who'd married a wealthy woman forty years older than he — to buy and run the magazine. Friend's money failed, and with it the review.

In the flat above the Pounds was a German whom Ezra suspected of harboring anti-French feelings. So, Pound and his protégé, George Antheil (the composer), practiced Antheil's latest works — with the two men striking blocks of granite and other atonal objects with sledgehammers and whatever else was handy. The cacophony finally "persuaded" the German to move.

When Pound moved to Rapallo, Italy, in December 1924, the American sculptor Janet Scudder moved in. Thus, Anaïs Nin notes in her diary of January 1926 that among her "famous" neighbors is Janet Scudder at 70-bis rue Notre-Dame-des-Champs. From here Scudder moved to 24 rue de Verneuil. A decade later (1934) Katherine Anne Porter took over the apartment at 70-bis.

75 • Alice Toklas's "pre-Stein" residence in Paris

In 1908 Alice Toklas and her close friend and traveling companion, Harriet Levy, moved into a four-room apartment here, directly across from number 70. Although the apartment was without a bathroom or an elevator, Toklas and Levy appreciated it after having lived in hotels for nearly a year.

Their only previous experience with something other than hotel rooms had lasted scarcely a week. When they first arrived in Paris in late September 1907, Alice and Harriet checked into the Hôtel Magellan, at 39 avenue Marceau. A short while later, they tired of hotel life and signed up for room and board at the home (on the rue de la Faisanderie) of a young bachelor whose mother was out of town.

Gertrude Stein heard about the arrangement and, although no improprieties were suggested or suffered, Stein grew alarmed, insisting that the two young women "leave the flat before any complications arise." By the end of the week, Alice and Harriet had moved back into a hotel — this time, the Hôtel de l'Universe on boulevard Saint-Michel.

Alice and Harriet left the Hôtel de l'Universe that summer when they traveled to Italy with Gertrude. Returning to Paris in September 1908, Alice and Harriet took a room at the Hôtel des Saints-Pères while they searched for a suitable apartment — which they found here at number 75. In 1910 Harriet returned to the United States, and Alice moved in with Gertrude and Leo Stein on the rue de Fleurus.

84 · Ford Madox Ford's apartment

Ford and his common-law wife, Stella Bowen, had separated by 1927, and Ford left his rue Denfert-Rochereau flat to do some traveling during much of 1926 and 1927. By mid-February 1928, he had settled into a spacious studio here on rue Notre-Dame-des-Champs. Ford left for New York in March 1928, returned to this apartment in April, and then gave up the apartment for the summer. Returning in the autumn of 1928, Ford took a flat on Vaugirard.

86 · Studio of Fernand Léger (and James McNeill Whistler)

Whistler occupied a rooftop studio here from 1892 to 1895. In 1921 Cameron Burnside, the official painter for the American Red Cross, lived and worked in this building. Fernand Léger, the friend of many expatriates and celebrated painter, had his studio here during the early twenties, prior to his moving out of Paris.

113 · The Hemingways' second Paris apartment (now gone)

In a flat overlooking a sawmill and small lumberyard Ernest, Hadley, and Bumby (John) lived at this address after their return from Canada in late May 1924. They first considered Ezra Pound's flat at 70-bis, but it was too cold for the baby. Then, they found this flat on the same street, a block off the boulevard Saint-Michel.

The whir of the circular saw and the pop of its single-cylinder engine caused Ernest to head around the corner to the Closerie des Lilas to do his writing. Their apartment was small and dark, with a narrow kitchen containing a stone sink and two-ring gas burner; a dining room not much larger than its heavy table; a small bedroom, where Ernest tried to work; and a master bedroom, off which was a tiny dressing room where the baby slept. The Hemingways kept this residence until their separation in the autumn of 1926.

AVENUE DE L'OBSERVATOIRE

39 • Bal Bullier (now gone; area under renovation)

Here, at the end of Notre-Dame-des-Champs, stood the largest dance hall in Paris: the Bal Bullier. The bronze statue of Marshal Ney with its back to the Closerie des Lilas was deliberately set facing the Bullier, which subsumed the spot (at what would have been number 43) where Ney was executed for his support of Napoleon.

Before its demolition, the Bullier was undoubtedly the most distinctive dance hall in Paris. A huge, garishly Arabesque building, it couldn't be missed. Moreover, unlike many of the other *bals*, the Bullier had a fairly sound reputation, since relatively few bar girls and apparently no Apache-pimps frequented this place.

Special dances were held at the Bullier, and some of them — like the annual Bal de l'Internat (Medical Students' Ball) — were nearly as libertine and raucous as the Beaux Arts students' annual Quatz'Arts Ball, after which they were modeled.

AVENUE GEORGES-BERNANOS

43 • Hôtel Beauvoir

The Beauvoir is the hotel where Hadley Hemingway stayed briefly in 1926, after Ernest announced that he wanted a divorce to marry Pauline. Hadley remained here until she found an apartment on the rue de Fleurus near Gertrude Stein's home.

BOULEVARD DU MONTPARNASSE

171 · Closerie des Lilas

Originally a country inn (*guinguette*) on the road to Orléans, this cafe "maintained all the traditions of the Old Latin Quarter," according to Jimmy Charters. Although it did not expand into a massive gathering and gawking spot like some of the other cafés on the boulevard du Montparnasse, the Closerie des Lilas was modernized in December 1925.

On 17 February 1922, a group of avant-garde artists and intellectuals (including André Breton, Erik Satie, Roger Vitrac, and Fernand Léger) scheduled a "Congress" at the Closerie. The purpose was "to determine the directives for the defense of the modern spirit." The proceedings of the Congress would then be published and broadcast throughout the Western World.

Among the groups invited to this Modernism Congress were the anarchic Dadaists, headed by Tristan Tzara. But Tzara, true to the spirit of Dada, wanted no part of the Congress or, for that matter, any kind of "movement." Dada was to be kept pure — heretical, impish, and unprogrammatic. Breton, a friend of Tzara's and the other Dadaists', pleaded with them to attend, but they refused.

Failing to appreciate Breton's efforts, the Congress organizers accused him of sabotaging the meeting. And, instead of a Congress, the affair turned into a mock trial of Breton, who was charged with fracturing the Modernist movement by antagonizing the Dadaists. Picasso attended, as did Brancusi, Matisse, Cocteau, and nearly a hundred others. Absent, of course, was Dada.

The upshot of this indictment of Breton was his breaking away from the Dadaists and other Modernists of the day. By 1923, his splinter movement became known as Surrealism, which drew heavily on the psychological work of Sigmund Freud. The "First Surrealist Manifesto" was published in December 1924. Thus, the Closerie is arguably the site of the inception of Surrealism.

If the Closerie effectively saw the birth of Surrealism, it also witnessed the death of the great banquets that had been traditional among French intellectuals, writers, and critics during the previous century.

In June 1925, the French literary journal *Les Nouvelles Littéraires* published a tribute to a living but neglected poet who called himself Saint-Pol-Roux-le-Magnifique. (His real name was Paul Roux. Because of the nature of his verse, some critics referred to him as the "Rabelais of poetry.") As in the previous decades, a vast banquet to honor the occasion was held on 1 July 1925 at the Closerie, where *vers et prose* soirées and dinners like this one had been traditional for nearly a century.

Responding to an anti-German remark that he'd overheard after dinner, André Breton (him again) rose to defend the honor of his German friend Max Ernst, who was present. Quarrels broke out, fruit was thrown, and a brawl ensued. Philippe Soupault, the French critic, swung from the chandelier, knocking over wine bottles, flowers, and table settings.

A crowd gathered outside, a few of whom joined the fracas. The amazed onlookers saw some of France's leading intellectuals and artists being arrested and others, mostly Breton's indefatigable Surrealists who were bloody from battle, being loaded into ambulances. This was the last grand banquet.

The Closerie des Lilas was also a Hemingway favorite: "It was one of the best cafes in Paris. It was warm inside in the winter and in the spring and fall it was very fine outside with the tables under the shade of the trees on the side where the statue of Marshal Ney was, and the square, regular tables under the big awnings along the boulevard." Hemingway added that "there were other good cafes to work in but they were a long walk away and this was my home cafe."

159 · Hôtel Venetia (no longer a hotel)

This hotel stood near the intersection with the avenue de l'Observatoire. Edna St. Vincent Millay and her mother stayed at the Venetia in April and May 1922 after moving from their rue de l'Université hotel. "We moved from the Intendance," she wrote her sister on 25 April 1922, using her slangy voice, "because it is so cust expensive, and are now in a cheap but not a very clean hotel . . . two minutes from this bleeding kafe [the Rotonde] and just around the corner from the beautiful Luxembourg gardens." This was the first time Millay had tried the Hôtel Venetia, having stayed at the Intendance and the Saints-Pères during her five-month visit the previous year.

Ernest Walsh had a room at the Venetia in August 1922, around the time when he and Ethel Moorhead reportedly met at the Hôtel Claridge — where she is said to have paid his hotel bills. According to Sylvia Beach's records, Walsh was actually living at the Venetia, which he gave as his address when he checked out a copy of Joyce's *Dubliners* from Shakespeare and Company. Specifically, Beach notes that "Miss Moorhead" returned the book that Walsh had borrowed.

Donald Ogden Stewart, already an established humorist when he came to Paris in the spring of 1923, was advised by John Peale Bishop to look up a young, unknown writer named Ernest Hemingway. Running into Hemingway at the Rendezvous des Mariniers on his first night in Paris, Stewart and Hem became instant friends. Since Ernest was leaving the next day to return to Switzerland, where he and Hadley had been skiing, he offered Stewart their flat on rue du Cardinal-Lemoine. Stewart gladly accepted.

When the Hemingways returned in May [Stewart's memoirs erroneously include Bumby, the Hemingways' baby, who wasn't born until October], Stewart moved to the Hôtel Venetia for the remainder of the summer and the fall. He chose this hotel, he says, because Edna St. Vincent Millay had stayed there, adding that "Elmer Rice must also have been one of the guests, for years later, when the curtain rose on a play of his about Paris, I cried out, 'That's my room!' "

In April of the following year (1924) Stewart returned to Paris and to the Venetia. Writing steadily for the next month, Stewart finished his humorous novel *Mr. and Mrs. Haddock Abroad*, parts of which he read aloud to friends at the Murphys' home on the quai des Grands-Augustins.

In July 1924, Stewart joined the Hemingway party at the *feria* of San Fermin in Pamplona. Stewart also spent the summer of 1925 in Paris, first staying in Montmartre with his Parisian mistress and then, after a few weeks with the Murphys in Antibes, back at the Venetia. In 1926, Don and his new wife, Bea, honeymooned in Europe. When they came to Paris that autumn they stayed at the Hôtel Les Antiquaires at 7 rue Montalembert, near the Pont Royal.

In late January 1925, Ernest Hemingway took a room in the Hôtel Venetia for a few days. He'd left Hadley and Bumby in Schruns, Austria, where they were skiing while he supposedly headed for New

York to confer with a new publisher, Charles Scribner. Admittedly in love with Pauline Pfeiffer, Ernest indulged his affections by secretly making a side trip to Paris to spend a few days with her. The Venetia, where he stayed, was about a block from the Hôtel Beauvoir, where a year and a half later Hadley took a room when Ernest announced that he wanted a divorce in order to marry Pauline.

157–159 · Au Nègre de Toulouse (now gone)

This modest café, which the Pounds and the Hemingways frequented when they lived on the rue Notre-Dame-des-Champs, offered exotic, inexpensive meals. The Friday *plat du jour* was the one in greatest demand: a couscous at 4.50 (25¢).

155 · Hôtel de Nice

The poet and critic Padraic Colum and his wife, Mary, stayed in this hotel during one of their many visits to Paris in the twenties. Merely by virtue of their good nature and popularity, the Colums advanced the cause of Irish nationalism and promoted Celtic lore. On later visits, the Colums lived at 6 rue Eugène-Manuel in Passy.

146 · The Jockey

Between March 1921 and November 1923, the building at number 146 — on the corner of Montparnasse and the rue Campagne-Première — housed the Académie du Caméléon, a literary and artistic cabaret founded by the sculptor Levet. Then, an ex-jockey named Miller leased the place and turned it into a moderately successful nightclub.

When Miller had to sell the club in 1923, reputedly to cover gambling debts, Hilaire Hiler — an American writer, musician, painter, and designer — took it over and redecorated the club, giving it a cartoonlike cowboy motif. By increasing the bar's appeal to the expatriates and the throngs of tourists who were inundating Montparnasse, Hiler had himself a hit.

"Hiler's Jockey," Robert McAlmon noted, "was, so long as he had it, an amusing and sociable hangout. Dramas and comedies and fights did occur there, but generally comedy and good will prevailed. . . . Jane Heap, Mina Loy, Clotilde and Laurence Vail, Mary Reynolds, Man Ray, Harold Van Dorn — among the French, Cocteau, Jacques

Rigaut, Radiguet, Louis Aragon, René Crevel, Marcel Duchamp, Kiki — almost anybody of the writing, painting, musical, gigoloing, whoring, pimping or drinking world was apt to turn up at the Jockey."

Hiler's success with the Jockey was such that Jed Kiley hired him to decorate his Montparnasse clubs, the College Inn and the Jungle, which Hiler did with similar success.

135 • Hôtel des Etats-Unis (now gone)

In late December 1929, Sergei Eisenstein, the Russian film-maker, returned to Paris and took a room at the Hôtel des Etats-Unis. (Since 1925 there had been three hotels of this name in Paris, but the one at 135 boulevard du Montparnasse was probably Eisenstein's. One biographer observes that the hotel was in the First Arrondissement, but none of the three hotels of this name — and several records confirm the name — was in the First. Moreover, the Montparnasse location fits better with certain other details of Eisenstein's biography at this period.)

Shortly after checking into the hotel, Eisenstein paid a visit to James Joyce to discuss filming *Ulysses*. Eisenstein was particularly intrigued by the montage possibilities of Leopold Bloom's interior monologues. Although Joyce was virtually blind at the time, he was captivated by Eisenstein's notions of cinematography. Later, Joyce claimed that the only two filmmakers who could handle *Ulysses* were Eisenstein and the German director Walter Ruttman.

On 17 February 1930, while he was still living at the Etats-Unis, Eisenstein gave a lecture at the Sorbonne on "The Principle of New Russian Cinema." Eisenstein's talk was most successful, but it did meet with some vociferous anti-Soviet heckling. Eisenstein left Paris in the summer of 1930 to make a trip to the United States.

RUE BOISSONADE

15 • Mariette Mills's studio

Mariette was a sculptor, whose bust of Robert McAlmon was shown at the Louvre in 1923. Heyworth Mills, Mariette's husband, made and repaired model ships. The Millses lived in a country home at Clairefontaine (near Rambouillet), but Mariette's studio here in Montparnasse was a hive of activity.

Painters like Picabia and Léger, composers like Satie, sculptors like Brancusi, and poets like Blaise Cendrars and Mina Loy all enjoyed the company of Mariette Mills, a woman who established long-lasting friendships. Another friend of the Millses' was Robert McAlmon, who used the studio as his residence during one winter. (McAlmon dates it as the winter of 1923–24, but it was probably his first winter in Paris, 1921–22.)

18 · Residence of Stella Bowen

The Australian artist Stella Bowen was Ford Madox Ford's common-law wife during his years as a Sussex pig farmer after the war. In November 1920 she bore him a daughter, Esther Julia ("Julie"). And, in 1923, Stella came to Paris with Ford, helping him with the *Transatlantic Review*, serving as hostess at his parties, and gaining acclaim in her own right as a painter. She seems to have encouraged Ford's affair with the West Indian writer Jean Rhys, who lived with Ford and Stella in Paris for several weeks in 1923–24. Ford and Stella separated in 1927, however, and Stella took up residence here.

RUE CAMPAGNE-PREMIERE

Number unknown · Hotel of the "Revue Nègre" troupe

(The hotel was described as being "just off" the boulevard du Montparnasse on the rue Campagne-Première. However, in the Bottins (*Annuaire du Commerce*) of the period, no hotel is listed on this street except the Istria, which is over a block from the intersection. One can only conclude that the hotel in question was private and unregistered.)

When Caroline Dudley brought the troupe of black American musicians and dancers to Paris in 1925, she is said to have reserved this entire hotel for them. Thus, this hotel was the first Paris residence of Josephine Baker, Sidney Bechet, Florence Mills, and others in the company. Later, virtually the whole gang moved to the

Hôtel Fournet on the boulevard des Batignolles, where they had much more freedom.

Black Americans, particularly jazz musicians, had been popular in Paris since World War I, when Jimmy Europe and other black troops brought their music overseas. The popularity of the entertainers continued throughout the twenties. In 1927, for example, an all-black show called "The Black Birds" opened at the Moulin Rouge. A review noted that the show was enhanced "by a red hot jazz band, the world famous jazz of the Plantation Club in New York." Over a hundred artists made up the Black Bird Company, including Broadway stars Adelaide Hall and Ada Ward.

But it wasn't just the black singers, dancers, and musicians who came, as Michel Fabre's study, *La Rive Noire*, reveals. Writers like Walter White and Gwendolyn Bennett, and intellectuals like James Weldon Johnson and Claude McKay, among others (some of whom are noted elsewhere) spent considerable time in Paris during the twenties. Many of them found new liberty in the City of Light. For instance, Jessie Fauset — who was one of the best-known black writers and served as associate editor of *The Crisis* — is quoted in the Paris edition of the *Chicago Tribune* (1 February 1925) as saying, "I have met more members of my own guild here in four months than in New York in four years."

3 · Rosalie's

(Morrill Cody places Rosalie's at number 13, which is surely in error, given the makeup of the street and other contemporaneous descriptions. In fact, Rosalie's was probably near the boulevard du Montparnasse corner — at number 3, as noted by Alain Jouffroy in *La Vie Réinventée: L'Explosion des Années 20 à Paris* [1982]. Neither the Bottins nor the telephone books for the period mention Rosalie's, which isn't surprising since it was a modest operation.)

Extremely popular among the expatriates and blue-collar workers, Rosalie Tabia's restaurant was identified only by her sign, CHEZ ROSALIE. The food was delicious, filling, and inexpensive, and Rosalie had a special fondness for the starving artists, since she herself had once modeled for Modigliani and Whistler.

Morrill Cody recalls that when "opening the door of Rosalie's one was often greeted with a pungent odor of fried onions and garlic, since the room inside had little ventilation. . . . One stepped down from the street level to the dark tiled floor. The room was big enough for several long wooden tables flanked by rough and hard benches without backs each of which accommodated up to eight persons if they were thin and sat close together."

No one except Rosalie, apparently, could make a go of the place. At least twice she was persuaded to sell the restaurant, only to buy it back each time (at a nice profit) when the new owners — who invariably sought to renovate the joint — went broke.

5 · Residence of Eugene McCown

Poor Eugene. This Missouri painter had many friends and boosters, but nobody seems to have known for sure how to spell his last name. The Paris edition of the *Chicago Tribune* spelled it "MacCown." Harry Crosby and Sylvia Beach, both atrocious spellers, write "McGowan." Jimmy the Barman and Morrill Cody spell it "MacCowan." However, "McCown" is probably correct since it's preferred by the meticulous Virgil Thomson, Eugene's close friend and fellow Kansas Citian. Oh, and McCown's portrait of Nancy Cunard, which is often reproduced, is brilliant.

7 · Residences of Matthew and Hannah Josephson and of Arthur Moss and Florence Gilliam

Matthew Josephson, writer and one of the editors of *Secession* and *Broom*, and his wife, Hannah, moved into a courtyard apartment here in December 1921. They returned to the States six months later, in July 1922.

Facing the same courtyard was the residence of Arthur Moss and his wife, Florence Gilliam. Together they started *Gargoyle* (1921–22), the first English-language little review on the Continent. Although supported by excellent writers, the review did not print much fiction or poetry. Instead, it tended to run art news, reviews of shows, and features on Parisian life.

Florence Gilliam later served as the Paris correspondent for two American theatre magazines and as drama reviewer for the *Tribune*. Some expatriates referred to Arthur Moss as "the sane man of the

[Latin] Quarter" because of his steadfastness, but Waverley Root called him "a malicious little man." In 1922 Moss and Gilliam moved to the carrefour de l'Odéon where they continued editing *Gargoyle* for a short while longer. They separated in 1930 and were divorced a year later.

9 • Artists' studios

This building contained over a hundred small studios made from doors, windows, and other materials salvaged from the World Exposition of 1889. For a brief time prior to the twenties, Modigliani lived here, as did the poet Rainer Maria Rilke and the American painter James A. McNeill Whistler.

11 • Residence of James Stephens and of Mina Loy

A gentle and widely loved poet, James Stephens was part of the Irish contingent of expatriates — along with Padraic and Mary Colum, Samuel Beckett, and James Joyce, who was born in Dublin on the same day as Stephens.

Stephens lived in a loft over a machine shop, according to Robert W. Service, who once subleased the apartment from his Irish friend. "When the various machines got going the place vibrated with a demoniac intensity. In an ear-shattering din we [Service and his wife] jiggled and joggled. . . . How could my landlord [Stephens] have written his radiant poetry in such a racket?"

Stephens was an excellent reader and storyteller. His readings were particularly noteworthy, according to reports, because he invariably *sang*, rather than read, his poems. "If you have a toothache or are in love," Stephens once observed, "you lose your time in trying to explain your sensations to those who have never suffered from toothache or from love."

Not including her studios or her lampshade shop, the English poet and artist Mina Loy had three residential addresses in Paris during the twenties: here, at 11 rue Campagne-Première; in the Namur Hôtel (rue Delambre); and also in a new building (erected in the mid-twenties) on the rue Saint-Romain. Loy had two daughters: Gioella, who later married the painter and art collector Julien Levy; and Fabie, who was born during World War I.

14 · Residence of Ludwig Lewisohn and Thelma Spear

Evidence suggests that the writer Ludwig Lewisohn and his mistress, Thelma Spear, who'd come to Paris with Lewisohn (when his wife wouldn't grant him a divorce), moved from their Passy apartment on rue Saint-Didier to this address sometime in the last half of the twenties.

(Lewisohn checked out books from Sylvia Beach using this address in the early thirties; also, several citations note that Lewisohn and Sisley Huddleston were neighbors — and Huddleston left his nearby boulevard Raspail address when he moved to the French countryside in late 1929 or early 1930.)

In any case, Lewisohn and Spear made friends with many expatriates, including Huddleston, the British writer. "Many evenings did we spend together," Huddleston notes, "in the former apartment of George Biddle. . . . With Thelma Spear as hostess, capital parties which gathered together the French, the German, the Jewish, and the American elite of Paris were given." Huddleston goes on to drop the names of Sinclair Lewis, Theodore Dreiser, Thomas Mann, Elmer Rice, Padraic and Mary Colum, Paul Robeson (who sang before a huge crowd at the Salle Gaveau on 29 October 1927), and a whole passel of others. This style of living did not seem to compromise Lewisohn's ability to produce penetrating cultural criticism and highly crafted fiction.

17-bis · The apartment of Eugène Atget

In 1899, when "Montparnasse was still a new neighborhood," the photographer Eugène Atget moved to this address, where he lived until his death on 4 August 1927. Living with him was his devoted companion, a former actress ten years his elder, Valentine Delafosse Compagnon.

The apartment was on the fifth floor and as bare and simple as their lives. (Atget is said to have reused scraps of paper over and over for his notes.) In the bedroom were a bed, washstand, mirror, and some family portraits. The dining room served as a darkroom, and Atget washed his prints in the kitchen.

By the early twenties, Atget had become rather shabby in his dress, virtually the personification of poverty. He preferred to photograph in the early morning, to catch the mist of dew. So, at daybreak the old artist would be seen shuffling down the streets of Paris, burdened with the weight of camera equipment and yet eager to photograph decaying historic buildings, ordinary street scenes, or lavish courtyard gardens. Still today, Atget's work belongs in the top rank of photographic art.

29 · Istria Hôtel

Wanting to be closer to his atelier at number 31, Man Ray moved from the Hôtel des Ecoles to a ground-floor apartment at the Istria sometime prior to December 1923. Kiki was living with him at the time. That same December, Marcel Duchamp returned from New York, and he and his current mistress, model Thérèse Treize, also moved into the Istria.

In the summer of 1927, William Carlos Williams and his wife, Florence, took their sons to Geneva and entered them in a Swiss school. Returning to Paris "for one final spree," they found a room in a cheap hotel. The room proved so unpleasant that they asked Robert McAlmon to help them find different lodgings. Since this was the summer of the American Legion Decentennial, hotel rooms were difficult to find. But McAlmon was nothing if not resourceful, and he got them a room at the Istria, where he was staying.

(Although Bill claimed that he and Flossie spent only one night in the cheap hotel, Sylvia Beach's notes indicate that they were registered for several days at the Hôtel Royal, 212 boulevard Raspail, which immediately follows their Geneva address in Beach's records.)

31-bis · Man Ray's atelier

Having shifted his interest from painting and sculpture to photography, Man Ray needed a place to work that would be more spacious than his tiny quarters at the Hôtel des Ecoles. So, in July 1922, Ray rented a studio in this building, although for the time being he kept his residence at the Ecoles. A little more than a year later he moved his living quarters to the Istria Hôtel next door.

In 1923 Ray encountered sculptor Berenice Abbott, whom he had known in New York. Seeing her to be *"mourant au faim"* (starving to death), Ray hired her as his assistant. Abbott worked for Ray the next three years, until she branched off on her own and took a studio on the rue du Bac. Ray stayed here, however, until 1929 when he moved both his residence and his studio to the rue du Val-de-Grâce.

18

AROUND MONTPARNASSE STATION

RUE DU DEPART

1–3 • Lavenue

(As a corner location on the place du 18-Juin-1940, the address is sometimes given as 68–70 boulevard du Montparnasse. Lavenue was both an elegant restaurant and a hotel. Oscar Wilde's first weeks of Parisian exile were spent here. Today the weather-worn word *Lavenue* is barely visible in the concrete facade above the tavern that has replaced the restaurant.)

In 1925 Ford Madox Ford, Nina Hamnett, and Robert McAlmon decided to hold fortnightly gatherings here to talk of art and such. Lavenue was reserved for the first meeting, which was designed to honor James Joyce. Someone, however, forgot to inform Joyce, who had to be fetched at the last minute. Needless to say, the evening was a flop, and any ideas for future sessions were quietly dropped.

26 • Piet Mondrian's residence (now site of Montparnasse Tower)

When the Dutch painter Piet Mondrian first came to Paris in December 1911, he lived here in the apartment of his friend Conrad Kickert, who was out of town. Mondrian came back to Paris in 1919, again taking Kickert's apartment. When Kickert returned the following year, Mondrian rented a room out near Montrouge. In 1921, however, a studio two floors below Kickert's opened up, and Mondrian was back at his favorite address, 26 rue du Départ, where he lived for fifteen years.

Consumed by his work, Mondrian did not spend much time in the Montparnasse cafés. His apartment was laid out geometrically, much like the paintings — including the various "Boogie-Woogie" works — that he was working on at the time. One visitor noted that Mondrian's apartment showed "an order that was balanced and cunningly calculated beyond perfection, a few squares of yellow and red and blue against vast stretches of white. The gramophone was red; so was the table. The wardrobe was blue. The plates yellow. The curtains red. . . ."

BOULEVARD EDGAR-QUINET

31 • Le Sphinx (now a doctor's office)

This *maison close*, or brothel, was operated by Marthe ("Martoune") Lemestre. For its grand opening in the late twenties, announcements were sent to nearly everyone in the district, inviting wives and mistresses as well as potential clients. Virtually the entire Quarter turned out for the free champagne and the tours of the upstairs bedrooms, which were starker and more strictly functional than the chromium-plated, Art Deco bar downstairs. The ultramodern bar outmatched the Coupole's, which up to then had been the latest word in brassy luxury. The Sphinx, incidentally, was the first building in all of France to install air conditioning.

Number unknown • The Gypsy Bar (now gone)

Situated near the spoked intersection of boulevard Edgar-Quinet, the rue du Montparnasse, and the rue Delambre, this bar was decidedly a step down from the likes of the Falstaff or the Dingo. It was foul-smelling and not at all conducive to conversation, leisurely or impassioned. Thus it should not be confused with Gypsy's Bar on the rue Cujas, which Joyce, McAlmon, Barnes, Liebling, and others frequented. This Gypsy Bar attracted a different clientele. When John Glassco stopped in one night, for example, he found it "full of hardfaced young lesbians and desperate looking old women whose spotted, sinewy arms rattled with jewelled bracelets. [One of these latter] was wearing male evening dress and a monocle."

60 · Popular spot for nightclubs (still is)

In the early twenties the club was called "Le Vertige." It then was given a salacious red decor and a new name: "Chants de Maldoror," after a long prose poem by Le Comte de Lautréamont (real name: Isidore Ducasse, 1846–70). This man and his verse were venerated by the Surrealists, who thus ransacked the club and attacked its patrons. Louis Aragon received a knife wound in the fracas. So, the club changed its name again and by 1930 was operating as L'Ange Bleu, in tribute this time to the film *The Blue Angel.*

RUE DU MONTPARNASSE

59 · Hôtel Unic

(In 1924, there were *four* Hôtel Unics registered in Paris, which, one might think, would hardly make them unique. The Unic at 151 rue de Rennes [now the Rennes-Montparnasse], which still displays an attractive Art Deco canopy, changed its name the following year, and thus only three Unics were listed in 1925. To complicate matters, the Unic Hotel here at 59 rue du Montparnasse was *not* one of those that were officially listed. This one was popular with the expatriates, however, because of its central location in Montparnasse. [Note: the Hôtel Unic currently at number 56 was not so-named in the twenties.])

In late March 1924, when Robert McAlmon got back to Paris from the south of France, he took a room here in this Hôtel Unic and reserved another for William Carlos Williams and his wife, Flossie. The Williamses were to return to Paris in May from a three-month tour of other parts of Europe. When they'd first passed through Paris back in January of 1924, the Williamses had stayed at the (expensive) Lutetia.

This stopover in Paris was a rich but hectic period for Doc Williams. Many of his friends from New York were in town, including Harold Loeb, Peggy Guggenheim, Mina Loy, Djuna Barnes, and the Vails, Laurence and Clotilde. Ezra Pound, Williams's former classmate at the University of Pennsylvania, came over from his new retreat in Italy.

Hilda Doolittle was also in Paris. Williams had known her while he and Pound were at Penn, during which time she was commuting to Bryn Mawr. Indeed, there are reports of Bill and Ezra's romantic rivalry over the tall, attractive redhead. H.D., as the poet became known later, was staying at the Hôtel Foyot with her consort, Bryher, McAlmon's wife. (At one time, but no longer, H.D. resided at 12 rue des Ursulines.) The presence of H.D. and Bryher added not only numbers but also a psychological tension to McAlmon's — and thus to Williams's — meanderings in Paris.

Things relaxed a bit when Bryher left for England and H.D. returned to Switzerland. McAlmon was emotionally and physically free to escort Bill and Flossie to various concerts and cafés.

When Williams left the Unic (and Paris) in June to sail home, he resumed work immediately on his manuscript of *In the American Grain*, which he'd brought to Europe with him but apparently hadn't touched. Since Williams completed and published the work soon after his return home, one can infer that Paris and Europe gave him the perspective or impetus he needed to finish this brilliant analysis of the American culture.

In October 1924, when Harriet Weaver, James Joyce's main financial supporter, came to Paris from London, she stayed in this Hôtel Unic. Since the hotel is a block over from the place de Rennes (now the place du 18-Juin-1940), McAlmon's reference to it in *Being Geniuses Together* as just "across the square" from Lavenue, the restaurant, is a bit misleading. Nevertheless, Weaver stayed here a month.

In May 1925, Weaver came back to Paris, intending to stay only "for a week" but staying three. Her residence in 1925 was in another modest hotel — at the end of rue Vaugirard on the place de la Sorbonne. Her final visit to Paris during the decade was in January 1928. Once again she stayed three weeks, two more than planned.

52 · Residence of Beatrice Hastings

In 1914, the English writer and editor Beatrice Hastings moved to Paris to write a weekly column ("Impressions of Paris") for the London periodical *The New Age*.

Although its founder and editor, A. R. Orage, tends to receive the credit, it was probably Hastings who first got Ezra Pound's essays published in *The New Age*. After she left the journal, Hastings continued to earn her living as a writer until 1916 when she "inherited a tolerable sum."

Soon after she arrived in Paris, Hastings was introduced to the painter Amedeo Modigliani by Nina Hamnett, the English model and artist. Hastings became Modigliani's loyal supporter, even though she recognized his capacity to exasperate even his most faithful friends. "Amedeo is a pig and a pearl," she once said.

Number unknown • Hôtel Jules-César

(This hotel was described as being situated between number 52 and the Falstaff, which was "a few doors down." No hotel of this name is listed in the various city registries for 1928, the relevant year in this context. A Hôtel Jules-César was registered in 1921 and a second one in 1925, but neither was on or even near the rue du Montparnasse. Assuming the name to be accurate, one can only conclude that the hotel was a private or otherwise unregistered enterprise — if Glassco's recollections, on which this entry is based, are reliable.)

When the young Canadian writer John Glassco came to Paris in 1928, he and Graeme Taylor took a room in this "charming hotel. It was neither comfortable nor clean nor warm [Glassco reports], but you never saw the proprietor, [and] there was always plenty of hot water. . . . The room cost twenty dollars a month and you could have breakfast in bed for fifteen cents."

42 • The Falstaff (now the Restaurant Falstaff)

Jimmy Charters, the famous Montparnasse barman, says: "From the strictly bartender point of view, the Falstaff certainly takes first place. I have always regretted that I left. The fine part of the Falstaff was the atmosphere, which was both gay and church-like at the same time. The Old English form of decoration, the wooden panelled walls, had a calming effect upon the heavy drinkers . . . ; yet it was a cheerful place where people enjoyed themselves and liked to sit about."

The patrons also liked the Falstaff. One customer noted that "it seemed on the whole better than the Dôme, which was often too noisy, than the Dingo . . . , which [was] too full of alcoholics. . . . Though these places were amusing and comfortable the Falstaff gained a special charm from the contrast between its rather stuffy oak panelling and padded seats and the haphazard way it was run by the bartender Jimmy Charters. . . . The Falstaff was owned jointly by two Belgian gentlemen who also shared a mistress, a very plump handsome grey-eyed woman called Madame Mitaine. The three of them sat quietly in the ingle of the fireplace every evening and did not interfere in any way, being content to count the cash when the bar closed at two o'clock in the morning. Jimmy ran the place on the principle that about every 10th drink should be on the house. . . ." Sound principle, that.

PLACE DU 18-JUIN-1940 (FORMERLY PLACE DE RENNES; GREATLY ALTERED)

5 · Restaurant des Trianons (now gone)

In the twenties, the Trianons was a classy restaurant, favored by expatriate writers when they had something special to celebrate. In May 1924, for example, Robert McAlmon threw a dinner here honoring William Carlos Williams.

In addition to Williams and his wife, also present at this dinner were James and Nora Joyce, Ford Madox Ford and Stella Bowen, Sylvia Beach and Adrienne Monnier, George and Böske Antheil (she was the former Elizabeth Markus, the niece of the writer Arthur Schnitzler), Mina Loy and one of her daughters, Laurence Vail and his sister Clotilde, Man Ray, Louis Aragon, Kitty Cannell, Bill and Sally Bird, Harold Loeb, and Marcel Duchamp. This crowd, some of whom had crashed the party, took up the "whole left wall of the plush restaurant." Only the Hemingways (back home for the birth of their son), it seems, missed this grand occasion.

Although usually on the borrow, James Joyce nevertheless kept a permanent table at the Trianons, where he took his evening meals and, at times, conducted business. In the spring of 1928, while the various backers and translators of the French version of *Ulysses* were at loggerheads, Joyce brought them all to the Trianons. Eventually Sylvia Beach, Adrienne Monnier, Stuart Gilbert, Valéry Larbaud, André Maurois, and Auguste Morel came to a mutually satisfactory agreement for publishing the book. (Monnier brought out the French version in February 1929.) Joyce referred to their agreement as the "Trianons Treaty."

BOULEVARD DU MONTPARNASSE

60 · Hôtel de Versailles (now gone)

When painter and sculptor Alexander Calder, the inventor of the mobile, came to Paris in late July 1926, he lived a month at this hotel, before finding a suitable studio on the rue Daguerre.

61 · Hôtel Edouard VI

This hotel was the residence of Cyril Connolly, a journalist for *The New Statesman*. Connolly wrote little fiction — one novel — but he was a good friend of Sylvia Beach and a staunch supporter of Shakespeare and Company. "In Sylvia Beach's bookshop," Connolly later recalled, "*Ulysses* lay stacked like dynamite in a revolutionary cellar." Connolly also knew Hemingway, and in London during World War II he gave a party where Ernest met a young writer named William Saroyan, who didn't show proper deference to Le Grand Papa (or so Papa thought).

AVENUE DU MAINE

14 · Jo Davidson's studio

In 1919 sculptor Jo Davidson rented a studio in this building where Kahlil Gibran had lived from 1903 to 1910. At first, Davidson sculpted *and* lived here. When his wife, Yvonne, came to Paris to join him, they found a furnished apartment on the rue du Bac. After the move, Davidson was able to use the entire space here — two rooms and a large balcony — as his primary studio.

Around the corner on what was then the impasse du Maine (now rearranged and called the rue Antoine-Bourdelle), Davidson had another studio in which he cut stone and worked on his American doughboy sculpture, a consuming, three-year project.

When the city of Paris decided to cut a new route for the street in 1931, Davidson's studio had to be demolished. And, since the sixteen-foot stone doughboy would have been too costly to move, it too was destroyed.

As a sculptor, Davidson worked fast, requiring only a few hours' pose from his subjects — which included (during these years) John D. Rockefeller, Clarence Darrow, Andrew Mellon, James Joyce, and Gertrude Stein.

In the thirties Davidson threw a large party in this studio. The event was significant for it was the first time James Joyce and Gertrude Stein ever met — even though they had shared interests, neighborhoods, and friends. The meeting between these two literary giants, who had dominated expatriate life in their respective ways, was cold and mercifully brief. Over the years, Stein had grown increasingly displeased that Joyce had never deigned to call on her.

Nevertheless, when Sylvia Beach approached Gertrude and offered to escort her across the room to Joyce, whose eyes were so bad that he could barely see, Stein finally consented.

"After all these years," she offered, coming up to the Irish novelist. "Yes," Joyce replied icily. When Stein noted that they lived in the same arrondissement, Joyce made no response, and Stein walked away. They never spoke — or met — again.

21 · Mina Loy's lampshade workshop

In this studio in 1927 Mina Loy, her daughter Gioella, and several other young women designed and painted the popular lampshades that Peggy Guggenheim was selling in Loy's rue du Colisée shop.

Next door to Loy's studio was that of Peggy Guggenheim's husband, Laurence Vail, who around this time was painting the large, room-divider screens that won him considerable attention. During the decade Vail married two of the most popular expatriates: Guggenheim and Kay Boyle. He seems, however, not to have been a particularly dedicated husband. For one thing, when Laurence's name is mentioned in letters or memoirs, one seems more often to find the name of his sister beside it than the name of his current wife.

RUE BLAISE-DESGOFFE

6 · Victoria-Palace Hôtel

When Katherine Mansfield arrived in Paris on 30 January 1922 for radiation treatments from Dr. Ivan Manoukhin, she took a room in the Victoria-Palace at the suggestion of her friend Anne Estelle Rice, the American painter. The hotel was rather costly and Mansfield, having separated from her husband, John Middleton Murry, was nearly broke, but she managed. At least her quarters here were considerably better than the barn near Fontainebleau in which she died almost exactly a year later.

During 1923–24 James Joyce and his family took rooms in this hotel. Harriet Weaver had turned a large inheritance (at today's rate: $825,000) over to Joyce, which enabled him to afford nearly a year's worth of the Victoria-Palace's luxury. Joyce was not one to scrimp.

RUE SAINT-ROMAIN

9 · Apartment of Djuna Barnes

With the money she earned by writing, Djuna Barnes bought an apartment here in one of two new (at the time) brick buildings, which are set in from the street and fronted by a quiet courtyard. Barnes and her companion, Thelma Wood, occupied a fifth-floor apartment — up stairway "D" — from the middle twenties until they parted in 1931. Prior to this residence, Barnes and Wood had lived in an apartment on the boulevard Saint-Germain.

By the time Barnes bought the apartment, she'd become fairly well known, having written several magazine pieces and a parody, *The Ladies Almanack*. In 1928, her first novel, *Ryder*, caused something of a sensation. She began work on her "poetic" novel, *Nightwood*, while in residence here, even though it was several years before she found a publisher for it.

The English poet Mina Loy also lived in this building late in the decade, having moved from her flat on rue Campagne-Première.

BEYOND MONTPARNASSE

OUT ALONG RUE BROCA

RUE BROCA

(Note: Prior to 1944, rue Broca ran all the way to the rue de la Santé and included the section now called rue Léon-Maurice-Nordmann, which today contains all numbers above the eighties.)

52 · Apartment of Walter Piston

Walter Piston "was by gift the best musician of us all. He had a good mind, too, and firm opinions," according to Virgil Thomson, who did not especially like Piston's music. Moving to Paris in 1924 with his wife, Kathryn, who was a dedicated painter, Piston studied under Nadia Boulanger and wrote several major works here, including "Three Pieces for Flute, Clarinet, and Bassoon," which premiered in Paris in 1925.

147 · Studio apartment of various expatriates

When Angela Martin, a former Ziegfeld chorus girl, and Daphne Berners, an Englishwoman who considered herself a *femme damnée*, moved out of this large studio in the spring of 1928 or 1929 (accounts differ), John Glassco and Graeme Taylor, two young Canadian writers, moved in. They were soon joined by Robert

McAlmon, who initially occupied a tiny storage room adjoining the studio, according to Glassco's (often inaccurate) memoirs.

McAlmon recalls the matter differently. "Lady Brett of *The Sun Also Rises*," he says, referring to Duff Twysden, "had acquired an American boy friend, much younger than she, and they discovered [this] huge bare studio on the rue Broca." Since they couldn't afford the rent, McAlmon took a lease on the studio and let Duff have the studio while he spent the summer in Nice. While there, McAlmon ran into Glassco and Taylor, whom he had known in Paris, and the three men shared a pension in Nice. "When I got back to Paris," McAlmon recalls, "it took more than gentle suggestions to get Lady Brett and her boy friend out of my studio." If McAlmon is correct, it would explain Glassco's claim that he found several unfinished portraits by Duff Twysden when he and Taylor moved in.

In any case, the painter Gwen Le Gallienne and Yvette Ledoux were living down the hall in the same building, and Hilaire Hiler's studio was just across the street.

BOULEVARD DE PORT-ROYAL

85 • Residence of William Shirer

When journalist William Shirer first came to Paris in late summer of 1925, he took a room in a pension beyond the courtyard of number 85. Later, he moved into the Hôtel de Lisbonne, a residence popular with the *Tribune* staff.

96 • Residence of Julian Bell

From the autumn of 1926 to the summer of 1927, Julian — the son of Bloomsburians Clive Bell and Vanessa Stephen — lived here at the family residence of his private tutor, M. Pinault. To secure this special tutorial arrangement for Julian, Clive had to use his connections with the Renoir family. (Clive, of course, knew the painter Pierre-Auguste Renoir, whose nephew was Clive's close friend and M. Pinault's colleague at the Sorbonne.) Writing his first major poetry and attending lectures at the Sorbonne, Julian was a student rather than a typical expatriate. (He was later killed in the Spanish Civil War.)

RUE DU FAUBOURG-SAINT-JACQUES

28 · Hôtel Médical

The Russian painter Marc Chagall first came to Paris in 1910. After staying briefly at 18 impasse du Maine (now rue Antoine-Bourdelle), Chagall moved to La Ruche on the passage de Dantzig. (La Ruche was a large, odd-shaped building fabricated from materials salvaged from the 1900 Exposition and converted into artists' quarters and studios.) When Chagall returned to Russia prior to World War I, he left over 150 paintings "locked" in his La Ruche studio with a twist of wire.

Returning to Paris on 1 September 1923 with his wife, Bella, and their daughter, Ida, Chagall checked into this hotel and raced over to La Ruche to retrieve his paintings. The wire was gone, and so were the paintings. During the war, the French government had assigned the studios to refugees from the occupied regions of France. Although the paintings were never recovered, it's unlikely that the refugees had taken them. In fact, some evidence points to Chagall's fellow painters, who simply may have been in need of canvas. Even more evidence, however, points to the poet Blaise Cendrars, whom Chagall forever suspected of taking and destroying the canvases. Chagall moved from the Hôtel Médical to Eugene Zak's studio early in 1924.

RUE MECHAIN

13 · Union Printery (now gone)

Failing to get some of her more obscure works published, Gertrude Stein decided to start her own press — the Plain Editions — and she hired the Union Printery to run off her first volume, an odd little work called *Lucy Church Amiably*. A thousand copies of this book, which Stein had completed in 1927, were ready for release by January 1931.

RUE DE LA SANTE

42 · Prison de la Santé (Maison d'Arrêt de la Santé)

Prior to World War I, Guillaume Apollinaire was held overnight in this prison after he'd been accused of stealing some *objets d'art* from the Louvre. He had indeed taken a few pieces, some stories say, in order to return them, thereby demonstrating the poor security in the museum.

In July 1929, Hart Crane spent some time in jail here after his brawl at the Café Select. Accounts differ, but one version says that Crane was in jail for only a matter of hours. Another version holds that Kay Boyle, the Crosbys, and other friends of his were out of town for weeks after Crane's arrest and were thus unable to help the poet out of his predicament.

The Paris edition of the *Chicago Tribune* reported that Crane was in jail several *days*, rather than weeks or hours. The story by reporter Edmond L. Taylor says that Crane was arrested July 4 and "is being entertained by officials of the police force and a public affair in his honor is planned for the near future. He is making an indefinite stay." Filed 10 July 1929, Taylor's story concludes by noting that Crane "was still there [in the Santé prison] up to a late hour yesterday. He may remain there for some time." All accounts agree, however, that Crane was eventually assessed an 800-franc fine and given an eight-day suspended sentence (like the *sursis* given E. E. Cummings).

55 · A la Bonne Santé

Hart Crane's friends — Harry Crosby, Roger Vitrac, and Whit Burnett (according to Crosby's diary) — awaited the poet's release in this bistro directly across from the jail. While waiting for him to emerge from the massive prison walls, they played checkers and drank beer. Crane came out looking "unshaved hungry wild" (Crosby's words). The welcome he received from his well-oiled friends was, shall we say, animated.

15 · The apartment of Morley and Loretto Callaghan

The Canadian writer and his wife moved here toward the end of "that summer in Paris," 1929. Their apartment was above a grocery store, but their Russian landlady spoke little French and no English. The summer was memorable for Callaghan, however, because of the boxing matches with Hemingway. At one sparring match, after settling on one-minute rounds, Morley and Ernest appointed Scott Fitzgerald timekeeper. Scott grew so absorbed in the fight that he forgot about the time and let a round go four minutes, to the advantage of the younger Callaghan. The bloodied Hemingway grumbled that Scott had done it on purpose.

BOULEVARD ARAGO

65 • Oliver Madox Hueffer's Paris apartment

Arriving in Paris on 3 September 1923, the English writer Ford Madox Ford moved in with his younger brother, Oliver Hueffer. (During the war, Ford had changed his surname from the German-sounding Hueffer.) With him was his common-law wife, Australian painter Stella Bowen, who in 1920 had borne him a daughter.

By this time the fifty-year-old Ford had had two careers, first as a successful and highly respected author and editor; then later as a less successful and virtually forgotten pig farmer in the south of England. Ford's literary career resumed with his move to Paris in 1923, for he once again became an important editor and novelist (starting with *Some Do Not*, the first of his Tietjens novels). And Stella received considerable notice in Paris as well, with three paintings in the 1923 Salon d'Automne.

While living with his brother, Ford got the idea for a little magazine, which he first referred to as *The Paris Review* but soon began calling the *Transatlantic Review*. A large, gregarious man who liked to throw parties and entertain friends, Ford needed a private residence. So, after three months, Oliver's wife rented Ford a *pavillon*-cottage for a nominal fee of 200 francs a month.

Behind some dilapidated studios between number 65 and the tennis courts at number 69, where Hemingway and Pound played tennis, Ford's cottage was tucked in back of a deep, bushy garden. Moreover, it wasn't far from the Santé prison, where the guillotine was still used on occasion, which added a gruesome tone to some of Ford's outdoor parties. (Public executions weren't banned in France until 1939.) Eventually, Ford's parties outgrew his small quarters, and like his prototype, Braddocks in *The Sun Also Rises*, Ford began renting various *bals musettes* — usually the one near the Hemingway residence on Cardinal-Lemoine — for his parties.

As of 1 January 1924, just before the first issue of the *Transatlantic Review* appeared, Ford moved his editorial office to Bird's Three Mountain Press at 29 quai d'Anjou. Ford maintained his personal residence in his boulevard Arago cottage, however, until a couple years later when he bought a flat on the rue Denfert-Rochereau.

Sometime in late 1923 or early 1924, Ford and Stella were joined in the cottage by Jean Rhys, whose husband, Jean Lenglet, had been extradited to Holland for illegally entering France. Born in the British West Indies in 1890 as Ella Gwendoline Rees Williams, Jean Rhys was given her *nom de plume* by Ford when he published her first story in the December 1924 number of the *Transatlantic Review*. Stella apparently encouraged Jean to become Ford's lover, for she lived with them for "many weeks" (in Stella's words). Ford was most supportive of Rhys's work, writing the preface, for example, of her first collection of sketches, *The Left Bank and Other Stories*. Her novel *Quartet* (published in England as *Postures* in 1928) is based on her life with Ford and Stella.

BOULEVARD AUGUSTE-BLANQUI

98 · Residence of Hadley Hemingway

In the autumn of 1927, after her divorce from Ernest and her brief residence near Gertrude Stein on rue de Fleurus, Hadley and her son, John, moved to a sixth-floor flat here, near the intersection with rue de la Glacière. American architect Paul Nelson, who designed the Lille Hospital, had a penthouse studio here.

The Hemingways' son, John, grew up to be called Jack; at the time, however, he was still known affectionately as Bumby. At preschool age, he played with his neighbor Julie Bowen, the daughter of Stella Bowen and Ford Madox Ford. And a frequent baby-sitter was Hadley's friend, Manuel Komroff, the future editor and *Esquire* writer. In addition to these friends, Hadley and Bumby often visited

Mr. and Mrs. John Gunther, who were living at the time in a flat adjacent to the Parc Montsouris.

EAST AND SOUTH OF THE MONTPARNASSE CEMETERY

BOULEVARD RASPAIL

248 • Residence of Sisley Huddleston

A correspondent for the *Christian Science Monitor* during the war, Huddleston became the chief correspondent for the London *Times* in the twenties. He lived for a while at 7 rue Corneille (above Le Cochon de Lait) near the Odéon, "under the shadows of the Café Voltaire." Soon after the Armistice, he moved here — at the intersection of boulevard Raspail and the rue Campagne-Première. By 1930, he'd settled in a "rural retreat" at Saint-Pierre-d'Autils.

According to some, Huddleston was inflated with self-importance. In reviewing one of his books, Elliot Paul wrote, "As I write this, I am haunted by the fear that Mr. Huddleston will find in it something which may be construed as complimentary to him. He is exceptionally adroit at this sort of thing. I, therefore, publicly disavow any such intention. If I have failed to make this clear, it is the fault of my technique."

RUE SCHOELCHER

11-bis • Principal residence of Anaïs Nin

Having lived in various places since their arrival in Paris in December 1924, Anaïs Nin and her husband, Hugh Guiler, finally settled down in this flat in August 1925. While Hugh worked in the Paris office of the National City Bank, Anaïs was dutifully recording her alternate periods of bliss and alarm as a wife consumed by her love for her husband. Her feelings for Paris also fluctuated, hating its "filth" one day and joyously praising its freedoms the next.

So devoted to and preoccupied by her husband was Nin during this period that she met very few people other than Guiler's business associates. It was some help when, by January 1926, her mother and brother moved into the ground-floor apartment facing hers. Still, she felt that "modern life does not affect us very much. In some ways Hugh and I are feeling more and more detached from it. . . ."

In August 1927, the American popular novelist and correspondent for the *Chicago Daily News*, John Gunther, and his wife sublet Anaïs's mother's apartment for a couple months. Anaïs increasingly enjoyed the company of new friends like the Gunthers — and some old friends as well.

As the value of their investments soared, Nin and Guiler were able to afford more lavish quarters. On 18 January 1929 Hugh signed a lease for an apartment in Passy, and Anaïs began to feel a "keen, particular pain at leaving our little apartment." On 15 April 1929, while the Passy residence was being prepared, Nin and her husband took temporary quarters at 13 square du Port-Royal.

At their temporary residence Anaïs's domestic tranquility was seriously threatened. One afternoon in May 1929, she and John Erskine, the American teacher and writer, were about to consummate an affair. Only Erskine's last-minute thoughts of his friendship with her husband prevented the adultery — by dampening Erskine's ardor, so to speak.

RUE BOULARD

2 • Hôtel Square

The writer Ken Sato took a room in this hotel, having left his rue Vavin residence. Sato's publisher, Robert McAlmon, claimed to like the way the Japanese writer "used the [English] language, particularly . . . the primitive 'No don't kill you; let me kill me or I kill the third man' sort of quality." McAlmon, however, was about the only one who liked the stuff.

RUE DAGUERRE

22 • Alexander Calder's first studio

After leaving the Hôtel de Versailles in August 1926, Calder took a studio room in a "small hotel run by a Swiss" for 450 francs a month. The room was painted "a sort of inoffensive gray with a little balcony with a bed on it." Calder lived and worked here for a year, until he returned to America in the fall of 1927.

RUE BOULARD

29 • Harry and Caresse Crosby's residence

The Crosbys lived here in *pavillon* number 1 (of seven) from the spring of 1924 to the summer of 1925. The tiny cottage lay beyond a high gate and down a picturesque pathway. But the house was "all front and no back," according to Caresse. The row of *pavillons* abutted a "high wall of a towering factory," and they were "one room deep, the stairs running up along the wall as on a backdrop."

Harry could not abide the commotion of Caresse's two children, Billy and Polleen, so they were exiled to the toolshed, just off the kitchen porch. Caresse had the shed converted into a nice little playroom for the children.

The Crosbys' maid during this period had two major duties: to take Polly back and forth to school; and, to place and collect Harry's bets on the horse races. For doing the latter, the maid automatically deducted 5 percent. From this *pavillon* the Crosbys moved to their best-known residence, on the rue de Lille.

RUE CELS

7 • Alexander Calder's second studio

When Calder returned to Paris in the autumn of 1928, he took "a ground-floor studio with a window" here. Calder owned an orange bicycle, which he peddled around the neighborhood for effect, wearing gray knickerbockers and bright red socks. While living here, he began to make his wire-sculpture circus toys.

Calder's work had received critical acclaim in both Paris and New York, but it wasn't selling very well. After entering various pieces in the Salon des Independents of 1929, Calder gave up this studio in June and returned to the United States. Less than a year later, however, he was back once more, taking a studio at 7 Villa Brune.

RUE FROIDEVAUX

69 • Gerald Murphy's atelier

Although both Gerald and Sara Murphy seemed to prefer Hadley to Ernest, when the Hemingways separated in 1926 Gerald offered Ernest the use of this studio, behind the Montparnasse Cemetery. Hemingway lived here through the spring of 1927, when he and Pauline Pfeiffer married and moved into their apartment on the rue Ferou. Meanwhile, Hadley had left the Hôtel Beauvoir and taken an apartment on the rue de Fleurus.

WEST OF THE GARE MONTPARNASSE

BOULEVARD PASTEUR

66 • Residence of Aaron Copland and Harold Clurman

During the winter of 1923–24, these two young Americans stayed with a French family here. Copland had already received some acclaim as a composer, and within a decade or so Clurman and his Group Theatre in New York would become an influential force in American drama.

RUE FALGUIERE

9 · Residence of Alfred Maurer (the Villa Gabriel)

An early American "modernist" painter, Alfy Maurer was one of Gertrude Stein's favorites before World War I. Stein believed, however, that Maurer was probably doomed forever to be a follower rather than an innovator. She was right.

RUE DE VAUGIRARD

148 · Paris–New York Hôtel

In 1929, Morley and Loretto Callaghan looked up Robert McAlmon here at the Paris–New York Hôtel. According to *That Summer in Paris*, the Callaghans stayed in this hotel until they found a place at 15 rue de la Santé.

Sylvia Beach's records, however, put the Callaghans elsewhere: first at 9 rue de La Michodière (Hôtel de Noailles); then at 2 square du Port-Royal, just around the corner from their final residence on the rue Santé, at number 15.

IMPASSE RONSIN

8 · The studio of Constantin Brancusi (now gone)

Today, a replica of Brancusi's workshop sits outside the northwest corner of Pompidou Center.

Though gregarious by nature, the experimental sculptor Brancusi lived alone here on the impasse Ronsin with his huge white spitz, Polaris. Brancusi had plenty of visitors, however. At a dinner in Brancusi's studio during the summer of 1923, for example, Harriet Monroe — the editor of *Poetry: A Magazine of Verse* — on her first and only trip to Paris, met the composer Erik Satie.

In late January 1924, Robert McAlmon brought William Carlos Williams (who'd just arrived in Paris) to visit Brancusi's studio, and a few days later Brancusi invited the two American writers back for one of his famous steak dinners.

RUE VALENTIN-HAUY

5 • Residence of Sergei Prokofiev

In October 1923, Prokofiev, his wife, and his mother (who died the following year) settled in "a small suburban flat" somewhere in Paris. According to a plaque on this building, the composer lived here from 1929 to 1935, although most biographers claim that he returned permanently to the Soviet Union in 1933.

During the twenties, Prokofiev was often away from Paris on tour as a concert pianist. "To be living in Paris," he said, "did not mean that one automatically became a Parisian or a Frenchman." Far more than most Russians in Paris, Prokofiev sympathized with the Soviets. Thus, he had little in common with fellow Russian expatriates like Stravinsky, although Prokofiev greatly appreciated the assistance that Diaghilev, for one, gave him.

7 • Apartment of Eugene and Maria Jolas

An engaging and hardworking couple with a baby daughter (Betsy), Eugene and Maria Jolas seemed to have no enemies, although some writers like Robert McAlmon felt Eugene's language to be too abstract and his interest in Surrealism a bit pretentious. Having resided for a while at 6 rue de Verneuil, the Jolases lived here at 7 rue Valentin-Haüy during the genesis of their little magazine, *transition*, in 1926.

After setting up the review's office on rue Fabert, the Jolases moved to the countryside in 1927 — before the first number of *transition* was issued. The move was prompted by a desire for seclusion and tranquility, and they found it in a lovely house at Colombey-les-Deux-Eglises, near Saint-Dizier, where *transition* was printed. After World War II, Charles de Gaulle obtained the house and used it for weekend retreats.

RUE BLOMET

45 • Joan Miró's studio (now gone)

There is now a small neighborhood park extending from number 43 to number 51, which contains a small bowling area (where number 45 would have been) and a large runabout area for children. The park includes a playfully fantastic sculpture by Miró on which kids obviously love to climb and slide.

A dedicated painter, Miró was so poor at times that according to reports he could afford but one lunch a week. Despite the failure of his work to sell, Miró's confidence was unshakable, and he refused to abandon or compromise his style of painting. His dedication was also evident in his ability to ignore his immediate neighbors. Next door, for example, lived the bohemian André Masson, a painter who periodically pursued "a systematic derangement of all senses" — by means of huge amounts of absinthe.

Miró's friend Picabia brought the Dadaist Tristan Tzara out to the studio, and soon an entire "Rue Blomet Group" was formed, including a reluctant Miró and enthusiasts like Picabia, Masson, Tzara, Michel Leiris, Robert Desnos, Jacques Prevert, and Antonin Artaud. Eventually, some of the Rue Blomet Group began to identify themselves with André Breton's Surrealists. Miró, however, remained Miró.

48 · La Bal Nègre

Located across from Miró's studio, this bar and dance hall was popular among Americans during the black craze initiated by Josephine Baker and the Revue Nègre troupe. There were surely more whites in grotesque blackface than blacks who frequented the place. In 1928, Eugene Jolas brought Harry Crosby and Kay Boyle together at the Bal Nègre — an odd meeting ground, no doubt, for three so distinct individuals.

REMOTE MONTPARNASSE REGIONS

These scattered, isolated sites defy incorporation into clusters.

RUE HALLE

24 • Residence of Mary Reynolds

Besides being a book binder of extraordinary skill, Mary Reynolds was an ardent supporter of the Surrealists, whose unofficial historian she became. Her husband had been fatally gassed during the war, so when Reynolds arrived in Paris in 1920 she was one of hundreds of thousands of war widows.

After moving from her first apartment on the place de la Sorbonne, Reynolds regularly opened her rue Hallé apartment for avant-garde salons for the Surrealists and other painters, like Villon, Rouault, and Léger.

A loyal and devoted friend of Marcel Duchamp, Reynolds was the painter's lover and confidante for nearly two decades. Even though in the twenties Duchamp moved many of his personal belongings into Reynolds's flat, they maintained separate residences — and, on occasion, separate lovers (in Duchamp's case at least). World War II finally separated them in 1940.

VILLA SEURAT

18 • Michael Fraenkel's residence

Following the winter of 1930–31, which he spent at the apartment of Richard Galen Osborn, a nearly destitute Henry Miller moved in with his new friend, Michael Fraenkel. Born in Russia and raised in America, Fraenkel had made enough money selling books by 1926 to enable him to retire to Paris and try writing. Thus, Fraenkel appears as the young writer Boris in Miller's *Tropic of Cancer.*

Walter Lowenfels was another young man who had retired from commerce (his family's butter business) to write, and it was he who brought Miller and Fraenkel together. In 1930, Fraenkel and Lowenfels — Villa Seurat neighbors since 1929 — founded the Carrefour Press.

The Villa Seurat is a short, private cul-de-sac with residences built specifically for artists. According to Miller's recollections, the street — which opened in 1926 — was "given up to quiet, joyous work. Every house contains a writer, painter, musician, sculptor, dancer, or actor."

RUE GEORGES-BRAQUE (UNTIL RECENTLY THE RUE DU DOUANIER)

Just off Montsouris Park • Home of Stephen and Sophie Green

During his Guggenheim year in Paris (1928–29), black poet Countee Cullen stayed here as a guest of the socially prominent Greens, using one of their rooms as a studio. A Phi Beta Kappa from New York University, Cullen was a deliberate writer, well trained in the English poetic tradition. His first book, *Color,* published in 1925, had marked the pattern for his subsequent work by interweaving his academic training and his racial awareness.

Although Cullen spent some time with white friends like the poet Allen Tate, he tended to prefer the company of black expatriates like the painters Ossawa Tanner, Palmer Hayden, and Hale Woodruff; the sculptor Augusta Savage; and the blues singer Alberta Hunter.

In the autumn of 1929, just before his third volume of poetry (*The Black Christ*) was published, Cullen was joined at the Greens' residence by Eric Walrond, another Guggenheim fellow. Born in British Guiana, Walrond had studied in the United States and had become a successful journalist before achieving literary acclaim with his collection of grim West Indian stories, *Tropic Death,* in 1926.

AVENUE DU GENERAL-LECLERC
(FORMERLY AVENUE D'ORLEANS)

101 • Residence of Marc Chagall (now gone; area remodeled)

Eugene Zak owned this studio and sublet it to his friend Marc Chagall from early 1924 until 1927. Chagall spent several months trying to recreate the paintings he'd lost in La Ruche. Perhaps his greatest coup during his Paris years was to win the assignment to paint the ceiling of the Opéra.

VILLA BRUNE

7 • Alexander Calder's third studio

When he returned to Paris in March 1930, Calder moved out here. Although he left the following December, he kept this studio, where he used to hold his little "circus" shows. After getting married in the States in January 1931, Calder brought his wife back to this lovely residence, with its glass front facing across a quiet, narrow lane onto a wooded stream.

RUE DIDOT

96 • Hôpital Broussais-Charité

Amedeo Modigliani died in this hospital from tubercular meningitis in January 1920. Upon seeing his body, the painter's model and lover, Jeanne Hébuterne, returned to her family's flat and leapt to her death. The cortege that followed Modigliani's coffin up rue Vercingétorix across Paris to Père Lachaise Cemetery included some of the most important artists of the century: Max Jacob, Picasso, Brancusi, Vlaminck, Lipchitz, Valadon, and Léger.

RUE VERCINGETORIX (AREA NOW COMPLETELY ALTERED)

3 • Residence of Berenice Abbott

Abbott first came to Paris in April 1921 "possessing six dollars, a slight knowledge of French, and a few friends." She was a sculptor, but she initially supported herself by taking odd jobs and by modeling for painters and sculptors. It wasn't until the winter of 1923, when she came back to Paris after a brief trip to Berlin, that she began to earn steady money — first as Man Ray's assistant and later as a photographer with her own clientele.

50 • Stuart Davis's studio

When the American painter Stuart Davis arrived in Paris in 1928, he took a studio out here, beyond the Gare Montparnasse. He liked Paris at once, noting that the "pressure of American anti-art was removed. You could starve to death quicker but you had the illusion that the artist was a human being and not just a bum." His lack of funds, however, forced him to return to New York in July 1929, where he discovered that the work of the young artists in America was "comparable in every way with the best of the work over there."

PASSAGE DE DANTZIG

2 • La Ruche

Located just off the rue de Dantzig, La Ruche was built just after the turn of the century as a central gathering hall for artists who wanted to live in an experimental commune. The building and its interior studios, which could serve as ateliers for as many as 120 artists, were made from the pavilions that were to be demolished after the 1900 Exposition. Designed by Eiffel (the tower man), La Ruche resembles a beehive — hence its name — with an octagonal exterior and "cubist" roof.

Located within ear and nose range of the slaughterhouses on rue de Vaugirard, the studios of La Ruche may not have been the best of places to work, but the company was surely inspiring. Living there for various lengths of time were such artists and writers as Fernand Léger, Max Jacob, Guillaume Apollinaire, Blaise Cendrars, Jacques Lipchitz, Ossip Zadkine, and Chaim Soutine. When he moved out of La Ruche just prior to World War I, Marc Chagall left behind some 150 paintings, which he never recovered.

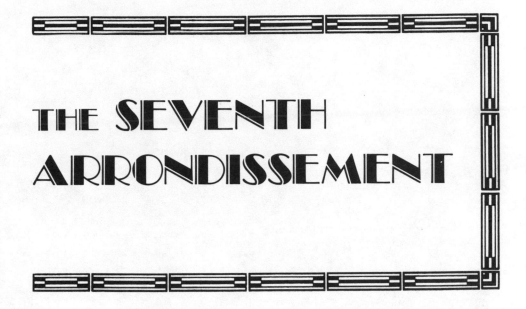

THE SEVENTH
ARRONDISSEMENT

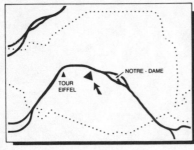

MAP 6

includes addresses from ...

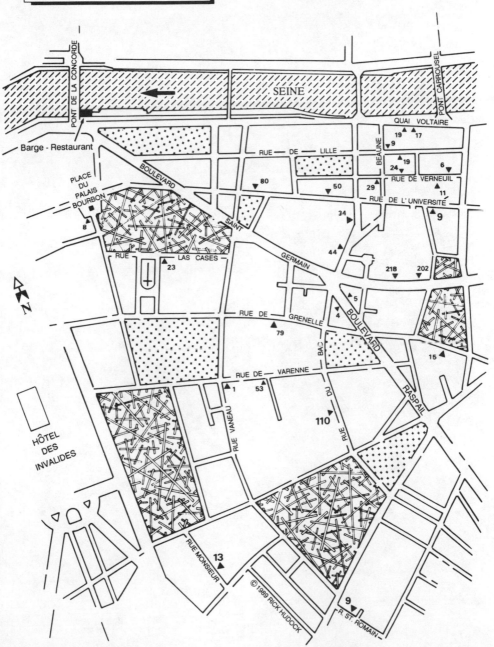

© 1989 RICK HUDOCK

THE INVALIDES
AND THE EIFFEL

QUAI ANATOLE-FRANCE

Pont de la Concorde • On the river below the Chamber of Deputies floated a restored barge made into a restaurant

Stravinsky's ballet *Les Noces* premiered on 13 June 1923, along with his *Pulcinella*, and to celebrate the occasion Gerald and Sara Murphy hosted a grand dinner on the barge the following Sunday, the seventeenth. Some forty artists, musicians, and patrons gathered for the event. Picasso was there, as were Sergei Diaghilev, whose Russian Ballet Company had staged the ballet; composer Darius Milhaud; artist and writer Jean Cocteau; Tristan Tzara; poet Blaise Cendrars; and Scofield Thayer, editor of *The Dial*.

Stravinsky arrived early to make sure his seating was satisfactory. It was: he was placed on the right hand of Princesse de Polignac, who'd commissioned the ballet. The dinner lasted all night. Instead of flowers, Sara Murphy piled small toys along the various place settings, and Picasso, for one, amused himself with the tiny cars and animals all evening. A program of musical compositions alternated with the dinner courses.

Jean Cocteau, who'd come dressed as a ship captain, wandered among the crowd whispering, *"On coule"* ("We're sinking"). At one point, some guests removed the enormous wreath commemorating the occasion, and Stravinsky, running the length of the room, dived through it. Exemplary, even for the Murphys who seldom did anything gauche, this dinner was the talk of Paris for years. It was the twenties counterpart of the famous Rousseau banquet in Picasso's studio a decade and a half earlier.

RUE DE L'UNIVERSITE

80 · Residence of Margaret Anderson

When Sylvia Beach canceled Anderson's rue de Grenelle address, she added this one — and apparently never had cause to change it, despite Anderson's having also stayed at the hotels Jacob and Bonaparte, among other places. Toward the end of the decade, Anderson and her companion, the former actress Georgette Leblanc, took an apartment on rue Casimir-Périer. "She [Anderson] not only arranged the apartment," Leblanc noted, "she prepares the days. Each one must fit into the week like an object in its box."

PLACE DU PALAIS-BOURBON

8 · William Bird's apartment

Besides operating a news service and serving as printer-publisher of the Three Mountains Press editions, Bill Bird was the friend and confidant of many expatriates. Bird's delightful wife, Sally, was a charming hostess, and their apartment, Lincoln Steffens recalls, "provided a place for rebels to conspire and play in."

RUE LAS-CASES

23 · Residence of Archibald MacLeish and family

Within the shadow of Sainte Clotilde, across from a splendid little park, the poet Archibald MacLeish and his wife, the soprano Ada — along with their six-year-old son and infant daughter — made their first home in Paris in September 1923.

The neighborhood was lovely, as was the building, but the interior was dirty and the living crowded. The apartment consisted of a small salon, a dining room, and three bedrooms — one that was rather comfortable and two bite-sizers for the kids. The cramped quarters may explain why MacLeish did not like Paris at first and called it "a degenerate metropolis" in a letter of November 1923. As noted elsewhere, apparently the MacLeishes soon moved to 86 boulevard Saint-Michel, probably before the winter of 1923.

RUE VANEAU

1-bis • Residence of André Gide

A celebrated writer by the twenties, Gide conscientiously supported the bookshops of Adrienne Monnier and Sylvia Beach. Without such generous gestures by influential French intellectuals and artists like Gide, operations like Sylvia's English bookstore and lending library could not have survived.

Nor, perhaps, the high level of literary art. Praising shops like Beach's and Monnier's, Sisley Huddleston wrote of the special mix they provided: "I have seen [these bookshops] thronged with [some] writers who, having given proof of their quality, such as André Gide and Valéry Larbaud, were addressed by others as *Maître*; and [with other writers who were] only beginning."

RUE DE VARENNE

53 • Residence of Walter van Rensselaer Berry

Walter Berry, Harry Crosby's cousin, moved into this fashionable townhouse in February 1921. He gave up his quarters at 14 rue Saint-Guillaume when he took over this lease from the American writer Edith Wharton.

Wharton and her husband, Teddy, who was twelve years older than she, had first moved to this house around 1910. (Edith was divorced from Teddy in 1913 — after he'd been institutionalized for psychological reasons in 1912.) Curiously, the "Residential Directory" of the *Franco-American Yearbook* lists this as her address in 1921, even though by then Wharton had been living for some time at the Pavillon Colombe, her home twelve miles north of Paris at Saint-Brice-sous-Fôret, Seine-et-Oise.

There is little persuasive evidence to support the rumors passed on by Caresse Crosby and others that Wharton kept a *pied-à-terre* here at 53 Varenne to be close to Berry, or that she and Berry employed a secret passageway for romantic assignations. They were acquaintances and may have been friends, but it's not very likely that Wharton and Berry were lovers, however alluring Caresse's speculations.

RUE DE GRENELLE

79 • Embassy of the U.S.S.R.

After she'd returned from Russia in 1925, Isadora Duncan and Victor Seroff, her new companion, attended receptions in the huge building hidden behind a fifteen-foot wall.

RUE DU BAC

110 • Residence of James McNeill Whistler, 1892–95

Although not of this generation (he'd died in 1903), Whistler was an experimental American painter whose dedication and unconventionality inspired many of the expatriate artists of the twenties. It's been said that attending the corpse of Marcel Proust were only two American presences: Man Ray in person (he'd come to photograph the body) and Whistler in spirit (on the wall hung one of his paintings).

In his poem "To Whistler, American," Ezra Pound acknowledges his indebtedness to Whistler:

> You also, our first great,
> Had tried all ways;
> Tested and pried and worked in many fashions,
> And this much gives me heart to play the game.

RUE MONSIEUR

13 • Home of Cole and Linda Porter

After their Paris wedding in December 1919, Cole and Linda Porter resided in Linda's pleasant house on the rue de La Baume, while also keeping a suite at the Ritz. A short while later, however, Linda sold the La Baume house and bought these more lavish apartments.

This residence, which reportedly cost a quarter of a million dollars, served as the Porters' Paris home for the rest of their lives. Linda's furnishings, along with the house's splendid location (including a gorgeous courtyard), made the residence a veritable Parisian showplace. Highbrow musicians like the composer Stravinsky, the pianist Rubinstein, and the conductor Golschmann mixed with popular performers like Beatrice Lillie and Fanny Brice at the Porters', where Elsa Maxwell was usually employed to oversee the appropriate social orchestration.

RUE MASSERAN

11 • Residence of Michael Arlen

Although he lived primarily in London during the decade after World War I, Michael Arlen had an apartment here during the latter part of the twenties. Having gained both fame and fortune from his novel *The Green Hat*, Arlen was resented by the expatriate *artistes*. They referred to him in terms usually reserved for Sinclair Lewis, whom they considered not only arrogant but, worse, commercial.

Noting that "many readers with ordinary intelligence find him fascinating," Alex Small in the *Tribune* adds that "some reason must exist for Mr. Arlen's phenomenal popularity." Arlen himself suggested that the explanation lay in his skill at selling cynicism to the cynics, pseudo-intellectualism to the pseudo-intellectuals, and snobbery to the snobs. "I'm not really a fashion," Arlen wrote. "I'm a disease — an international disease. Nobody likes me. Most of the people who read me say: 'How horrid, or how silly, or how tiresome.' And yet they read me."

Small's *Tribune* piece also notes that Arlen's real name is Dikran Kouyoumdjian. Presumably born in Bulgaria, Arlen once proclaimed, with his usual self-assurance, "Yes, I am an Armenian — the only known survivor of that race."

15 • Jo Davidson's residence

Between his short stay on the rue du Bac and his 1925 move to the rue Leconte-de-Lisle in Passy, the American sculptor — along with his wife, Yvonne, and his children — lived in a "small house on the corner of the rue Duroc and the rue Masseran."

This residence was the Davidsons' favorite. "It was a beautiful house," he notes. "On the ground floor to the left of the entrance was a large salon with three windows giving on a garden and three on the street. To the right was a dining room with frescoes by Le Fauconnier. The floor above had a small library as well as bedrooms and bath and the top floor was for the children and their governess."

AVENUE DE LOWENDAL

5 • Librairie Six (now gone)

In December 1921, Man Ray's first Paris exhibition was held in Philippe Soupault's tiny bookstore here. The show exhibited such works of "anti-art" as Ray's tack-studded flatiron (which he titled *Cadeau* because it was a gift to Soupault). Nothing sold — neither the metronome with the moving eye (*Object to Be Destroyed*), the jar of ball bearings in oil (*Export Commodity*), nor any other Dada creation. Subsequently Ray turned to photography, a field that allowed him to be just as zany and inventive — and, better yet, financially successful.

In the late summer of 1922, John Rodker and Iris Barry took over part of the Librairie Six while they worked frantically to bring out a second printing of 2,000 copies of James Joyce's *Ulysses*. Since the book had to be smuggled past the customs officials into both England and the USA, its sales were impressive. The first printing, sponsored by Sylvia Beach's Shakespeare and Company, was released in February 1922. The second, a less expensive edition, was issued in October 1922, under the aegis of Harriet Weaver's Egoist Press. Rodker and Barry's speed, however, had a cost: over 200 errata had to be acknowledged when the issue appeared.

RUE CHEVERT

6 • Residence of Mrs. E. G. Colton

The name "Mrs E. G. Colton" actually referred to the celebrated anarchist Emma Goldman. By marrying James Colton, a Welsh acquaintance she barely knew (and never lived with), Emma Goldman got herself a new name — and along with it came a new British passport and renewed freedom to travel.

Goldman spent most of the first half of the decade in England and the second half at her Saint-Tropez cottage, "Bon Esprit," which Nellie and Frank Harris and Peggy Guggenheim purchased for her. Goldman did visit Paris occasionally, and after staying at the Hôtel Terraso, she began using the apartment here at 6 rue Chevert. (It may not have been until the early thirties that she used this address. Sylvia Beach first refers to this address when "Mrs. Colton" checks out Eugene O'Neill's *Mourning Becomes Electra*, a play published in 1931.)

RUE FABERT

40 • *transition* office; Hôtel de la Gare des Invalides (now gone)

Conceived by Eugene Jolas and Elliot Paul in 1926 and issued from 1927 to 1938, *transition* bore the influence of Freudianism and German Expressionism. Mostly, though, the journal was open to all kinds of experimental writing and innovative thinkers.

At first Paul and Jolas used the dining room table in the Jolas apartment for their daily editorial meetings. Later, upon Maria Jolas's insistence, they rented a fourth-floor room in this hotel to use as an office. (The operation required separate quarters still later, when the Jolases moved their residence to the French countryside.)

Looking out the only window in Room 16, Jolas and Paul could see the splendid Esplanade des Invalides below and, in the dim distance to the north, Sacré Coeur. At the end of the first year, Robert Sage — who, like Paul, was a writer for the *Tribune* — was named associate editor, and his wife, Maeve, hired on as secretary.

The editorial policy of *transition* explicitly intended to offer "an opportunity [for American writers] to express themselves freely [and] to experiment." The editors also invited foreign authors and previously unpublished writers to submit manuscripts. *Transition* was to be an outlet for "new words, new abstractions, new hieroglyphics, new symbols, new myths. . . ."

The first number contained over twenty works, including Joyce's "Opening Pages of a Work in Progress" (*Finnegans Wake*), a poem by André Gide, Gertrude Stein's "An Elucidation," poems by Hart Crane and Archibald MacLeish, and a story by Kay Boyle plus her review of William Carlos Williams's *In the American Grain*. Later, *transition* would introduce writers like Katherine Anne Porter, Allen Tate, and Henry Miller.

Published from 1927 to 1938, the review was accurately named, for it covered the "transition" from *les Années Folles* ("the crazy years," i.e., the twenties) to *les Années Difficiles* ("the difficult years," the thirties). No number appeared in 1931, and only one issue — a 400-pager — in 1930. Subscriptions to *transition* never exceeded 1,000, and the most copies of any issue numbered 4,000. Hardly a money-maker, the magazine's deficits were recouped out of Jolas's pocket and from voluntary contributions by friends.

QUAI D'ORSAY

61 (renumbered; formerly 67) • The American Church

This neo-gothic, nondenominational church was completed in 1929, prior to which the congregation had met at 21 rue de Berri. The new Paris *Herald* building took over the rue de Berri location in December 1930.

SQUARE DE ROBIAC

2 • James Joyce residence

James Joyce and his family lived in an apartment here, just off 192 rue de Grenelle, from 1925 to 1930 — longer than anywhere else in Paris. During this period Joyce wrote much of his "Work in Progress," *Finnegans Wake*.

Joyce occasionally gave readings from his new material. When Eugene Jolas and Elliot Paul were working on the first number of *transition*, they cautiously asked Sylvia Beach to find out from the sometimes-imperious Joyce if he'd let them run something from his "Work in Progress" in their new review. So, one Sunday afternoon in mid-December 1926, Beach and her friend Adrienne Monnier took Jolas and Paul to the Joyce apartment, where he spontaneously read from a section he was then writing. The very first number of *transition* led off with "Opening Pages of a Work in Progress."

On other occasions, Joyce's readings were less spontaneous and open. For example, in 1927 shortly after he'd written the "Anna Livia Plurabelle" section of *Finnegans Wake*, Joyce sent formal invitations to some twenty friends (including Padraic and Mary Colum, Hemingway, Bill and Sally Bird, Stuart Gilbert, Sylvia Beach, and Robert McAlmon) for a reading of "Anna Livia" at a three-thirty tea the first Wednesday in November.

During the summer of 1929, after dining at the Trianons, James and Nora Joyce brought their companions — Robert McAlmon and Morley and Loretto Callaghan — back to this apartment for drinks. Joyce played for them his prized recording of Aimee Semple McPherson, in which she coos seductively, "Come, come on to me. . . ." The Reverend McPherson's solicitous tones appealed to Joyce.

Noting that he was approaching "the close of my Paris career," Joyce moved briefly into the Hôtel Powers (52 rue François-I) on 11 April 1931. When he left for London a few days later, Joyce's proposed "week or two" in Paris had lasted almost exactly ten years. He wasn't gone from Paris long, however. He soon returned and in effect re-upped for a second ten years.

RUE DE MONTTESSUY

9 • Address of Elliot Paul

Although Paul's most beloved and best-known address was at the Hôtel du Caveau on the rue de la Huchette, about which he wrote so movingly in *The Last Time I Saw Paris*, Paul had an apartment here before he discovered the Caveau.

14 • Residences of Harold Loeb, Kitty Cannell, and Mary Butts

Early in October 1923, after his prestigious little magazine, *Broom*, had folded, Harold Loeb moved into a flat adjacent to Kitty (Kathleen) Cannell, his fellow writer and, for a while, his companion and mistress. He lived here the next several years, although he traveled considerably. During his first months in residence, Loeb worked on the manuscript of his novel *Doodab*, which had been accepted by Liveright in 1923. Following Loeb's revisions, the novel was published in 1924.

Loeb is unflatteringly portrayed as the "arrested adolescent," Robert Cohn, in Ernest Hemingway's *The Sun Also Rises*, and some of Kitty Cannell's traits are reputedly ascribed to the character Frances Clyne.

Mary Butts, the English writer, also lived in this building during the mid-twenties, though she wasn't one to stay put for very long. Mary was a tall, lovely, and outgoing woman with carrot-red hair, and for a period she was especially preoccupied by occult matters. Although she never described the affair in detail, Butts supposedly spent an unpleasant summer at Aleister Crowley's black-magic temple at Cefalu.

"[Mary] could stir up others with drink and drugs and magic incantations," her friend Virgil Thomson notes, "and then when the cyclone was at its most intense, sit down at calm center and glow." Thomson called her "the storm goddess" because of her ability to provoke ecstasy and unrest in those around her, including the usually unflappable Virgil Thomson.

Butts had once been married to publisher John Rodker and later lived with Cecil Maitland, who died in 1927. After Maitland's death, she married artist Gabriel Atkin and moved back to England. No one who knew Mary Butts ever spoke of this fascinating woman indifferently.

AVENUE ELISEE-RECLUS

2 • Apartment of John Rodker

Poet, printer, and former husband of Mary Butts, John Rodker made several trips to Paris from London during the twenties.

Besides this address, Sylvia Beach had one for him at the Hôtel du Pavillon on the rue de Verneuil and another at 30 boulevard Marbeau near the Bois de Boulogne. After starting up two presses in London following World War I, Rodker came to Paris in 1922 to work on Harriet Weaver's second edition of Joyce's *Ulysses*.

AVENUE CHARLES-FLOQUET

1 • Residence of Virginia Gross

The wife of Christian Gross, First Secretary of the American Embassy, and a sugar millionairess in her own right, Virginia was from the Crocker banking family of California. Willing to spend money to gain entrance into the international social set, Mrs. Gross found George Antheil, Ezra Pound, and Virgil Thomson most happy to oblige her. In July 1926, she underwrote four weekly concerts of Antheil and Thomson material (and one piece by Pound). She opened all four of the reception rooms in her apartment here at number 1 and brought in the requisite pianos and musicians, including the conductor Vladimir Golschmann. At the last concert, Mrs. Gross was seen rubbing elbows with two princesses, a duchess, and three Italian marchesas. Mission accomplished.

8 • Residence of James and Nora Joyce

Having lived at number 26 during the winter and spring of 1922–23, the Joyce family returned to the avenue Charles-Floquet when they left the Victoria-Palace Hôtel in 1924. Here, the Joyces — including Lucia, Giorgio, and "a biscuit-colored cat" — had the entire fifth floor to themselves. They were becoming quite domesticated.

BOULEVARD DE GRENELLE

6 • Vélodrome d'Hiver (torn down in 1959)

Ernest Hemingway and others — including Allen Tate, Sylvia Beach, and Adrienne Monnier — came out here periodically to watch the six-day bicycle races. No one watched all six days, of course. Rather, after dinner or a show, a group of elegant revelers might catch a limo to the Vel' d'Hiv' to end the evening. Depending on the mood, some wealthy spectator might offer a prize to one of the racers. When the awards weren't thought sufficiently generous, the regular, poorer audience (*les populaires*) would shout insults up to the wealthy set, calling the bejeweled ladies "*poules de luxe*," for instance.

RUE AUGUSTE-BARTHOLDI

2 · Apartment of Richard Galen Osborn

In December 1930, Henry Miller was jobless and veritably destitute. Fortunately, he made friends with Richard Galen Osborn, "who [Miller says] rescued me from starvation in Paris and set my feet in the right direction." Miller spent the winter here in Osborn's studio, which looked out upon the Eiffel Tower. In the spring of 1931 Miller moved in with another newfound friend, Michael Fraenkel, who lived on the Villa Seurat.

ALONG THE CHAMPS-ELYSEES

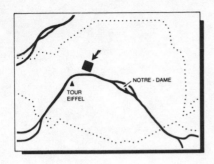

MAP 7

includes addresses from ...
22. Around Concorde
23. The Gaveau and the Claridge

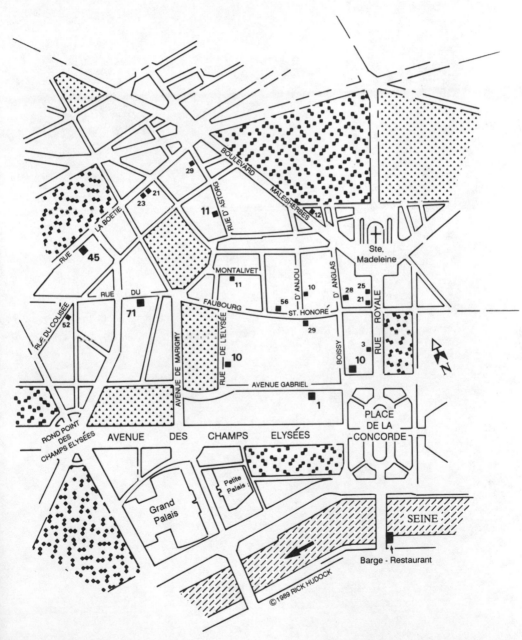

© 1989 RICK HUDOCK

AROUND CONCORDE

PLACE DE LA CONCORDE

10 · Hôtel Crillon

Before and during World War I — up to her arrest in 1917 — Mata Hari was supposed to have lived periodically in this plush hotel. The hotel had two entrances, particularly useful (one supposes) for spies. One entrance led into the *place* near the French Ministry of War and the other into the rue Boissy-d'Anglas, near the French president's palace.

Following World War I, American diplomats headquartered at the Crillon, where they considered secret terms and agreements in preparation for the Versailles Peace Conference. So much for the first of Wilson's Fourteen Points: "open covenants openly arrived at." The activity, intrigue, and tension at the Crillon increased when President and Mrs. Wilson arrived, even though the President's private residence was at 11 place des Etats-Unis, which was near the embassy offices.

The *New York Times* sent sixty-year-old novelist Gertrude Atherton to cover the talks. Familiar with Paris from previous visits, Atherton always preferred the Crillon, where she first stayed almost a half-century before.

While preparing for the talks in 1919, Colonel Edward House, President Wilson's personal emissary, placed a request to Washington for a dozen code books. Curiously, the State Department promptly sent twelve code *clerks* — including a gangly James Thurber, who dutifully reported to the Crillon. Told they wanted code books, not code clerks, the befuddled Thurber was immediately assigned to the U.S. Chancellery, next to which he found a little *pension* where he lived until returning to America in February 1920.

Thurber's account of the incident is priceless. The State Department had compiled a new code especially for the peace talks. The code had certain flaws, however. For example, there was no code word for "America," and the code groupings themselves were sometimes transparent. "Love," to illustrate the matter, was generated in code form as "LOVVE." According to these new code groupings, Thurber notes, "books" and "clerks" may very well have differed only by a single letter — say, DOGEC (for "books") and DOGED (for "clerks").

But what complicated the matter was the fact that a Naval officer had taken over the diplomatic communications at the Crillon, and he used the Navy's code, not the new State Department code. Thus, his communiqués were received in Washington by State Department personnel who could not read them. The State Department people replied with "bewildered and frantic queries" — in their own code of course, which the Navy couldn't unravel. All communication, needless to say, between the Peace Conference officials at the Crillon and the State Department in Washington came to a halt, until the Naval personnel in Paris agreed (presumably in standard English) to use the new State Department code. That's when Colonel House's staff in the Crillon requisitioned a dozen code clerks, uh, *books*. And Thurber showed up.

In 1921, after working for a short while in "The Sunwise Turn," the Greenwich Village bookshop owned by her cousin Harold Loeb, Peggy (Marguerite) Guggenheim took off for Paris. She checked into a room at the elegant Crillon, before moving on to the equally sumptuous, but newer, Hôtel Plaza-Athénée on the avenue Montaigne.

In February 1923, Isadora Duncan and her husband, the Russian folk poet Sergei Esenin, were staying at the Crillon when Esenin had another of his "momentary fits of madness" (Isadora's words from the *Tribune* of 28 February). "He wanted to go back [to Russia]," Isadora is quoted as saying, "so I sent him. . . . He can smash things up in Moscow and no one will care because he is a poet." Esenin eventually committed suicide.

Publisher William Randolph Hearst and Marion Davies stayed at the Crillon during their visit in September 1928. Upon their return, Hearst's newspapers ran a story exposing a secret British-French agreement, which embarrassed the French government. When Hearst came back to the Crillon in late summer 1930, the story goes, he was politely informed that he was "an enemy of France" and instructed to leave within four days. Departing at once, Hearst fired off a letter to the *New York Times*, saying, "I told them [the French officials] I did not want to take the responsibility of endangering the great French nation, that America had saved it once during the war, and [that] I would save it again by leaving it."

Others who stayed at the Crillon:

- General John J. Pershing, after the war;
- Fred and Adele Astaire, who came to Paris for a couple of weeks' respite in January 1924 after their Broadway show *For Goodness Sake* played London (under the title *Stop Flirting*). The Astaires brought two other shows overseas in the twenties: the Gershwins' *Lady Be Good* in 1926 and *Funny Face* in 1928;
- Film stars Douglas Fairbanks and Mary Pickford, who honeymooned in the Crillon's Imperial Suite in 1920, and other stars like Tom Mix and Jackie Coogan used the Crillon during their visits to Paris.

AVENUE GABRIEL

1 • Théâtre des Ambassadeurs (new building there now)

When Josephine Baker and "La Revue Nègre" hit Paris, many clubs employing black performers sprang up. Les Ambassadeurs was one of the most glamorous. In 1926, for instance, its management brought over the entire sixty-three-member troupe of the Cotton Club in Harlem.

RUE ROYALE

3 · Maxim's

In the twenties even more than today, Maxim's was the restaurant Americans tended most to identify, rightly or wrongly, with Parisian haute cuisine.

21 · Café Weber (now gone)

The Weber, a restaurant Thomas Wolfe mentions frequently in his journals, stayed open late — endeavoring, according to one account from the period, "to keep alive the tradition of [the] after-theatre supper."

25 · Taverne Royale (now gone)

In this café-bar Thomas Wolfe composed some of the journal entries that went into Eugene Gant's "Paris Diary" in *Of Time and the River*. During his several visits to Paris in the twenties, Wolfe spent many hours at the Taverne Royale — lonely and loving it.

RUE BOISSY-D'ANGLAS

28 · Le Boeuf sur le Toit (now gone)

Following the war, an Alsatian named Louis Moysès (variously spelled as Moÿses and Moïse) ran a popular restaurant on rue Duphot. Some accounts say it was called La Cigogne, but more reliable records list it properly as the Bar Gaya. In any case, it specialized in foi gras de Strasbourg, and its clientele included Les Six, Lady Cunard, and Igor Stravinsky. Jean Cocteau claimed he and Raymond Radiguet ate there every night. Eventually, Cocteau approached Moysès about starting a business together, and the result was Le Boeuf sur le Toit ("The Ox on the Roof"), a cabaret that proved to be a spectacular success.

Moving the club from the rue Duphot to this location at 28 rue Boissy-d'Anglas, Cocteau staged a memorable Grand Opening for the new and larger Boeuf sur le Toit on 10 January 1922. In the audience that night were Picasso, Brancusi, Marie Laurencin, and dozens of other artists and celebrities. Later, Le Boeuf sur le Toit moved again (to rue de Penthièvre), but its height of popularity was reached here in the twenties.

Cocteau was the principal impresario of the cabaret. He was sometimes called Le *Veuf* sur le Toit — "the widower," instead of "the *ox*," on the roof. The club's name has a variety of explanations, but its proximate source was the tango-ballet Cocteau and composer Darius Milhaud had written for the Théâtre des Arts.

The cocktail pianists Jean Wiéner and Clément Doucet were said to have "played like angels and looked like Mutt and Jeff." Popular with artists and socialites, Le Boeuf sur le Toit also capitalized on the new craze for American jazz. Its bandleader was Vance Lowry, a black American saxophonist who was influenced by the work of Fletcher Henderson. Lowry's jazz band attended the 1923 funeral of Cocteau's protégé, novelist Raymond Radiguet — who, with two novels to his credit, died at the age of twenty from typhoid fever.

Robert McAlmon claims to have gone to Le Boeuf sur le Toit "almost daily" in 1922 to dance with some of the women who patronized the club — among whom were Flossie Martin, Nina Hamnett, Mary Butts, and Eileen Lane.

RUE DU FAUBOURG-SAINT-HONORE

29 • Coco Chanel's townhouse (through a *passage*)

When Coco's socialite friend and sometime lover, Misia, married her third husband, the artist José-Maria Sert, Coco benefited doubly. The talented Serts designed and painted the interior of her townhouse. Moreover, since José was a highly regarded painter and Misia had posed for some of the greatest artists of Montmartre (Renoir, Toulouse-Lautrec, Bonnard), the Serts proved a valuable connection to the art world.

Through them, Coco met many expatriates, including Sergei Diaghilev, whom she would always revere, and Picasso, who had a room in this townhouse for a while, as did Misia, of course.

56 • Helen Scott Agency

Although primarily a travel bureau, Helen Scott's business was to fill American demands and to answer American questions.

Helen Scott's staff could find peanut butter for you, buy your husband or wife a last-minute gift, or give you reliable information about doctors, apartments, schools, designers, or hotels.

Caresse Crosby, in fact, called the operation "Helen Scott Will Get It for You," for it was Scott's agency that obtained a baby elephant for Caresse to ride "practically undraped and wholly uninhibited up the Champs-Elysées" to the raucous Quatz'Arts Ball of 1926 (at least according to Caresse's memoirs).

RUE D'ANJOU

10 • Jean Cocteau's apartment

A stately building with spacious, silent stairs, this was Cocteau's Parisian residence — except during his period of mourning at the Hôtel Bonaparte after Raymond Radiguet's death.

Cocteau's butler invariably told the callers at 10 rue d'Anjou that the multi-talented artist was not in, for Cocteau usually hid himself away in a nearby hotel to work. Madame de Chivgny (Madame de Guermantes in Marcel Proust's *Remembrance of Things Past*) lived one flight below Cocteau, and thus Proust also could be found at times climbing these quiet stairs.

BOULEVARD MALESHERBES

12 • Hôtel Florida (now operating as the Hôtel Waldorf)

Scott and Zelda Fitzgerald stayed here briefly in late April 1925 after their return from two months on Capri. The odd-looking car they'd been driving to Paris broke down in Lyon, where they abandoned it. Supposedly Zelda had commanded the top to be removed from their new Renault because she preferred open motorcars. The customizing had been crudely done with a welder's torch.

A few days after checking into the hotel, Scott invited his new friend, Ernest Hemingway, to go with him to Lyon to retrieve the Renault, while Zelda, who wasn't feeling well, remained abed in the hotel. Hemingway's acidic version of the trip appears in *A Moveable Feast*.

By May 12, the Fitzgeralds had moved out of the Florida and into their flat on rue Tilsitt.

RUE MONTALIVET

11 · Residence of William and Louise Bryant Bullitt

Leaving their rue Desbordes-Valmore apartment, William and Louise (Bryant) Bullitt had moved to this residence by March 1926. Louise Bryant was John Reed's widow, a poet, and a journalist of considerable reputation. During this period, she actively supported the work of the black writer Claude McKay, who shared her interest in the Soviet Union.

Meanwhile, Bullitt was traveling to Vienna periodically to undergo psychoanalysis with Freud. A man of many talents and interests, Bullitt would later serve as the first U.S. Ambassador to the Soviet Union and as Ambassador to France. In 1926, Harcourt Brace published his novel, *It's Not Done*, which he dedicated to "Louise Bryant, my wife."

Louise, Bill, and their infant daughter returned to the United States in September 1926. Less than a year later, Louise was back in France alone — and Bill, in Vienna with Freud. And tragedy was about to strike.

RUE DU FAUBOURG-SAINT-HONORE

71 · Harry and Caresse Crosby's residence, winter 1923–24

Leaving their apartment on the Ile Saint-Louis, the Crosbys leased this flat from Princess Marthe Bibesco, a friend of Harry's cousin Walter Berry. The wife of Prince Georges Bibesco, Marthe was one of three princesses Bibesco living in Paris in the twenties, and they all seemed to have some special talent.

Marthe Bibesco was the author of *Le Perroquet Vert*. Elizabeth Asquith (daughter of Lord Oxford) married Prince Antoine Bibesco, the former Rumanian Minister in Washington, and was "the gayest and most charming of the [three Bibesco princesses]," according to one observer. The third was less well established and displayed more of a sober, philosophical bent, but her lineage traced back to Marshal Ney on her mother's side. Prince Antoine and Princess Elizabeth Bibesco resided on the quai Bourbon, Ile Saint-Louis, and thus were the Crosbys' next-door neighbors during the summer of 1923, although Princess Marthe is the only Bibesco Harry and Caresse mention.

The Crosbys lived in Marthe Bibesco's flat from September 1923 to the spring of 1924, paying 50,000 francs (about $2,200) in rent for the half-year. One entered the building by passing through a splendid arcade and into a gorgeous courtyard. The quarters were equally lavish. There was a carpet of silver-gray, light-green wall hangings, rose wallpaper, and a large bedroom with a mirrored wall. The Crosbys assumed charge of the princess's entourage, including her driver, cook, governess, and two maids. When the princess returned to Paris in early 1924, the Crosbys moved briefly to rue Boulard.

RUE DE L'ELYSEE

10 · The American Library (now gone)

By 1929 the American Library Service (a branch of the American Expeditionary Force) had converted its wartime library into a 37,000-volume public library. The offices and books took up two floors of this romantic old building overlooking the French president's palace. During 1929 an estimated 2,750 persons held library cards, but fewer than a thousand (995) of the holders were Americans, which indicates the popularity of the library among the British and French. The library director was Burton Stevenson, who had served as general director of all ALS libraries before taking this choice post.

THE GAVEAU
AND THE CLARIDGE

RUE D'ASTORG

11 · Hôtel Astor

Sergei Eisenstein, the Russian filmmaker, arrived in Paris early in November 1929 and stayed at this hotel until leaving for a brief visit to England at the end of the month. When he returned to Paris after Christmas, he took a room at the Hôtel des Etats-Unis in Montparnasse.

29-bis · Daniel-Henry Kahnweiler's Galerie Simon (now gone)

Following World War I, Daniel-Henry Kahnweiler opened a new gallery here. Prior to the war, Kahnweiler had done well for — and by — many of the most innovative artists, including Picasso and Matisse. During the war, however, most of Kahnweiler's paintings were confiscated and auctioned off while he was in self-imposed exile. With a German name and French sympathies, Kahnweiler found only Spain and Switzerland hospitable during the Great War.

Some of the more experimental writing of the twenties — pieces by Raymond Radiguet and Gertrude Stein, for instance — were issued under the aegis of "Les Editions de la Galerie Simon."

RUE LA BOETIE

21 · The gallery of Paul Rosenberg

In the teens, Ambroise Vollard and D. H. Kahnweiler were Picasso's principal dealers. After the war, Rosenberg handled most of the Picassos for sale to the public.

23 · Picasso's studio (building still there; studio gone)

This was Picasso's studio after World War I. Having married Olga Koklova in 1918 and fathered a son (Paulo) in 1921, Picasso settled down a bit in the twenties, though he traveled a lot to attend exhibitions of his work.

45 · Salle Gaveau

At three in the afternoon on 26 May 1920, an outrageous "Festival Dada" was held in M. Gaveau's concert hall. Among some nineteen items, the bill included "Le Célèbre Illusioniste Philippe Soupault" (in actuality, Soupault was not an illusionist but a Dada intellectual, if that's not a contradiction in terms), "Le Rastaquouère André Breton" (another intellectual; the big word designates a foreigner who lives very well and whose source of income is unknown), and Tristan Tzara's "Vaseline Symphony."

In an article praising Tzara, Ford Madox Ford described Dada as "a movement which, conducted with much and salutary extravagance, did a great deal towards bringing international minds back from the contemplation of after-war circumstances to the consideration of the Arts. . . . It was as if, worried as were our minds by the endless details, the endless alternatives of tidying up the trench and wire-soiled map of the world, the odd manifestoes of Dada really burst themselves upon our attentions."

The Dadaists themselves, however, usually refused to go any farther than to say Dada was "anti-Art," although occasionally one or another might be prompted to issue some deliberately ambiguous or nonsensical manifesto.

On 5 May 1926, a concert by exclusively American composers — Aaron Copland, Virgil Thomson, Walter Piston, and George Antheil — was held in the Salle Gaveau. The *Tribune*'s reviewer hated it, calling the concert "a presumptuous parading of immaturities."

The *Trib*'s reviewer of this All-American Concert was Irving Schwerke, himself an American — and a pianist. He observed, "The public exhibition of their pointless cacophonies can have done no good to the cause of American music, and I for one regret that the concert took place."

The performers included soprano Ada MacLeish (the wife of the poet Archibald MacLeish) and Copland, who played the piano. "The hall," Schwerke noted, "which held a large audience at the beginning of the concert, held a small one at the end."

On October 16 of the same year (1926), the Gaveau was the site of an evening of works by George Antheil. Reported to be in the hall that evening were James Joyce, Max Jacob, Sergei Diaghilev, the members of Les Six, Adrienne Monnier, and Sylvia Beach.

"Mr. Antheil," noted the sympathetic Elliot Paul, "was forced repeatedly to rise and bow at the conclusion of his Symphony in F." And, "in order to beautify for the eye that which was designed for the ear, Paul Poiret [the fashion designer] reserved front seats for his mannequins," Paul's *Tribune* review noted.

In *Four Lives in Paris* (1987), Hugh Ford maintains that Antheil was in Tunis at the time — not taking bows at the Gaveau. Ford notes that "it is possible Paul did not even attend the concert." Ford also suggests that the illustrious audience, including Poiret's mannequins, was the product of Elliot Paul's fertile imagination.

Ford's claims are probably incorrect, for the chronology is jumbled in the Antheil section of this otherwise admirable work. In *The Life and Music of George Antheil* (1983), Linda Whitesitt quotes letters from Antheil to his patron, Mrs. Mary Louise Bok. Their dateline places Antheil in Paris around the time of the October concert or immediately thereafter.

RUE DU COLISEE

52 · Mina Loy's lampshade shop

The poet Mina Loy operated her famous lampshade shop here in 1927 and 1928. Loy had developed a way of painting the inside of lampshades so that the electric bulb within produced quaint, scenic effects on the shade. One of her creations, for example, recreated the earth aglow on the lamp's surrounding glass globe. Another depicted a convoy of old schooners sailing around the lamp.

Loy's shades proved to be an instant success. Enthusiastically supportive, Peggy Guggenheim set her up in a shop here on the rue du Colisée. The demand was so great that Peggy volunteered to wait on customers in the shop, while Mina and her two daughters painted the shades in her studio out on the avenue du Maine.

Although Loy had obtained the proper patents, her techniques were widely copied and soon the large department stores were marketing less expensive imitations. In the face of this heavy competition, Loy's business soon failed. And she returned to her writing.

RUE DE LA BAUME

3 · House of Linda Lee Thomas

Divorced from Edward Thomas in 1912, Linda lived in this exquisite little house until shortly after her marriage in December 1919 to the American songwriter Cole Porter. Cole and Linda returned here following their honeymoon in Italy and the south of France. Then, they sold the house and bought an even more splendid one on the rue Monsieur.

Cole and Linda first met at a wedding reception at the Hôtel Ritz in early 1918. Eight years older than he, Linda was then thirty-five and a celebrated divorcée. She had married into money (Edward Thomas was heir to a big publishing concern) when she was eighteen, and the terms of her divorce brought Linda a handsome settlement from her playboy husband.

RUE FREDERIC-BASTIAT

8 · Hôtel de Berri

One of the residents of this hotel during the second half of the twenties was Miss Juliet Shelby, better known by her Hollywood name, Mary Miles Minter.

After the murder of director William Desmond Taylor in 1922, Minter's career plummeted. Like Mabel Normand, Minter was initially a suspect and, though innocent, was compromised by salacious revelations in the press during the murder trial.

Up to that time Mary Miles Minter had made a sizable fortune as Hollywood's virginal young sweetheart. Minter, however, had unwisely turned her money over to her mother, Charlotte Shelby, who took a whopping 30 percent of the gross as her fee. In 1926, Mary Miles Minter sued her mother for $1,345,000, but curiously she settled out of court for a paltry twenty-five grand, deliverable a year later.

Reduced to these straits, Minter sought refuge in Paris and the Hôtel de Berri, where she could afford to live a star's life on a starlet's income.

RUE LA BOETIE

89 • Hôtel Excelsior

This was the residence of Miguel Covarrubias, the Mexican artist who designed the opulent sets for "La Revue Nègre" when it opened in 1925. Covarrubias also designed the famous banana "skirt" for Josephine Baker.

110 • La Licorne (now gone)

This gallery, owned by Dr. Girardin, carried many pieces of modern art during the twenties, including several by Joan Miró — which didn't sell.

AVENUE DES CHAMPS-ELYSEES

74 • Claridge Hotel (main entrance now on rue de Ponthieu)

Many American movie stars and other celebrities chose to stay at the Claridge, which was called a "flamboyant palace" of a hotel. Among them were Peggy Joyce, Mae Murray, Fatty Arbuckle, Pola Negri, Adolph Zukor, Eddie Cantor, Jack Dempsey, and Estelle Taylor, Dempsey's new bride. And, during her most successful years — those prior to 1920 — Isadora Duncan stayed at the Claridge whenever she passed through Paris.

In an unpublished song, "Omnibus," from the 1928 *La Revue des Ambassadeurs*, Cole Porter's lyrics hint at another possible explanation for the hotel's reputation — its discretion:

> That building there, upon the right,
> Is the famous Hotel Claridge.
> It's where the ladies go at night,
> When they get fed up with marriage.

One prominent resident of the Claridge was Ethel Moorhead, who had been active in the woman's suffrage movement in England. Moorhead was also a practicing writer, painter, and editor.

The story goes that Moorhead spotted a pale, ill-fed American in the Claridge bar who caught her sympathy. When she struck up a conversation with him, she learned that the young man was a veteran named Ernest Walsh. He was unable to pay his hotel bills, apparently, because his Army pension checks were being misdirected to California. So, Moorhead covered his debts, and they began to consider publishing a little review together.

Most versions of this story imply that Walsh was registered at the Claridge. In fact, Sylvia Beach's library records indicate that he was staying in Montparnasse at the Hôtel Venetia in August 1922, which is about when he and Moorhead met. Drinking at the Claridge bar while actually living in cheaper quarters elsewhere would not have been a foolish thing for a young American male to do. Nevertheless, the 1923 records from Adrienne Monnier's bookshop reveal that Walsh was installed in the Claridge within a year.

The magazine Walsh and Moorhead started as a result of their encounter at the Claridge was called *This Quarter*, and it ran from 1925 to 1932. After visiting Scotland and traveling the Continent — and, for Walsh, making a trip to California — Moorhead and Walsh returned to Paris in October 1924 for a couple of months. This may have been when they set up an editorial office for their new review at 338 rue Saint-Honoré. During Walsh's term as editor, *This Quarter* published major works like "Big Two-Hearted River" (spring 1925), for which Hemingway was paid 1,000 francs ($50).

When Walsh died in 1926, Moorhead tried to edit the review

herself, but she was forced to let several months pass without an issue. In 1929, she hired Edward Titus as editor. Under Titus, the magazine resumed regular publication, but his cautious editorial policy caused the magazine to lose much of its appeal, importance, and — alas — audience.

RUE DE BERRI

21 • (new) Paris *Herald* building

During most of the twenties this spot was occupied by the American Church, before it moved into its new, neo-gothic building on the quai d'Orsay.

In December 1930, the Paris *Herald* moved here from the rue du Louvre. These accommodations were necessary because the *Herald* had grown into a major newspaper, printing sixteen to twenty pages daily with frequent supplements and a rotogravure section on Sundays. The new *Herald* building was nine stories high and designed in the form of an H, with one courtyard opening in the front and one in the back.

THEATRE DES CHAMPS-ELYSEES

AVENUE WINSTON-CHURCHILL

Grand Palais

Traditionally, the Salon des Beaux Arts et Artistes Français was the most prestigious — and conservative — of the painting exhibitions held annually in the Grand Palais. It opened on the first of May and ran through June. The Salon d'Automne, which opened on the first of November and ran through mid-December, was more avant-garde. Early in the century, for example, Gertrude Stein saw her first Matisse, Braque, and Picasso paintings at an Autumn Salon.

By the twenties a third Grand Palais show had established itself: the Independents — or, officially, the Salon des Société des Artistes Indépendents. During the twenties this exhibition usually ran from February into March. Since it presented works by unaffiliated artists, some of whom had never exhibited before, the Independents was open to virtually anyone at all.

At the Independents of 1923, Gerald Murphy showed his huge, oversized painting of an ocean liner, which baffled the officials. They didn't know if, where, or how they should hang it. ("If you think mine is too large," Murphy responded, "I think the others are too small.") Murphy contributed to the Independents again the next year, showing a six-foot-square precisionist rendition of the insides of a watch. Also shown in the 1924 Independents was Joan Miró's *The Farm*, a painting Ernest Hemingway later bought as a birthday present for his wife, Hadley.

QUAIS BETWEEN PONTS ALEXANDRE III AND DE L'ALMA

The International Exhibition of Decorative and Industrial Arts opened on 18 July 1925. The enormous exhibition, whose name abbreviated to "Art Deco," was held in stalls and buildings along both sides of the River Seine. Originally scheduled to open in the midteens, the exhibition was postponed when war broke out in 1914. Most of the exhibitors simply put their designs and pieces into storage and brought them out in 1925, when the exhibition finally opened. In effect, Art Deco had been on hold for over a decade.

RUE JEAN-GOUJON

33 • Anglo-American Press Association (now gone)

This was a hangout for journalists — correspondents like Guy Hickok, Paul Scott Mowrer, Lincoln Steffens; editors like Elliot Paul, Lewis Galantière, Al Laney; and stringers like Ernest Hemingway. Some writers used this club as their mailing address (writer-publisher John Rodker in 1925, for example). Others preferred using the Guaranty Trust Bank or Sylvia Beach's bookstore.

Before moving around the corner to 38 cours Albert-Première, where it is today, the International Chamber of Commerce also operated out of this rue Jean-Goujon address. Perhaps the best-known employee for the International Chamber of Commerce was Lewis Galantière. A Chicagoan, Galantière helped find accommodations for many Americans who came to Paris in the early years — Pound, Anderson, Hemingway, and others.

AVENUE MONTAIGNE

25 • Hôtel Plaza-Athénée

Modernized in 1920, the Hôtel Plaza-Athénée afforded its clients the latest comforts. Gloria Swanson, for one, chose the Plaza-Athénée whenever she required accommodations in Paris.

Peggy Guggenheim and her mother were in residence at the Plaza-Athénée in 1921 when friends introduced Peggy to Laurence Vail. Soon thereafter he made an attempt to seduce her in her room. Afraid her mother might walk in on them, Peggy agreed to accompany Vail to his apartment on the Left Bank (rue de Verneuil). "He was surprised by my lack of resistance," she recalls. "That was how I lost my virginity. It was as simple as that." Peggy was twenty-three at the time. After they married, Laurence and Peggy traveled constantly, but when they happened to land in Paris, they usually stayed at the Lutetia rather than the Plaza-Athénée.

In December 1925, Rudolph Valentino came to Paris and spent a month at the Plaza-Athénée. Meanwhile, back in New York his wife was processing their divorce — much to his chagrin. Valentino's arrival at the Gare du Nord that December brought some 2,000 Frenchwomen out into the winter cold to see him, even though his most recent film, *The Eagle*, had just opened to hostile reviews. When the English painter Nina Hamnett introduced Valentino to James Joyce, the men had to confess that they'd never heard of each other.

6 · Hôtel Théâtre des Champs-Elysées (now Hôtel Montaigne)

When A. J. Liebling, journalist and travel writer, arrived in Paris in October 1926, he stayed in this hotel for a week, until he realized that he'd used up virtually all the money he'd been allotted for the entire year. In November, his funds sufficiently replenished to allow him to remain in Paris, Liebling moved to the cheaper Hôtel Saint-Pierre, which was near the Sorbonne where Liebling had enrolled and was occasionally attending lectures.

15 · Théâtre des Champs-Elysées

The site of many memorable events of the twenties, this theatre of 2,200 seats was built between 1911 and 1913. Across the street was the popular Bar du Théâtre, which attracted the performers and the lively after-show crowds. The facade of the theatre was designed by sculptor Antoine Bourdelle, who taught at the Grand Chaumière. The principal feature of Bourdelle's relief *Meditation of Apollo and the Muses* was inspired by Isadora Duncan.

In the autumn of 1923 Gerald Murphy received an invitation from his friend Fernand Léger, the painter, to create an American ballet. Murphy's work was to be staged in this theatre by the Swedish Ballet Company as a curtain raiser for Darius Milhaud's *La Création du Monde*.

Murphy contacted his Yale classmate Cole Porter, who was living in Paris, and they drafted *Within the Quota*, a thirty-minute musical satire. So impressive were Murphy's sets and Porter's music, which was orchestrated by the French musician Charles Koechlin, that Léger reversed the order of performance and used the Milhaud piece as a curtain raiser. Murphy painted a backdrop showing a huge Hearst newspaper with the headline "Unknown Banker Buys Atlantic." "C'est beau, ça," a pleased Picasso told Murphy backstage on opening night, 25 October 1923.

In 1925, under the new management of André Daven, the Champs-Elysées booked a group from America — from New York's Harlem, to be exact. Thus, at 9:30 P.M. on 2 October 1925, Josephine Baker, dancing in nothing more than a few feathers, was catapulted to fame in "La Revue Nègre." Saxophonist Sidney Bechet was in the company, which had arrived in Paris on September 22 — just ten days before the opening. Dancing to "Yes Sir, That's My Baby," Baker introduced the Charleston to her jubilant audience.

Adrienne Monnier, who saw an early performance of "La Revue Nègre," gushed, "Doesn't Josephine Baker all by herself give the liveliest pleasure, the most amazing that can be imagined? With her get-ups, her grimaces, her contortions she kicks up a shindy that swarms with mocking enticements. . . ."

Janet Flanner's first-night review also raved: "Josephine Baker has arrived at the Théâtre des Champs Elysées . . . and the result has been unanimous. . . . Covarrubias did the sets, pink drops with cornucopias of hams and watermelons. The music is tuneless and stunningly orchestrated and the end of the show is dull, but never Miss Baker's part." John Dos Passos, incidentally, had helped paint the set.

The Théâtre Champs-Elysées was also the site of the official premiere of George Antheil's *Ballet Mécanique* on 19 June 1926. Since there'd been several "semi-private premieres" before this opening — one at the Salle Pleyel and a Friday-the-13th performance at the Conservatoire (November 1925) — some of the audience knew what to expect.

In *The New Yorker* (24 October 1925), Janet Flanner described the preview she'd seen: "It is really very wonderful. It sounds like three people: one pounding an old boiler, one grinding a model 1890 coffee grinder, and one blowing the usual seven o'clock factory whistle and ringing the bell that starts the New York fire department going in the morning. It's good but awful." Flanner's review of the preview that she'd seen, however, doesn't quite capture the full chaos on the official opening night.

Present at the premiere that night in 1926 were Harry and Caresse Crosby, Constantin Brancusi, Sergei Koussevitsky (the Russian composer), and James Joyce wearing a black eye patch. "I would rather have seen Joyce than any man alive," Harry Crosby noted in his journal that evening. "Did not like the Ballet Mécanique but liked Antheil and the verve with which he played. It was exciting and there was hooting and whistling and cat calls and wild applause and cries of silence Taisez-vous, Taisez-vous, and always the mad music."

The conductor was Vladimir Golschmann, who Anthiel observed "is the last final dot of perfection; his conducting technique is a thing most beautiful to behold." Also present were T. S. Eliot with his current patron, Princess Marguerite de Bassiano (née Chapin); Ezra Pound, accompanied by a stunningly dressed Djuna Barnes; Sergei Diaghilev; Dr. and Mrs. William Carlos Williams.

Antheil's *Ballet Mécanique* — which was not a ballet at all, but a somewhat musical composition — employed eight pianos, a Pleyel player-piano, automobile horns, anvils, oil drums, xylophones, assorted machines, and a couple airplane propellers.

Fistfights broke out during the concert, and many people called for their money back. At one point during the commotion, Ezra Pound bounded onto the stage and shouted, in French, "Silence, imbeciles! Get [shifting into English] the hell out of here if you don't like it! Or at least show some elemental manners!"

The mechanized music continued during Pound's tirade, since even Antheil or conductor Golschmann apparently couldn't stop the cacophonous mechanical contraptions. Toward the end of the performance, when the airplane propellers got up speed, they raised such a wind, Stuart Gilbert says (and William Shirer, who was also present, confirms), that a man's toupee blew off.

One woman leaving the concert noted to Bill Williams that "the subway seems sweet after that." If, as Williams believed, part of Antheil's intention was to teach his audience members to attend to sounds — to reawaken their ability and willingness to listen — then, he felt, the woman's comment demonstrated that the concert had been a resounding success (so to speak).

In the *Tribune* the next morning, a sympathetic Elliot Paul reported that "the combatants filed out peacefully" and that Antheil was greeted with "uproarious applause" by the (presumably tiny) audience that remained to the very end.

The next month (July 1926) sanity returned to the Champs-Elysées. "Paul Whiteman and his orchestra took their first Paris audience by storm," the *Tribune* reported. Whiteman's orchestra introduced an enraptured full house to George Gershwin's *Rhapsody in Blue*.

The Champs-Elysées was also where Charles Lindbergh's autograph was auctioned off in May 1927 for $1,500.

2 • Hôtel Elysées-Bellevue (now gone)

Sinclair and Grace Lewis took three rooms in this hotel ("as far as possible from the Dôme and other haunts") on 1 December 1924. While here, he celebrated his fortieth birthday (Grace was in Switzerland) and saw the publication of *Arrowsmith*. Two days later (7 March 1925), rejoined by his wife, Lewis left for Marseilles.

RUE DE MARIGNAN

10 • Residence of Mary Cassatt

One of America's finest painters, Mary Cassatt lived in a fifth-floor apartment here for the last forty years of her life. (She died in 1926.) Outspoken and somewhat aloof, Cassatt visited Gertrude Stein's salon one evening in 1908 and saw the modernist work of Matisse, Picasso, and others. Cassatt told the friend who'd taken her to Stein's salon, "I have never in my life seen so many dreadful paintings in one place; I have never seen so many dreadful people gathered together, and I want to be taken home at once." Ironically, both Cassatt and Stein were born in Allegheny, Pennsylvania, and lived most of their lives in Paris.

RUE DE LA TREMOILLE

14 • Hôtel La Trémoille

When H. L. Mencken visited Paris in 1929, he stayed here. Avoiding the Left Bank crowd, Mencken made only one visit to the Café Dôme. Generally unimpressed with Parisian life, the celebrated editor and journalist wryly noted that "the cafés of Paris dangerously outnumber the pissoirs."

AVENUE GEORGE V

31 • Hôtel George V

Edna Ferber, one of America's best-selling novelists, chose to stay at the posh George V during her spring 1929 swing through Paris. In 1925 she'd won a Pulitzer for her novel *So Big*, which pretty much describes the size and impressiveness of this hotel.

This hotel was the site of Nadia Boulanger's "Morning Musicales," which were sponsored by the Princesse Edmond de Polignac — Winaretta Singer, of the sewing-machine fortune. These regularly scheduled programs of music and champagne brought together some of the most fashionable women of Paris.

AVENUE DES CHAMPS-ELYSEES

99 • Fouquet's (restaurant)

Ever able to spend money he didn't have, James Joyce liked to eat here whenever he could — which he did with increasing frequency in the late twenties and thirties. This restaurant was even more elegant and expensive than his previous favorite, the Trianons. To this day the mere mention of Joyce's lavish tips inspire Fouquet's headwaiters to heights of story-telling eloquence.

THE ETOILE AND NORTH TO THE WAGRAM

RUE DE PRESBOURG

4 · Hôtel Beau-Site (remodeled)

When Gerald and Sara Murphy first arrived in Paris in September 1921, they took a suite of rooms in this hotel on rue de Presbourg, a street that rings the south side of the Arc of Triumph. After a brief stay here, they moved to a flat on the rue Greuze.

AVENUE DES CHAMPS-ELYSEES

133 · Hôtel Astoria (gone; 131–33 is now a Publicis Drugstore)

Jules Glaenzer, a friend of George Gershwin's and a vice-president at Cartier, threw a huge party in the summer of 1929. Among those whom Glaenzer invited was the young Broadway composer Richard Rodgers. Catching a liner out of New York, Rodgers came to Paris, checked into the Hôtel Astoria here, took in the festivities, and returned to the States — all in a matter of a few days. The American soprano Grace Moore lived in the Astoria that same summer, when she debuted in *La Bohème*.

RUE DE TILSITT

14 · The apartment of F. Scott and Zelda Fitzgerald

Scott and Zelda signed an eight-month lease on this fifth-floor walk-up near the Etoile and had moved in by 12 May 1925. This was the famous "summer of 1,000 parties and no work." Though nicely situated, the apartment was dark, grim, and garishly furnished with eighteenth-century imitations. "Early Galleries Lafayette," one observer called them. Generally pleased, Zelda didn't mind the "servant problems" (there were no servants). Nor did she object to the mucus that Scott found on the wallpaper. Hygiene, she felt, didn't matter in Paris since no one ever stayed home.

At this time Fitzgerald was beginning to resign himself to the sad fate of his masterpiece, *The Great Gatsby*. Although some of the first reviews (cabled to him in early May) had praised the work, harsher notices were now coming in. Worse yet, sales were so bad that he could only hope that the total would reach 23,000 copies — the number Scott figured would cover the advances he'd already received from Scribners.

Despite their many months in Paris, Scott and Zelda ever remained American tourists, refusing to be assimilated into a Parisian way of life. One story tells of Scott's entering a celebrated French restaurant, shoving aside the waiter's offered menu, and demanding — in very clear and pointed English — a club sandwich. Few American expatriates would have been so audacious, although many of them, no doubt secretly a bit homesick, probably longed for something as plain and simple *and American* as a club sandwich. The purity of Fitzgerald's innocence at times could be downright endearing, as Glenway Wescott's memorial attests: Scott, Wescott said, "was our darling, our genius, our fool."

Although they traveled frequently — most often to Gerald and Sara Murphy's Villa America at Cap d'Antibes — Scott and Zelda kept this residence until their lease ran out in January 1926. They returned briefly to Paris in late June, when Zelda's attack of appendicitis required her to enter the American Hospital in Neuilly, and Scott rented a room nearby. They left Paris in July 1926, not to return until 1928, when they rented an apartment on the rue de Vaugirard.

RUE BREY

3 · Hôtel Wagram

When Ben Huebsch, the influential New York publisher, came to Paris in 1920, he took a room in this hotel. Huebsch's visit to Paris was indicative of his vanguard interest in literary and artistic developments.

His one-man publishing company, B. W. Huebsch, Inc., played a major (and, today, underappreciated) role in American literary history during the first decades of the twentieth century. Gorham Munson, for instance, calls Huebsch "one of the makers of the favorable climate . . . for American literature in the Twenties." It was Huebsch who published Gorky, Strindberg, Romains, and Bergson in the States. He was the U.S. publisher of Joyce's *Dubliners* and *Portrait of the Artist* in 1916. And, most important, in 1919 when no other publisher would take the manuscript, Huebsch brought out Sherwood Anderson's *Winesburg, Ohio*, a work that changed the course of American fiction. Along with Liveright and Knopf, the Huebsch publishing firm was distinguished by its taste and its receptivity to new, if unorthodox, writers. In 1925, B. W. Huebsch, Inc., merged with the newly formed Viking Press.

RUE BEAUJON

Number unknown • Apartment of Josephine Baker

In 1926 Josephine Baker and the "Revue Nègre" troupe moved on to Berlin, with plans of later playing Moscow. In Berlin, according to Josephine, she became the protégée of Max Reinhardt, the theatre impresario.

When an offer came from Paris to star in "La Folie du Jour" at the Folies-Bergère for 27,000 francs (about $1,350) a month, Josephine had three choices. She could stay with Reinhardt in Berlin, go with the troupe to Moscow, or return to Paris. The twenty-year-old dancer chose the last, since it effectively made her a legitimate, independent star. With such an income, "La Bakair" — as the French called her — could afford whatever residence she desired. She selected an apartment here, on the rue Beaujon, near the Etoile.

Josephine was notorious for receiving friends and strangers in her apartment, so her residence was a popular place. After her nightclub, Chez Josephine, opened in 1926, taxicab drivers claimed that if a fare requested "chez Josephine," they had to ask whether he meant the club or Baker's apartment.

AVENUE DE FRIEDLAND

47 · Hôtel Campbell

The poet John Peale Bishop and his wife spent most of 1926–33 in Europe (their three children were born overseas). During these years, their principal residence was the Château de Tressancourt at Orgeval, Seine-et-Oise, outside the city. Their first year or so, however, was spent in Paris.

Having moved from their square Alboni residence by 4 July 1927, the Bishops were settled in this hotel, where John learned that a short story of his won a $5,000 prize from Scribners. His wife's family money notwithstanding, these funds helped him pay the plumbers and electricians who were remodeling the Château de Tressancourt. By the end of October 1927, the château was ready, and the Bishops moved in. In March 1930, they were back in Paris (at 4 rue Mignard) when the twin boys were born.

In his *Collected Essays* Bishop observes, "If I ever find myself the father of an extraordinary youth, I shall [not send him to college at all, but] lock him up in a library until he is old enough to go to Paris."

AVENUE HOCHE

15 · Anaïs Nin's residence

Leaving their pension on rue d'Assas, Nin and Hugh Guiler, her husband, spent February and March 1925 here in a one-room apartment of a bachelor friend. In April they moved to rue Pauquet and then, in August, settled down for a few years in a flat on rue Schoelcher.

RUE DU FAUBOURG-SAINT-HONORE

252 · (The new) Salle Pleyel

Occupying a location on the rue de Rochechouart for over half a century, the Pleyel Company opened their new *salle* here in

1927. The new Pleyel was the largest concert hall in Paris, seating 3,000 and housing sixty studios.

Accordingly, the Salle Pleyel concerts that occurred prior to 1927 — those of Ezra Pound, George Antheil, Aaron Copland, Olga Rudge, Ada MacLeish, and other expatriates — all took place in the old hall on Rochechouart.

The need for a new concert hall — indeed, for several concert halls — is demonstrated by the statistics compiled by Irving Schwerke, the music critic for the *Tribune* from 1921 to 1934. During the 1925–26 season, New York City offered 1,156 musical performances; Paris, over twice as many: 3,394. In 1927–28, the ratio was similar: New York, 1,218 musical performances; and Paris, 2,978.

RUE DARU

12 • Saint Alexandre Newsky (Russian Orthodox Church)

This was Stravinsky's church, of Byzantine design, where in 1918 Picasso married Olga Koklova, a dancer with the Ballets Russes. Across the street at number 13 is the Ville de Petrograd, a quaint café favored by Russian expatriates.

AVENUE DE WAGRAM

39 • Salle Wagram

The Quatz'Arts Ball, an annual orgiastic costume party sponsored by the Beaux Arts students, was often held in this huge hall. In 1926 and 1927, for instance, Harry and Caresse Crosby attended the ball here as patrons of the atelier Defrasse et Madeleine.

For the 1926 ball, which was held on the evening of June 18, Harry and Caresse opened up their rue de Lille apartment and hosted a dinner for "their" atelier. Harry describes the subsequent preparations for the ball: "costumes are being prepared and C[aresse] tries on hers and she is passionate with bare legs, bare breasts, and a wig of turquoise hair . . . (my costume a frail red loin-cloth and a necklace of three dead pigeons)."

Once properly attired — that is, having reached the proper state of undress — the entire group paraded up the Champs-Elysées, Caresse on top of a baby elephant rented for the occasion. Inside the hall, riding topless in a "dragon's mouth," her "figure showing like the prow of a ship," Caresse won first prize. "My breasts helped," she said.

At the 1927 ball, held on June 10, Harry carried a bag of ten snakes to go with his necklace of dead pigeons (he'd increased the number from three to seven). Climbing up to the attic loge, Harry dumped out the snakes, which "dropped down among the dancers and there were shrieks and cat-calls and there was a riot . . . and beside me sitting on the floor a plump woman with bare breasts [was] absorbed in the passion of giving milk to one of the snakes."

RUE DES ACACIAS

49 · Les Acacias (gone; area remodeled)

Located next door to the Grand Hôtel Les Acacias, at number 47, this elegant and aristocratic dance hall was the brainchild of the dancer Harry Pilcer, who turned the operation over to Maurice Chevalier in the early twenties. The hours from five to seven in the evening were reserved for *thés dansants* ("tea dances"), which were genteel affairs, relatively speaking, where women could find discreet gigolos or meet their current lovers. At night, cabaret acts entertained the ballroom dancers. In 1926 Josephine Baker performed here a few times as a favor to the new American manager, Elsa Maxwell.

Also on the rue des Acacias

The following celebrities are said to have been living on this street in 1925: Gloria Swanson, Pearl White, Norma Talmadge and Joe Schenck, Rex Ingram, Parker Reed, Betty Blythe, and Sessue Hayakawa, the Japanese actor.

Gloria Swanson first came to Paris in 1924, along with a Paramount crew, to make *Madame Sans Gene* (released in 1925). While in Paris, she met and married the Marquis Henri de la Falaise de la Coudraie. The nephew of the man behind the Hennessy cognac fortune, the marquis was Pearl White's ex-lover.

Another reputed resident on Acacias, Pearl White had come to Paris to make her last film in 1924 (released in the United States as *The Perils of Paris* and in France as *Terror*). Her story is particularly sad, for following this film she is said to have dropped a half-million dollars at the Chemin-de-Fer tables, lost nearly as much on her stable of race horses, become an opium addict and alcoholic, consorted randomly with gigolos, and ballooned severely in weight. She had been hospitalized for various problems several times. Although she bought a villa in Cairo, Egypt, in 1927, White spent most of her last years at her country estate at Gazeran near Rambouillet. She died at the American Hospital in Neuilly on 4 August 1938.

RUE PIERRE-DEMOURS

6 · Hôtel Regent's Garden

Actress, writer, and daughter of a famous actor, Cornelia Otis Skinner lived here in the summer of 1921, while she studied voice in Paris. Eventually, she joined the troupe with which her father, Otis Skinner, toured.

RUE JADIN

14-bis · Temporary residence of Stephen Vincent Benét

In 1925, former Senator Simon Guggenheim and his wife established the John Simon Guggenheim Memorial Foundation with an endowment gift of three million dollars. The Guggenheim Foundation awards were worth $2,500, a sum designed to allow the recipients to dedicate a year to their work. Among the first Guggenheim fellows were Aaron Copland, Norbert Wiener, Linus Pauling, Roger Sessions, and Stephen Vincent Benét.

Benét's Guggenheim enabled him and his wife to return to France for the year 1926–27. The Benéts were living in this apartment when their son was born on 28 September 1926. By the following January, they'd moved to 89 avenue de Neuilly (now avenue Charles-de-Gaulle) in suburban Neuilly. In March 1927, Benét received a six months' renewal of the grant, and by November 1927, Benét and his family had returned to Paris, taking an apartment on the rue de Longchamp.

BOULEVARD PEREIRE

56 • Sarah Bernhardt's residence (now gone)

The celebrated actress Sarah Bernhardt died here at the age of sixty-nine on 26 March 1923. Attending the Divine Sarah during her last moments were her son, her grandson, a granddaughter, and several friends. She was buried in the rosewood coffin that she'd purchased thirty years before. It was lined with mauve satin. Believing that "death must hold no terror for me," Bernhardt occasionally slept in the coffin — a practice that caused the phrase *"le cercueil de Sarah Bernhardt"* to refer to anyone with a particularly macabre sensibility.

PASSY

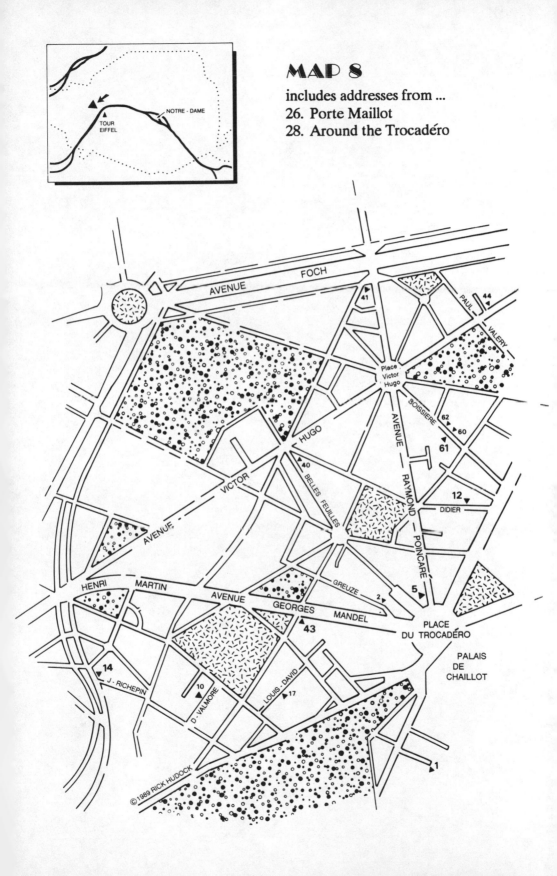

MAP 8

includes addresses from ...
26. Porte Maillot
28. Around the Trocadéro

PORTE MAILLOT

RUE PERGOLESE

10 · The final Paris residence of Scott and Zelda Fitzgerald

When Scott and Zelda returned to Paris from Cannes in October 1929, they took up residence in an apartment here at 10 rue Pergolèse, unaware that it'd be their last extended stay in the city. By all accounts, there was a delirious tension between the Fitzgeralds at this time, and their excesses were most likely a kind of psychological defense. "Nobody knew whose party it was [Zelda wrote]. It had been going on for weeks. When you felt you couldn't survive another night, you went home and slept and when you got back, a new set of people had consecrated themselves to keeping it alive."

Zelda was hospitalized briefly in April 1930, her mental problems having grown severe. By late May 1930, she was in the sanatorium at Les Rives de Prangins (Switzerland) and Scott, although he hadn't been granted visiting rights, was staying nearby in Geneva. When Zelda was released in September 1931, she and Scott returned to Paris and spent four days at the Majestic Hôtel. It was the last time they saw Paris.

RUE LE SUEUR

15 · Residence of Mr. and Mrs. Eugène Laurence Vail

These are the parents of Laurence Vail and his sister, Clotilde. (An artist of some repute, Laurence was Peggy Guggenheim's first husband and Kay Boyle's second.) Eugène Vail was French-American, and his wife was a wealthy New Englander.

Although the children, Laurence and Clotilde, were American citizens, they were raised in Europe. Clotilde, who had a special talent for singing blues, lived at this address with her parents while her brother traveled Europe as Peggy Guggenheim's husband.

RUE PICOT

Number unknown • Pauline Pfeiffer's flat

This "new and strange girl" (Hemingway's phrase), who openly resolved to have Ernest Hemingway for her husband, lived on this street while she worked part-time for the Paris edition of *Vogue* magazine.

Pauline was much more assertive and stylish than Hadley Hemingway, whom she strategically befriended. At their first meeting, Ernest apparently was more impressed by Pauline's sister, Jinny, than by Pauline. Nevertheless, within eighteen months of their meeting, Ernest had separated from Hadley and was preparing to marry Pauline.

AVENUE FOCH (WAS AVENUE DU BOIS-DE-BOULOGNE UNTIL 1929)

41 • Home of Pierpont Morgan Hamilton (Whatever's there now is guarded by men with bullet-proof vests and automatic weapons)

When J. P. Morgan's nephew Pierpont ("Peter") Hamilton and his wife, Marise, separated in 1926, Peter offered this elegant house to Archibald and Ada MacLeish and their children for the winter, rent-free. MacLeish had only to pay the wages of the servants and staff. So, except for a week skiing in Switzerland with Ernest and Hadley Hemingway, the MacLeishes lived in these unusually lush quarters from September 1926 through February 1927. In a letter to his mother, MacLeish boasts playfully that he and Ada had three bathrooms and a mechanical piano in their twelve-room apartment, plus a butler, a chef, a governess, five maids, and a chauffeur.

AVENUE VICTOR-HUGO

44 • Residence of Louise Bryant Bullitt

When Louise Bryant returned to France in late autumn 1927 and took up residence here, her husband, William Bullitt (the future U.S. Ambassador to the U.S.S.R. and to France), went to Vienna, where he was to be treated by Sigmund Freud. Although Bill listed this address with Sylvia Beach as his own, he and Louise were living their own lives by then. Bill was suffering mild psychological disturbances, and Louise was drinking heavily. She had cause. The previous March she'd learned that she was suffering from Dercum's disease, an incurable and grotesque illness in which parts of the body bloat up and become tumorous. By 1930, the year they were divorced, Louise had returned to the States and moved back again to Paris, where she found an apartment on the rue d'Assas.

NEUILLY-SUR-SEINE

Several expatriates lived in Neuilly-sur-Seine, a suburb just beyond the city limits of Paris at Porte Maillot. Among them were the poet Stephen Vincent Benét, the writer William Seabrook, and the filmmaker King Vidor, who lived in the Villa Trianon at 49 boulevard d'Inkermann. A friend of the Fitzgeralds, Vidor visited Sylvia Beach and inscribed a photo for her, dating it 22 June 1928. The most important address in Neuilly, however, was 63 boulevard Victor-Hugo, the location of the American Hospital, whose medical staff in the twenties was headed by the American doctor Edmund L. Gros.

OLD EMBASSY AREA

RUE DUMONT-D'URVILLE

29 · Majestic Hôtel

George Gershwin; his sister, Frances; his brother, Ira; and Ira's new wife, Leonore, stayed in this hotel just south of the Etoile during their 1928 visit to Paris. The entourage arrived on March 25 and, except for a couple weeks in Vienna, remained here until they returned to the United States on 20 June 1928. This was Gershwin's last holiday abroad. Although he presumably worked on the blues section of *An American in Paris* while at the Majestic (and in Vienna), most of the composition was written immediately after Gershwin had returned to New York. He later claimed that the only inspiration he got in Paris for *An American in Paris* was the taxi horns.

During this stay in Paris, Gershwin attended a sadly inept performance of *Rhapsody in Blue*, a satisfactory dance version of the same piece — performed at the Théâtre Champs-Elysées by the Ballets Russes (choreographed by the dancer Anton Dolin) — and an impressive evening of works by various composers at the Opéra, including Gershwin's own recently completed Concerto in F.

After Zelda Fitzgerald's first breakdown and her subsequent release from a Swiss sanatorium on 15 September 1931, she and Scott made a final visit to Paris and spent four days at the Majestic before returning to the States.

RUE JEAN-GIRAUDOUX (FORMERLY RUE PAUQUET)

22 · Residence of Anaïs Nin

In early April 1925, Anaïs Nin and her husband moved into a flat here, leaving their room on the avenue Hoche. In August, to Nin's great glee, they found a larger and more permanent residence on rue Schoelcher, and they moved as soon as they could. Actually, they left this pleasant building with its wrought-iron balconies a week *before* their September lease on the Schoelcher residence actually started.

RUE LA PEROUSE

2 · Pension of Miguel de Unamuno

After King Alfonso of Spain was deposed in September 1923 and Primo de Rivera had installed himself as dictator, an order exiling Salamanca philosophy professor Don Miguel de Unamuno was issued on 21 February 1924. From the prison on Fuerteventura (Canary Islands) where he spent four months, Unamuno was allowed to sail for Paris on 9 July 1924.

By September he'd settled into a tiny room in a pension here at number 2. Possessed by despair and death wishes, Unamuno felt that Paris was inhabited by Philistines "who believe that animation and gesticulation pass for true emotion." Despite his malaise, every afternoon Unamuno walked to the Café Rotonde and met with his Spanish friends, who included the young filmmaker Luis Buñuel.

After the discussions, Buñuel and the others walked Unamuno back to his pension, where the professor had a small bedroom on the second floor. He had a single chair, which he offered to his guests, while he sat on the edge of his bed. "Books were piled everywhere," one visitor recalled. "Piles of them stacked on the hearth reached to the mantelpiece and those on the mantelpiece reached to the ceiling."

Eager to leave Paris, Unamuno was escorted to the city of Hendaye on the French border by his friend Eduardo Ortega y Gasset at the end of August 1925. (An odd friendship, Unamuno and Ortega's. During the Spanish Civil War in the last half of the thirties, Unamuno would declare himself in support of Franco, whereas Ortega was ever a staunch leftist.) In 1930, after the collapse of Rivera's dictatorship, Unamuno returned to his beloved Spain.

AVENUE KLEBER

37 · Galerie Au Sans Pareil

Having moved from the rue du Cherche-Midi by 1920, the Au Sans Pareil housed the first important Dada exhibition — the "Exposition Dada" of Max Ernst, which ran from the end of May to early June 1921.

AVENUE D'IENA

2 · Private residence of American ambassador

In 1925 this became the home of the U.S. ambassador, causing Sisley Huddleston to remark in 1928 that "only recently has the United States Ambassador been fittingly housed." The building was a gift to the American government from Ambassador Myron T. Herrick, who bought it in 1924 with $200,000 of his own money. The building had once belonged to former French President Grévy.

Myron T. Herrick had been President Taft's appointment in 1912; thus, when Woodrow Wilson, a Democrat, was elected President, Herrick dutifully tendered his resignation, and Wilson named William Graves Sharp to replace Herrick.

According to one report, Sharp didn't show up until four o'clock on the morning of 3 September 1914 — at the height of the Marne crisis. German troops were on the veritable outskirts of Paris. Herrick sternly refused to turn the ambassadorial offices over to Sharp, claiming, "The Embassy is like a ship in a stormy sea. I'm on the bridge and I shall not leave until we get into calmer waters." Apparently, the waters didn't calm till December, for that's when Herrick finally turned the embassy over to Sharp.

When Harding assumed the presidency in 1921, he reappointed his fellow Ohio Republican Herrick to the post he loved. Fluent in the language and conscious of French tradition, Ambassador Herrick deliberately chose to arrive in Paris on Bastille Day: 14 July 1921. It was a shrewd, symbolic gesture, and acts like that made Herrick one of the most popular American ambassadors to France in this century. There's even a street named after him.

It was at this residence that Ambassador Herrick held a press conference for a red-eyed Charles Lindbergh on 22 May 1927 at three o'clock in the morning. The exhausted pilot, too excited to sleep, talked to the press from the edge of his bed, wearing baggy pajamas that he'd borrowed from Herrick.

The next day Herrick solidified his standing with the press and public by holding a formal press conference in the residence. Outside, a wild throng blocked the entire avenue, hoping to get a glimpse of the man who flew the Atlantic in a plane called *The Spirit of St. Louis* — which was not, for the French, an allusion to a Missouri city.

RUE DE CHAILLOT

5 · U.S. Chancellery (American Embassy Offices, 1913–33)

Until late 1933 this building housed the offices of the U.S. Embassy, including the ambassador's office, which occupied a large, bright room on the second floor facing the street. It was outside this building that Isadora Duncan stood in silent vigil one night, holding a burning candle to protest Sacco and Vanzetti's death sentences.

In the winter of 1918 James Thurber, a code clerk for the State Department, was dispatched to work here in the chancellery. He lived in a small pension around the corner, until February 1920, when he returned to the States. Curiously, the "Residential Directory" of the *Franco-American Yearbook* gives this as his address in 1921, even though by then Thurber had been in America for over a year. In the autumn of 1925, Thurber returned to Paris, though he was no longer in public service.

RUE HAMELIN

44 · Union Hôtel Etoile

Marcel Proust, who'd lived in this building since 1919, died here on 18 November 1922. Two days later, his brother, Dr. Robert Proust, summoned Man Ray to photograph the body of the celebrated French writer. The other "presence" in the room at the time was also American: a painting by James McNeill Whistler.

AROUND THE TROCADERO

TO THE NORTH

RUE BOISSIERE

60 · Residence of Louis Bromfield

In addition to residing at the Hôtel de l'Odéon and the apartment on the boulevard Flandrin, Louis Bromfield and his wife and children also lived here briefly.

Bromfield's second novel, *Possession*, which he'd finished just before leaving the States for Paris late in 1925, proved to be such a financial success that he was eventually able to lease a former monastery and its surrounding gardens near Senlis, thirty-five miles north of Paris. This rural estate became the primary residence of the Bromfields for nearly a dozen of the fifteen years they spent in France between the wars.

61 · American Women's Club

Housed in a three-story white stone building, the club offered its 1,200 members (as of 1929) a library, lounges, assembly rooms, a mirrored ballroom, and a dining room that looked out upon a lovely garden. The eleven bedrooms on the third floor were used by American women who were traveling alone. The club sponsored exhibitions, lectures, and recitals appropriate for expatriate American women. It was all quite proper. Gilbert White, whose conduct normally was Bohemian (to say the least) but whose painting was traditional and conservative, frequently accepted invitations to exhibit his work and give talks at the Women's Club. He called it the W.C.

62 • Burton Rascoe residence

When Burton Rascoe resigned as literary editor of the *New York Herald Tribune* in 1924, he had a three-month break before beginning work as columnist for the Editors Features Service. Impulsively, Rascoe withdrew a sizable sum from his savings account, bought two transatlantic tickets, and phoned his wife. Pack — we're off for Paris.

Hearing of the Rascoes' plans to spend October through December in Paris, Mrs. Mary Rumsey (daughter of financier E. H. Harriman) insisted they use her apartment here, on the second floor of 62 rue Boissière. She even cabled her housekeeper "to kick Augustus John [the famous English painter] out if he is still there — he has been there long enough."

The Rascoes, that is, were able to spend their Parisian interlude in lavish accommodations: a living room and bedroom facing the street, a vestibule leading to a "largish dining room" with a fireplace, and "that great rarity in a Paris apartment — a modern bathroom with a real porcelain tub as well as the inevitable bidet and a toilet." The housekeeper "treated [the Rascoes] to service such as [they] had never known before."

A few days after the Rascoes' arrival in October 1924, Ernest Hemingway took Burton to meet Gertrude Stein, who looked just "as Sherwood Anderson told me [Rascoe] she looked, like the wife of an Iowa corn doctor."

Because of Burton's previous position as a literary editor, the Rascoes knew virtually every American and English writer in Paris, and those whom they didn't know knew them. Their days gave them no pause. Nor, apparently, did they seek it.

RUE SAINT-DIDIER

12 • Residence of Ludwig Lewisohn

In 1924, the American writer Ludwig Lewisohn resigned from the staff of *The Nation* and sailed for Europe with Thelma Spear.

Lewisohn had been unable to obtain a divorce from his wife and had just written a transparent account of his dilemma in *The Case of Mr. Crump*, which Edward Titus published in 1926.

After extended stays in Berlin (where Lewisohn had been born) and Vienna, Lewisohn and Spear decided to try Paris, although Lewisohn says, "We had never heard of the Café du Dôme, [and] the Carrefour of Montparnasse was an unknown country to us." They loved it.

Lewisohn and Spear rented this "little service-flat . . . off the Avenue Kléber [with] excellent steam heat and a perfect bathroom." Both Lewisohn and Spear thrived on Parisian life, even during the last part of the decade when they were living in their rue Campagne-Première apartment, where life was considerably more hectic than it was here in pacific Passy.

RUE DE LONGCHAMP

36 • Residence of Stephen Vincent Benét

By November 1927, Benét, his wife, and their infant son had moved here from Neuilly. In August 1928, Benét made a quick trip back to the States, but he returned by October and intensified his efforts to finish his poem "John Brown's Body." "I shall finish it," he said, "or explode in loud fragments." The Benéts kept this residence until they left Paris in March 1929 — just about the time "John Brown's Body" received the Pulitzer Prize.

AVENUE RAYMOND-POINCARE

In 1936, the section of avenue de Malakoff that runs from the place Victor-Hugo to the Trocadéro was renamed avenue Raymond-Poincaré.

5 • Residence of Jules Glaenzer

George Gershwin came to Paris in April 1923 and stayed here with his friend Jules Glaenzer, who was an executive at Cartier. Glaenzer took Gershwin to the Montparnasse cafés, Montmartre nightclubs, and even a lavish Parisian bordello. On 27 April 1923, the day of his departure, Gershwin drew a sketch of himself in Glaenzer's guestbook and wrote, "In mourning at leaving Paris."

RUE DES BELLES-FEUILLES

40-bis • Early home of the Crosbys (now a bank)

After their New York wedding in September 1922, Harry and Polly (later, Caresse) Crosby stayed at the Hotel de l'Université, just down from the Hôtel Jacob. Tiring of hotel life, Polly "found fashionable housing" here in a large, impersonal flat. By mid-June 1923, they had moved into the Princess Bibesco's apartment on the Ile de la Cité.

TO THE WEST

RUE GREUZE

2 • Apartment of Gerald and Sara Murphy

Arriving in Paris in 1921, the Murphys first took rooms in the Hôtel Beau-Site, but they soon moved into this flat and stayed until they'd finished renovating their sixteenth-century apartment on the quai des Grands-Augustins.

While living here, Gerald learned that a fire had destroyed most of the Russian Ballet's scenery, so he traveled out to the 20th arrondissement and volunteered his services as a set painter. (He had been studying painting under Natalia Goncharova, one of the designers for the Ballets Russes.) While working on the sets for *Scheherazade*, *Pulcinella*, and other ballets, Murphy met Diaghilev and several other notables — including Braque, Picasso, and Derain — who were pitching in to help Diaghilev's ballet company build and paint new sets.

RUE LOUIS-DAVID

17 · Residence of the Dayang Muda of Sarawak

Sarawak was a British Crown Colony in northwest Borneo, ruled by a rajah. Gladys Palmer, of the Huntley and Palmer (English) biscuit fortune, married the brother of the Rajah of Sarawak and thus became Dayang Muda (i.e., a "Princess") of Sarawak.

After bearing him six children, the Dayang Muda divorced her husband in the twenties and returned to Europe. She first visited England, and then she and her Scots cousin, Archibald Craig (Archie was a friend of Kay Boyle's), moved into this apartment on Louis-David in Paris.

In May and June 1928, Kay Boyle lived in a room here on the fifth floor to be across the hall from the Dayang Muda, who had commissioned Boyle to write her biography.

When Gertrude Stein and Alice Toklas called on Boyle and the princess that May, the unlikely gathering was tense and quiet. The silence was finally broken when Raymond Duncan, an acquaintance of Archie Craig's, suddenly burst uninvited into the apartment. Stein was surprised — and pleased — to see Duncan, whom she knew (Raymond had once reminded her that they had been childhood neighbors in Oakland, California), and the tension mercifully relaxed.

This meeting was Boyle's first encounter with Isadora Duncan's brother. Boyle and her daughter, Sharon, moved into Duncan's Neuilly commune that July — perhaps after briefly residing at 201 rue d'Alésia, as Sylvia Beach's and Adrienne Monnier's records independently indicate. To earn her keep, Boyle was required to clerk in Duncan's fabric shops on rue Saint-Honoré and boulevard Saint-Germain.

RUE CORTAMBERT

16 · Residence of Julien Green

Born of American parents, raised in Paris, and sent to the University of Virginia, Julien Green is nevertheless usually considered a "French" writer, since he wrote in French. A close friend of

Gide and others, Green frequently set his novels in the American South. His most popular novel, *Adrienne Mesurat* (1927), won considerable acclaim in England under the title *The Closed Garden*. He lived here from 1916 to 1932.

AVENUE HENRI-MARTIN

43 • The residence of the Princesse de Polignac

This mansion, which has housed the administrative offices of the Singer Foundation since 1928, was the incomparable residence of the Princesse de Polignac. She was the former Winnaretta Singer of the sewing-machine family. Her brother, Paris Singer, lived for a while with Isadora Duncan and was the father of one of Isadora's children.

When she was twenty-eight, Winnaretta married Prince Edmond de Polignac, who was fifty-nine. The prince conveniently died prior to 1920, leaving Winnaretta a princess and entirely free. The princess used her funds and her influence well. She was a generous and imaginative supporter of the fine arts, sponsoring art shows, commissioning exhibitions, and opening her home for various cultural occasions.

Her afternoon and evening salons were as free, gay, and enviable as anything Natalie Barney could offer. One evening in 1927, for instance, the princess's guests were entertained by a piano duet by Igor Stravinsky and Sergei Prokofiev, two men who rarely played together and, given their opposing political views, seldom had much time for each other.

RUE JEAN-RICHEPIN (FORMERLY RUE EMILE-AUGIER)

14 • Studio of Francis Picabia

Actually this house, which dates from 1913, was the residence of Germaine Everling, his mistress, but Picabia regarded it as his studio. One of the first painters to promote Dada in Paris, Picabia was also one of the first to abandon it (1921). Margaret Anderson had made Picabia the Paris editor of her *Little Review*, but "all we ever got out of him," she said, "was a 'Picabia' issue." Picabia moved to Provence in 1925.

RUE DESBORDES-VALMORE

10 • Residence of William and Louise Bryant Bullitt

William Bullitt married Louise Bryant in Paris on 10 December 1923, shortly after his divorce from his first wife. At the time, Louise was well known as the widow of writer John Reed. Her new husband would become famous in the thirties as the first U.S. ambassador to the U.S.S.R. and, subsequently, as ambassador to France. But in the twenties Louise was the celebrity: a poet, a journalist, and a former Greenwich Villager.

Ardent supporters of George Antheil and regular participants in Montparnasse café life during the twenties, Bill and Louise Bullitt lived in three different residences during their Paris years. At first they rented a house owned by the American writer Elinor Glyn, who had bought it in 1913.

From 1924 to 1925, during which time their daughter, Anne, was born, they lived in this charming house at 10 Desbordes-Valmore. Set back some ten feet from the street, the building is neatly fronted by a small garden of trees, shrubs, and flowers.

TO THE SOUTHWEST

AVENUE DE CAMOENS

1 • Residence of Laurence and Margaret Benét

When Stephen Vincent Benét visited Paris for the first time early in September 1920, he stayed here at the home of his Uncle Larry, the managing director of La Société Hotchkiss et Cie (a munitions firm). Laurence Benét's apartment afforded one of the finest views of the Seine and Eiffel Tower in all of Paris. Later, Stephen Vincent Benét took a room in Montparnasse, but he still used this as his mailing address.

Benét's visit to Paris was most productive — and not just for the poetry he wrote. During this period he met his wife-to-be, Rosemary Carr, at the Paris apartment of his friends Richard and Alice Lee Myers. In June 1921, Benét returned to the United States in order to marry Carr. In November of the same year, he and Rosemary were back in Europe on their honeymoon. In 1926, Benét and his family returned to France once again, when Stephen had received a Guggenheim Award. They took an apartment on the rue Jadin.

SQUARE ALBONI

10 · An early residence of John Peale Bishop

When they arrived in Paris in 1926, the poet Bishop and his wife took up residence here, according to Sylvia Beach's records. By the summer of 1927, while their permanent residence outside Paris was being readied for occupation, the Bishops had moved to the Hôtel Campbell on the avenue de Friedland.

RUE RAYNOUARD

21 · American Ambulance Field Service Headquarters

Prior to World War I, medical science had discovered the process for typing blood, which meant that transfusions could now save lives that once would have been lost — *if* the wounded could be gotten to hospitals in time. Coincidentally, the development of the gasoline engine and inexpensive auto production meant motorized ambulances — that is, the potential for speedy trips from the front lines back to the medical centers.

One problem remained. Where were France, Belgium, and Italy to get ambulance drivers? The war was consuming the supply of young, able-bodied men. Ideally, the drivers would be mechanically inclined, since even Sunday recreational motorers in those days frequently had to "get out and get under." Where could such a pool of drivers be found?

Easy. In the technologically advanced countries that were still neutral — especially the United States, which had an abundance of adventurous young men. They were eager to drive for the Allies, too, since they weren't allowed to fight the Central Powers for them.

Accordingly, the American Ambulance Corps was founded, and its Field Service headquarters was located here. Many American expatriate writers got their first exposure to Europe when they were dispatched from this building as volunteer Red Cross or Norton-Harjes ambulance drivers. Among them were John Dos Passos, E. E. Cummings, Ernest Hemingway, Julien Green, John H. Lawson, Louis Bromfield, Sidney Howard, Malcolm Cowley, Harry Crosby, William Seabrook, Slater Brown, Robert Hillyer, and Dashiell Hammett. Walt Disney lied about his age so he could volunteer, but he didn't get to serve.

A new building has replaced the original AAFS quarters, but a plaque marks the spot, noting that some 2,437 American volunteers drove ambulances under the French flag. (This figure, presumably, wouldn't include the drivers who were assigned to Italy — Hemingway, for instance.) During the three-year period before the United States officially entered the war, the American drivers carried 400,000 wounded men, and 127 of the volunteer drivers died.

VOIE GEORGES-POMPIDOU (WAS QUAI DE PASSY)

12 • Residence of Paul Claudel

One of the most important French writers of the early twentieth century and a friend of Adrienne Monnier, who introduced him to Sylvia Beach, Claudel was a Roman Catholic convert with inclinations toward mysticism. By no means part of the Bohemian life of Montparnasse, Claudel considered James Joyce to be "an enemy of God." Son Excellence Paul Claudel also served as the French ambassador to Japan.

RUE LYAUTEY

3 • Radiation Clinic of Ivan Manoukhin (now gone)

Just off the rue Raynouard in a chic neighborhood, Dr. Ivan Manoukhin set up his clinic for treating tuberculosis by X-raying the spleen. When the British writer Katherine Mansfield heard of the doctor's widely advertised, if radical, methods, she came to Paris (from Switzerland) for treatments. On 31 January 1922, the day after she had moved into the Victoria-Palace Hôtel, Mansfield signed up with Manoukhin, who prescribed twenty-five X-ray sessions. She completed fifteen and stopped.

Recently estranged from her husband, John Middleton Murry, Mansfield ended the treatments partly because of her inability to afford Manoukhin's fee. In addition, she was growing suspicious of the effectiveness of his methods. Mostly, however, her decision to abandon Manoukhin's therapy was based on the severe radiation sickness the X-ray treatments were causing her.

After a brief visit to England, Mansfield returned to Paris and decided this time to try the popular hypnotherapy cures of Dr. Georgei Gurdjieff. In October 1922, Mansfield checked into the Hôtel Select on the place de la Sorbonne and enrolled in Gurdjieff's Institute for the Harmonious Development of Man.

Later, she moved to the doctor's commune housed in Le Prieure ("The Priory"), a château near Fontainebleau. From his diagnosis of Mansfield, Dr. Gurdjieff concluded that she needed to breathe a richer air, so he assigned her to sleep in the barn. Mansfield died at Le Prieure a couple months later, on 9 January 1923.

Mansfield's fate notwithstanding, expatriates like Solita Solano, Kathryn Hulme, and Jane Heap idolized Gurdjieff and periodically attended his institute. Margaret Anderson, the founder of *The Little Review*, and her companion, the former actress Georgette Leblanc, lived at the institute for several months in 1924, returning for briefer stays during the subsequent years. Jean Toomer, the black American writer, attended the institute in the summer of 1924 and several summers thereafter. Toomer became a Gurdjieffian instructor in New York and Chicago.

RUE RAYNOUARD

74 · Studio and apartment of Romaine Brooks

(Beatrice) Romaine Goddard Brooks was born in the United States and educated in Europe, and her interest in art — like her circle of friends — was also international. Leaving her quai de Conti flat, Brooks moved to this apartment, where she produced some of her most interesting work.

Designed in 1925 according to her own specifications, Brooks's residence consisted of ten top-floor rooms with high ceilings reaching up one and a half stories. A lifelong friend and lover of Natalie Barney's, Brooks lived on the floor above Natalie's sister, Laura. Unlike Barney's celebrated residence on the rue Jacob, Brooks's quarters were bright, open, and sparsely decorated with priceless art objects. She also placed several of her own paintings — mostly of women wearing hats, neckties, and monocles — on easels along the apartment walls. After visiting her one afternoon, the Fitzgeralds described Brooks's studio as "a glass enclosed square of heaven swung high above Paris."

RUE DE BOULAINVILLIERS

12 • Tristan Tzara's residence (now Hôtel Eiffel Kennedy)

When Tristan Tzara brought his Dada movement from Zurich to Paris on 17 January 1920, he took a room in the hotel here. In July 1921, Tzara left for three months of travel in Europe, and Man Ray moved into his room.

Arriving in Paris from New York on Bastille Day 1921 (or so he claimed), Ray was impressed with "quiet residential Passy" and with this "Hôtel Meublé," as a sign in the window indicated. Ray eventually learned that the sign referred to the fact that the rooms were *furnished* ("*meublé*"). Three weeks later, Ray left Tzara's hotel room to take free lodgings in a garret in Yvonne Chastel's apartment on the rue de La Condamine in Montmartre.

RUE DE L'ASSOMPTION

5 • James Joyce's residence

On 15 July 1920, the Joyces left the Hôtel Lenox, which Ezra Pound had found for them, and moved here to a three-room flat that was provided by his translator, Madame Ludmilla Bloch-Savitsky. The accommodations were too cramped for Joyce, however. He called the place "a matchbox." He and his family returned to the Lenox three and a half months later, on 1 November 1920.

While Joyce was living here, Tristan Tzara was at 12 rue de Boulainvilliers. Thus, from July through October 1920, the two former Zurich residents were living within shouting distance (half a block) of each other. Actually, given the way the buildings are situated, the two residences are in direct line of sight of each other. In this small and remote neighborhood, they surely shopped at some of the same markets and walked the same streets. Yet, there's no evidence that Tzara and Joyce ever saw — or even knew — each other at the time.

AVENUE DE VERSAILLES

9 · Home of Jean Prévost

After leaving the Chez Rieder on the place Saint-Sulpice, where he was living in 1927 (and probably before), Jean Prévost moved to an apartment out here. He was still serving as Adrienne Monnier's assistant editor on her journal *Le Navire d'Argent* (subtitled "Revue Mensuelle de Littérature et de Culture Générale"), the first number of which came out in June 1925.

RUE CHAMFORT

2 · Apartment of Olga Rudge

Olga Rudge, a concert violinist, lived out here virtually secluded in a quiet neighborhood far from the noise of Montparnasse. Nevertheless, Rudge was Ezra Pound's protégée and lover. With the help of George Antheil, Pound composed some violin concertos for her. Pound also organized and supervised many of her concerts. Speaking of her innovative work, the *Tribune* observed, "Her experiments in the newer music spring from inner conviction, not from an ambition to achieve notoriety."

RUE LECONTE-DE-LISLE

6 · Jo Davidson's residence

As Davidson's success as a sculptor grew, he required more living space than his avenue du Maine studio and the rue Masseran cottage afforded. So, around 1925 he bought this house near the Bois de Boulogne. Deciding to enlarge and remodel it, Jo and Yvonne added bedrooms, bathrooms, and a second studio-workshop.

Yvonne Davidson had taken up dress designing, and her fashions by this time had proved so successful that she was able — and virtually obliged — to open a new shop just off the Champs-Elysées.

QUAI LOUIS-BLERIOT (WAS QUAI D'AUTEUIL)

124 · Residence of H. G. Wells

The famous English writer H. G. Wells used this address during his infrequent trips to Paris in the twenties. Known to be moody and seldom to suffer either fools or reporters, Wells was spotted one day coming out of the Hôtel George V "full of good food and fine wine" by a *Herald* reporter. Caught off guard and in an agreeable mood, Wells consented to a brief interview. When asked about "the Communist menace," Wells replied in secretive tones and exaggerated furtiveness that he suspected the YMCA of being the international force behind the worldwide Communist movement. The *Herald* quoted him the next day, and Wells was livid. Splutter in protest though he may, the great writer couldn't deny having said it.

ISOLATED, REMOTE SITES IN PASSY

BOULEVARD FLANDRIN

25 · Louis Bromfield's residence

The American writer Louis Bromfield came to Paris late in 1925. Despite his intentions to stay only a short while, Bromfield and his family remained in Europe until World War II. Among their residences in Paris was this "large glass apartment overlooking the Bois." Bromfield noted that he was "regarded, with the Fitzgeralds, as vulgar for liking heat and bathrooms."

Hardly an experimental stylist, Bromfield once said that he wrote "the Victorian novel with trimmings." In a piece on the writer in the *Tribune* of 13 June 1926, Alex Small observes, "When he was a soldier [during World War I], Mr. Bromfield spoke . . . of becoming an innkeeper at Compiègne. It seems a pity that he did not; he would have been a charming host and stood out as a genius in a trade which counts few geniuses. And even if he is a very good novelist, the world could easily get along without one of the number, or even several."

BOULEVARD SUCHET

47 · Elegant residence of Anaïs Nin and Hugh Guiler

After waiting six months, Anaïs Nin and her husband, Hugh Guiler, finally moved into these splendid quarters directly across from the Bois de Boulogne on 17 July 1929. The delay notwithstanding, the apartment was still without gas, hot water, electricity, and a telephone when they moved in. Hugh's shrewd investments had brought them here, and the stock market crash a few months later eventually drove them away.

After the stock market collapse, Hugh and Anaïs searched for a house in the country, and on 18 August 1930 they signed a lease on a house at 2-bis rue Mont Buisson in the village of Louveciennes, just outside Paris. Anaïs says she "was enthusiastic." Her feeling was prompted to some extent, no doubt, by the 25,000 francs a year they were saving on rent alone. Nevertheless, her enthusiasm was not totally sincere. She admits in her private journal that she was "broken-hearted about the other [i.e., this boulevard Suchet] home. Though from now on I won't mention the subject again." They left this Passy apartment on 3 October 1930.

AVENUE ERLANGER

4 • Residence of Philippe Soupault

One of the first experimenters with automatic writing, Soupault was perhaps the zaniest of the zany Surrealists. For example, he was said to have halted a late-night bus by putting a chain across the street. When it stopped, he entered and officiously proceeded to interview each of the passengers, writing down dates of birth and other meaningless statistics. Maybe you had to be there.

RUE DE VARIZE

Number unknown • Sinclair Lewis's flat

In mid-June 1927, Sinclair ("Red") Lewis persuaded the mistress of a London friend to move in with him here in a rue de Varize flat — on which he'd taken a three-month lease. Lewis invited Ludwig Lewisohn and Thelma Spear to a house-warming party on the night of June 23rd.

By 1927, according to Lewisohn, Red Lewis "was in flight from himself." He does seem to have been unable to sit still for anything like a sustained relationship. He spent most of his days and nights drinking and carousing with a variety of friends like Marc Connelly,

Stephen Vincent Benét, George Slocombe, and William Lyon Phelps. The mistress also proved too demanding for the restless Lewis. So, before the month was out, he was begging the young poet and novelist Ramon Guthrie to travel to Munich with him. By the first of July, with two and a half months to go on his lease, Lewis had hit the road, and the mistress was back in London with her original lover.

MONTMARTRE
AND
CLOCKWISE

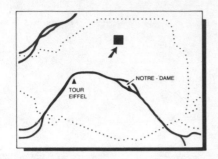

MAP 9

includes addresses from ...

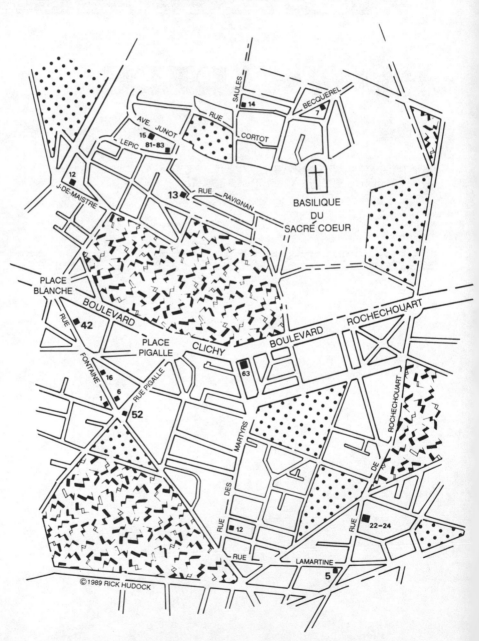

©1989 RICK HUDOCK

30

CLICHY

RUE D'EDIMBOURG

18 · Residence of Vladimir Golschmann, conductor

According to George Antheil, Maistro Golschmann conducted (if that's the word) the premiere performance of Antheil's *Ballet Mécanique* at the Théâtre Champs-Elysées. Other commentators do not mention Vladimir Golschmann in reference to this performance, but they do refer to him as the conductor of Antheil's Symphony in F (a.k.a. the Second Symphony), which was on the same program with the *Ballet Mécanique* that evening of 19 June 1926.

The following October, Golschmann also conducted a program of Debussy, Stravinsky, and Antheil — the Symphony in F again and an earlier Antheil work, *The Sinfonietta* (for five instruments). Obviously, Antheil thought very highly of Golschmann, who was later to be the conductor of the St. Louis Symphony.

RUE DE BERNE

20 · Virgil Thomson's early Paris residence

Thomson first came to Paris in June 1921 as a member of the touring Harvard Glee Club. Thomson had a scholarship, which meant that he was able to remain in Paris when the rest of the Glee Club had to return home. He initially stayed with a French family, which may have been at 38 rue de Provence, an early address that Sylvia Beach lists for him. However, in order to be relatively close to the studio of

Nadia Boulanger, under whom he was studying, Thomson took a room in this residential hotel (i.e., apartment building) at 20 rue de Berne.

Thomson's fellow composer Roy Harris referred to the place as "a whorehouse," and Thomson himself admits that it was inhabited "like all that street, by daughters of joy." For a dedicated musician, though, such a situation proved convenient, since having neighbors who worked all night meant they wouldn't object to his late-hours piano practice.

When his scholarship expired the next year, Thomson went back to America. In 1925 he returned to Paris and moved into this same apartment building, where he lived through autumn 1927. Then, he took a room at the Hôtel Jacob briefly before moving to his permanent residence at 17 quai Voltaire.

BOULEVARD DES BATIGNOLLES

23 • Hôtel Fournet (now gone)

Josephine Baker and most of the "La Revue Nègre" troupe quietly moved from their Montparnasse hotel to this one in Montmartre. André Daven, the manager of the Théâtre des Champs-Elysées, was a stern watchdog who kept a close eye on the black Americans. Out here it was more difficult for Daven to keep track of them.

RUE BALLU

36 • Apartment of Nadia Boulanger

One of the rooms in the apartment of this influential musician and teacher contained two concert grand pianos, a full-sized church organ, some overstuffed chairs, and other assorted furniture.

Boulanger tutored all day, sometimes starting at seven in the morning and continuing until midnight. She encouraged her coterie — which included Aaron Copland, Roy Harris, Virgil Thomson, and the group known as Les Six — to discuss composition theory, as well as to practice rigorously.

Besides being a private tutor, Boulanger played the organ at the Sainte Madeleine church, taught at the Conservatoire, and gave lessons during the summer at Walter Damrosch's American Conservatory of Music in Fontainebleau.

RUE NOLLET

48 · Hôtel Nollet (listed in 1921, but not after 1925)

Especially popular with musicians, this hotel housed an assortment of artists in the early twenties: composer Vittorio Rieti, professional traveler Gaétan Fouquet, violinist Yvonne de Casa-Fuerte, composer Henri Sauguet, and painter Max Jacob.

15 · Langston Hughes's garret (now a residential hotel)

Langston Hughes, twenty-two, a prize-winning black poet from Harlem, arrived in Paris 23 February 1924 with $7.00 in his pocket. During his first month, while he was futilely looking for work and virtually starving, Hughes put up in a Montmartre hotel room of a Russian *danseuse*. When he finally landed a dishwasher's job in Le Grand Duc, he rented a garret here at 15 rue Nollet.

In July 1924, however, Hughes unwisely — but with characteristic generosity — allowed a drug addict to move in with him. A few days later, Hughes quietly moved to a flat on the rue des Trois-Frères, beyond the Bastille. Hughes left Paris in August to tour Europe with friends. By October, he was back, for that was when the well-known black poet and editor, Jessie Fauset, arrived in Paris and looked him up to get his advice about traveling through the south of France.

Hughes returned to New York on 10 November 1924. In his pocket when his ship docked was 25¢, which he used to take the A-Train back to Harlem.

Total cost for Hughes's eight and a half months: $6.75.

RUE DE LA CONDAMINE

22 · Residence of Yvonne Chastel

In August 1921, Man Ray moved from Tristan Tzara's hotel on Boulainvilliers to an attic loft here in Chastel's home.

Yvonne Chastel had been the first wife of painter Jean Crotti, whom Ray had known in New York. She was also a close friend of Ray's Dada buddy Marcel Duchamp — the man who painted *Nude Descending a Staircase.*

In November or December 1921, when Duchamp went to New York, Ray left this garret and moved to the Hôtel des Ecoles on the rue Delambre in Montparnasse.

AVENUE DE CLICHY

52 · Residence of Jacques Benoist-Méchin

In the early twenties, Jacques Benoist-Méchin moved from his home at 8 rue Brémontier to this address, near Montmartre Cemetery. A music student barely out of his teens, Benoist-Méchin was a favorite of Joyce's and Antheil's. He presented ("played" is hardly the word) part of Antheil's *Ballet Mécanique* during one of its previews.

It was Benoist-Méchin to whom Joyce once observed, speaking of all the allusions and puzzles in *Ulysses*, "It will keep the professors busy for centuries arguing over what I meant."

31

MONTMARTRE

RUE DUHESME

9 • Residence of George Slocombe

During 1923–24, red-bearded George Slocombe, friend of many expatriates, both American and British, lived in a flat out here, well beyond Sacré-Coeur. Slocombe was affiliated with Bill Bird's news service, the Consolidated Press Association, while working as correspondent for the London *Daily Herald* (12 rue Vivienne). Subsequently, Slocombe moved completely across town to 5 rue Schoelcher, opposite Montparnasse Cemetery.

AVENUE JUNOT

15 • Home of Tristan Tzara

In 1926, Tristan Tzara, the exponent of Dada, and his Swedish wife, the poet-painter Greta Knutson, moved into this new stone-and-mortar house that they had commissioned from Adolf Loos, the innovative Viennese architect.

RUE LEPIC

81–83 • Moulin de la Galette

A famous dance hall during La Belle Epoque of the previous generations, this landmark at the crossroads of Junot and Lepic —

and Montmartre generally — had fallen out of favor with the expatriates of the twenties.

RUE JOSEPH-DE-MAISTRE

12 · Hôtel Terraso

Following her deportation from America to the Soviet Union in 1919 and her subsequent disillusionment with Bolshevism, the anarchist Emma Goldman lived primarily in England. (Later, after her marriage, she settled in the south of France.) She also made occasional visits to Paris.

In 1926, she married a longtime, but not particularly close, friend, James Colton, a Welsh miner in his sixties. It was a marriage of convenience, for they didn't live together, nor did they intend to. Indicative of their relationship is Goldman's inscription in the copy of *Living My Life* (her autobiography) that she gave to him: "To James Colton — brave comrade and staunch friend, affectionately, Emma Goldman, Paris, Oct. 1931." He was, remember, her husband.

With a Welsh husband, Goldman could get a British passport and could therefore travel more freely. Prior to 1925, she usually stayed here, in the Terraso, when she came to Paris. After her marriage, she used an apartment on the rue Chevert and the name Mrs. E. G. Colton.

RUE RAVIGNAN

13 · The Bateau Lavoir

Picasso's famous studio was located at number 13, but it was the entire complex of studios — including numbers 11 and 13-bis — that gave this building its laundry boat (*"bateau lavoir"*) shape. Picasso worked here during the Fernande Olivier years, from 1904 until 1909, the year he moved to a studio on boulevard de Clichy. He kept the studio until 1912, when he and Fernande officially separated.

The Bateau Lavoir was the site of the famous banquet to honor the painter Henri Rousseau in 1908. Some details, minor ones, are clear.

Max Jacob, for example, had recently fought with Picasso and didn't attend the banquet; therefore, his studio served as the men's cloakroom. Jacques Vaillant was not in town, so his studio was used for women's coats.

Other details are more elusive. According to Gertrude Stein's account of the evening, the guest list included Marie Laurencin, Guillaume Apollinaire, Georges Braque, Germaine and Ramon-Antonio Pichot, André Salmon, and of course "Le Douanier" himself. (Rousseau, despite his nickname, was never a "customs officer.") Somehow, Stein notes, the caterer didn't show up, and they had to make do with buckets of rice.

According to André Salmon's recollections, however, the food was provided by victualers along the rues Lepic and Ravignan. The account by Fernande Olivier, Picasso's mistress and apparently the mastermind behind the dinner, agrees more often with Salmon's version than with Stein's, but even Fernande's has its inconsistencies.

We'll probably never know for sure who spilled what wine on whom, who delivered which speeches, or who struck whom for what reason. Even the precise date of the dinner is disputed. All tellers agree, though, that it was a memorable evening — a benchmark event against which the passing of time and friendships is measured. In that way, the Rousseau banquet was like the opening night of Stravinsky's *Rite of Spring* in 1913. By the twenties, both occasions had reached the status of myth.

RUE DES SAULES

14 · Le Lapin Agile

Located at the intersection of rues Saint-Vincent and des Saules, this popular café, half hidden by acacia, was once called the Cabaret des Assassins. Between 1908 and 1914, it was a favorite hangout for writers and painters. The expatriates of the twenties like the Fitzgeralds or the Crosbys may occasionally have made a sentimental trip out here, but otherwise this once-famous café held little attraction for anyone but Montmartre locals.

RUE BECQUEREL

7 · Apartment of Salvador Dali and Gala Eluard

A friend of the Spanish writer Federico García Lorca and the Spanish filmmaker Luis Buñuel from their days together at the Madrid School of Fine Arts, the Surrealist painter Salvador Dali first traveled to Paris in 1927, where he met two other countrymen: Pablo Picasso and Joan Miró. In March 1929, Dali followed Buñuel back to Paris in order to help with the filming of *Un Chien andalou*. (The following year Dali would write and help shoot Buñuel's second film, *L'Age d'or*.)

After living briefly on rue Vivienne, Dali and Gala — the wife of the Surrealist poet Paul Eluard — moved into an apartment here, at 7 rue Becquerel. On 18 November 1929, two days before the opening of his first one-man show in Paris, at Camille Goemans's gallery, Dali and Gala fled on a "voyage of love" to Barcelona, where they remained for a month. Meanwhile, back in Paris Dali's paintings were the rage. All eleven of them that were exhibited at the Galerie Goemans were sold, and they brought 6,000 to 12,000 francs ($225 to $500) apiece.

BOULEVARD ORNANO

68 · Home of Ramon Guthrie

Having served as an ambulance driver, the poet and novelist Ramon Guthrie became a flyer when the U.S. joined World War I. Although his plane crashed, his life was spared, and he stayed on in France for a while to adjust and to study. After a period back in the States, Guthrie had returned to Paris by the mid-twenties and had taken an apartment out here by the Clignancourt Métro. During Sinclair Lewis's periodic swings through Paris, Red would invariably check in with Guthrie, one of his few true friends.

32

PIGALLE

RUE FONTAINE

Number unknown • Chez Josephine

Although she continued to perform as a dancer in the larger nightclubs, Josephine Baker opened her own club on the rue Fontaine 14 December 1926. Night after night customers would fill her club, hoping Baker would show up after performing at the Casino de Paris or some other large cabaret — and she often did. During this period Josephine was dancing at least ten hours a day, counting her appearances at the Folies-Bergère, the Acacias, and here, at Chez Josephine.

On occasion, according to Baker, she would also step in for the black American woman she'd hired as cook. Chez Josephine offered a menu of both standard nightclub fare like Cordon Bleu and soul food like chitlins and black-eyed peas.

Leaving Paris for a world tour in 1928, Josephine reluctantly closed her club. Montmartre — especially the areas around the places Blanche and Pigalle — was getting pretty rowdy by then.

42 • André Breton's apartment (new building since 1930)

A passionate intellectual and theorist, Breton was a friend and supporter of most of the major artists of the period. He was a champion of Dada until he broke from it in 1923 and formed the Surrealist movement.

In the autumn of 1922, Breton moved into a fourth-floor apartment here. His walls were covered with paintings by Picasso, Braque, Chirico, and Seurat.

16-bis • Au Zelli's (now a new building)

Up at the corner of the rues Fontaine and Douai, Joe Zelli filled a window with photographs of his entertainers and bar girls (topless). A huge electric sign drew the customers to the window, from which they could easily spot Zelli's club a half-block down rue Fontaine.

An ostentatiously alliterative description dating from 1926 reveals the spirit of the nightclub's unique owner: "Joe [Zelli] is a great, grinning, good-time guy, and he will give you a gladsome hour. And there are 740 girls, more or less, to dance with, and every one is affectionate, hungry, thirsty, and broke. . . . Joe is worth a million dollars now. All made in 7 years — and with personality. Nothing else. Go into Zelli's in 1927 [next year]; open 3 bottles of wine. Stay away 3 years, come back, and Joe will rush to meet you and call you by your first name, and you will love it."

6 • Le Palermo

The 1925 *Bottin* lists a club spelled as "Kilex'o" here. This is most certainly a typo for "Kiley's." The telephone books for 1927, 1928, and 1929 list Le Palermo here at number 6.

Discharged from the U.S. Army in 1918, Jed (Gerald) Kiley wrote briefly for the Paris edition of the *New York Herald* before becoming a nightclub owner. His club, Le Palermo, was so popular and financially successful that he opened another club, the College Inn, in Montparnasse. Kiley's success here in Le Palermo was due in part, no doubt, to the frequent appearance of his most famous customer, the Prince of Wales — one of the world's most celebrated and beloved Prince-Designates.

In April 1929, Jack Landorff opened the Cotton Club here, based on the success of a similarly named club in Harlem. He booked as his headliner Alberta Hunter, the black blues singer who had sung in Paris in 1927, and she received her usual raves: "[Alberta Hunter] is billed like a circus. . . . Her opening was a tremendous success, and whether it be variety, musical comedy or cabaret, Miss Hunter can always hold her own" (Ivan Browning, *Chicago Defender*, April 6, 1929).

Despite Hunter's singing "Chiquita" in French and her heavily demanded "Why Do I Love You" from *Showboat*, the Cotton Club folded shortly after it opened, and by the end of May, Alberta Hunter was back in the States.

1(?) • Bricktop's

The exact address of Bricktop's nightclub is listed in none of the standard works (the various *Bottins*, phone books, tour guides, directories, commercial registries). One writer refers to it as being on rue Fontaine, adding that it was "diagonally across the corner from Zelli's," which was not (alas) on a corner. Bricktop herself speaks of it as "across the street" from her old club, Le Grand Duc, which was at 52 rue Pigalle. Such descriptions would most likely place Bricktop's at or adjacent to 1 rue Fontaine.

Bricktop's passport gave her name as Ada Smith du Conge. In her not-entirely-reliable autobiography (written with James Haskins), Bricktop claims she was christened Ada Beatrice Queen Victoria Louise Virginia Smith. In any case, she arrived in Paris in May 1924 and began working immediately as a singer and dancer at Le Grand Duc. A year or so later she opened a club called The Music Box, which was located at the intersection of rue Pigalle and cité Pigalle. That club failed, however, and Bricktop returned to the "Duc" until she'd recovered financially.

Deciding to open another club in 1926, Bricktop sought sufficient backing this time, and she secured an investment from Elsa Schiaparelli. She also had a better location — this spot on the rue Fontaine, near Zelli's. When Cole Porter advised her to avoid such a banal name as The Music Box, Bricktop asked him for a suggestion. "Simply Bricktop's," Porter said with a shrug.

Bricktop's was an overnight sensation. It was supposedly at this club that Mabel Mercer, a mulatto from Staffordshire, England, established her theme song, an exquisite rendition of "Bye-bye Blackbird." Here, too, Sidney Bechet and Louis Armstrong are said to have jammed through early-morning hours. And, most notoriously, it was here that Bricktop's black piano player, Leon Crutcher, is reported to have been shot and killed. (This incident appears in

McAlmon and Boyle's *Being Geniuses Together*, but there's no mention of it in Bricktop's memoirs.)

RUE PIGALLE

55 · Hôtel de Paris
When the black singer Alberta Hunter first arrived in Paris in August 1927, she stayed with friends (Nettie and Glover Compton) in an apartment on rue Victor-Massé. Hunter soon came to like the new freedom — and attention — she found in Paris and moved into this hotel on Pigalle. Also in residence at the time was the black opera singer Caterina Jarboro (real name: Catherine Yarborough). Hunter resumed her old rivalry with Bricktop, bowled over audiences with her impeccable blues, and generally conquered wherever she went — which was off to the French Riviera in early December 1927.

52 · Le Grand Duc (diagonally across from Bricktop's)
Owned by a French nobleman, George Jamerson, who reputedly had gangland connections, Le Grand Duc has been described by more than one observer as "a dive." Few of the expatriates were regulars here, although people like Fred and Adele Astaire stopped in on occasion, as did Clifton Webb and Mary Kay. Most expatriates preferred the clubs run by Joe Zelli, Jed Kiley, Bricktop, Frisco, or Josephine Baker.

According to Bricktop, who was brought to Paris specifically to sing at Le Grand Duc, the place consisted of one small bar and twelve tables. The club was managed by a black American, Gene Bullard, who'd been in France since 1914. Bullard had received many medals for his service during World War I, including the French Legion of Honor.

During the spring and summer of 1924, the black American poet Langston Hughes washed dishes and waited tables here. Hughes's dishwashing job at Le Grand Duc may have been menial, but it was considerably better than the first work he'd found.

Hughes had arrived in Paris on 23 February 1924, and he nearly starved his first month in the city. At one point he even resorted to writing his mother for money, only to learn that his stepfather was seriously ill and that she was starving as well.

Finally, Hughes found work as a doorman at a small club on rue Fontaine, but he discovered that he was to be the club's bouncer as well as sidewalk shill. The first fight the Harlem poet witnessed — and was supposed to stop — involved two women who'd armed themselves with broken bottles. When Hughes saw them waving the jagged glass toward each other's eye shadow, he decided to forsake his five-francs-per-night pay (25¢) and quit. Shortly thereafter, he landed the dishwasher job at the Grand Duc, which at least paid well enough for him to rent an attic room on the rue Nollet.

RUE DES MARTYRS

12 • Frisco's (now gone)

This popular Montmartre nightclub was established for "Frisco" — the Jamaican Jocelyn Augustus Bingham — by his friends, Bricktop and Josephine Baker, who was like a daughter to him. A dancer and piano player, Frisco was also an excellent host. As a result, his club did a very nice business: "The Ritz [Hôtel]," he recalled years later, "sent me five tables [of customers] every night."

BOULEVARD DE ROCHECHOUART

63 • Cirque Médrano (now gone; new buildings here)

Among the performers in this popular circus was Barbette, a transvestite from Round Rock, Texas, whose real name was Vander Clyde. A high-wire trapeze performer, Barbette drew much acclaim. "For his triumphal entry in his first scene," Janet Flanner notes, "he wore, besides his diaphanous white skirts, fifty pounds of white ostrich plumes." Cocteau and the Dadaists took naturally to the Médrano — and to Barbette.

33

TOWARD THE *TRIB*

RUE SAINT-LAZARE

Gare Saint-Lazare

Most of the Americans who came to Paris in the twenties got their first view of the City of Light from this station, the usual destination of the Le Havre–Paris boat trains.

Nathanael West tells of coming out here to pick up newly arrived young American women. Spotting a likely prospect or two, West says he'd pretend that he thought they were distant cousins whom he'd been sent to meet. When the resulting "misunderstanding" was cleared up, West may have just found himself a date who'd spring for lunch, or perhaps more, in return for West's showing her around Paris. West was indeed lonely and poor during his Paris months, but it's not very likely that the reticent West actually practiced such a brazen ploy.

RUE DE CLICHY

16 • Casino de Paris

This nightclub had a slightly better reputation for good taste than its nearest rival, the Folies-Bergère. Still, it had its risqué edge. Josephine Baker danced here in her 1930 revue, "Paris Qui Remue," wearing little more than a towering headdress.

RUE DE MOGADOR

25 • Théâtre Mogador

In 1927 Isadora Duncan gave her last public performance here. The receipts were a paltry 12,000 francs or about $500, which would have covered little more than the rental of the theatre.

Duncan's life had grown increasingly tragic over the previous decade or so. Her children, by Gordon Craig and Paris Singer, had drowned in the Seine. Her husband, Sergei Esenin, a schizophrenic Russian poet, had returned to St. Petersburg and hanged himself in the very hotel room where he and Isadora had honeymooned. And now, in 1927, her skills as a dancer had been compromised by age, alcohol, and amour. "My life," she observed, "has known but two motives — Love and Art — and often Love destroyed Art, and often the imperious call of Art put a tragic end to Love."

In late March 1928, the Gershwins sat through a botched performance of *Rhapsody in Blue* here at the Mogador. At least Frances, Ira, and Lenore (Ira's wife) did. George waited out the second half of the concert in the bar.

RUE DE ROCHECHOUART

22 • The "old" Salle Pleyel (now gone)

Established in 1860, this concert hall was the site of some of the more experimental musical productions of the twenties.

One of the oddest no doubt was the concert Ezra Pound arranged in July 1924 to display the talents of Olga Rudge, the violinist he was promoting. The evening, according to reviewer Irving Schwerke, himself a pianist, offered "an explosion of uncontrolled modernity."

Pound contributed compositions for violin and for violin and voice. More than one acquaintance has described Pound as tone-deaf, although Pound himself tried to play several different instruments — some as exotic as was his sense of musical harmony. Pound's unmusical ear may not have mattered on this occasion, though, since the Pleyel's program indicates the performers' assignments: "Miss

Olga Rudge (violinist) . . . , Mr. George Antheil (hammerer of the clavier), and Mr. Ezra Pound (at the pages)."

On 16 September 1925 a small, invitation-only preview performance of Antheil's *Ballet Mécanique* was given in the Pleyel. It was underwritten by Natalie Barney, and the audience included James Joyce, the Hemingways, and Janet Flanner, who described the event in her October 24 column in *The New Yorker*.

24 · Pleyel studio (now gone)

During the early twenties Igor Stravinsky lived in Anglet, near Biarritz, until he and his family moved to Nice in 1924. Much of Stravinsky's business, however, was conducted in Paris. At first he stayed at the Hôtel Meurice whenever he came to the city.

Things changed when the Pleyel Company began negotiating with Stravinsky for the rights to transcribe his works for the "Pleyela," a patented mechanical piano. (He had reached a similar agreement a few years earlier with a London player-piano company.) To strengthen its bargaining position the company allowed Stravinsky the use of its studios at his will. On 27 August 1922, during the negotiations, Stravinsky advised a friend to write him at his "Pleyel address at 24 rue de Rochechouart," which was this studio next door to the Pleyel Concert Hall at number 22. In 1923, Stravinsky signed a six-year contract with Pleyel.

RUE LAMARTINE

5 · Offices of the Paris edition of the *Chicago Tribune*

This building on Lamartine actually belonged to a French newspaper, the *Petite Journal*. On one of its floors, Jay Allen ran the foreign-news desk of the *New York Daily News*. But this address was most famous for housing the Paris edition of the *Chicago Tribune*, whose offices were in fact reached through the back entrance to the building, off rue Cadet.

Unlike its powerful rival, the *Herald*, the *Tribune* had no operations plant of its own, so it shared printing presses as well as quarters with the *Petite Journal*.

The spacious ground floor of the *Petite Journal* building was used as an exposition hall. Entering through the front doors on the rue Lamartine, one might encounter a cage of trained seals or, most strikingly, a professional faster — much like the hunger artist of Kafka's story.

In addition to these working quarters, the *Tribune* maintained an editorial office at 420 rue Saint-Honoré and an information office at 5 rue Scribe. When tourists arrived in Paris and registered at the information office, their names were run in the *Tribune* the next day, letting their friends know they were in town. The *Trib*'s "Arrivals" was one of its most devoutly read sections. The rival *Herald* also registered new arrivals — out of an office at 49 avenue de l'Opéra.

More than the *Herald*, the *Tribune* was the newspaper read by the Left Bank expatriates. As the brainchild of the eccentric and stern Colonel Robert R. McCormick, the *Chicago Tribune* began publishing an Army Overseas Edition in 1917 and continued, with some modification, after the war. William Shirer described the *Tribune* as "the world's zaniest newspaper," adding that it was "not at all what its owner, the lordly Colonel Robert Rutherford McCormick, intended it to be and thought it was."

Among the writers on the *Tribune* staff at various times were Waverley Root, Morrill Cody, James Thurber, Wambly Bald, Eugene Jolas, Elliot Paul, and Shirer. During the summer of 1925, Thurber took a $12-a-week job writing headlines and translating French news stories (and making up hilarious items of his own) for the paper.

Should Thurber or Shirer find himself in possession of only a brief cable-dispatch of stateside news, he sometimes felt an impulse to complete the story by means of his fertile imagination. Thus, an entire Yale-Harvard football game could issue forth *ex nihilo*, complete with dazzling plays and postgame interviews, from nothing more than a cabled final score. Heaven help the reader when Thurber and Shirer were working on a story *together*.

Others who worked at times for the *Tribune* in various capacities were Henry Miller, Harold Stearns, Oscar Riegel, John Chapman (later drama critic for the *New York Daily News*), William Bridges, and Virgil Geddes. As Al Laney of the rival *Herald* concedes, "The *Tribune* was a lively paper, now and then brilliant, but" — Laney hedges, his loyalty showing — "it was not [widely] read."

THE EXPATRIATES
A Selected Bibliography of Their Works

The following bibliography lists the major literary works that were composed or published in Paris during the twenties, as well as the expatriates' principal memoirs about the period. This bibliography also mentions works that were not written in Paris (for example, Fitzgerald's *The Great Gatsby*) but that nevertheless were influenced by or exerted an influence on the writer's tenure in Paris.

This list does not include biographies or surveys written by literary critics or historians. Neither does it mention all the works by people who visited Paris during the decade. Thus, for instance, Willa Cather's *One of Ours* is listed, for it draws upon Cather's two-month visit to Paris in 1920; but, Cather's other novels of the decade are not noted here.

Adams, B. M. G. *England* (Paris: Three Mountains Press, 1923). *Fiction*
Aldington, Richard. *The Eaten Heart* (Paris: Hours Press, 1929). *Poetry*
Anderson, Margaret. *My Thirty Years' War* (New York: Covici, Friede, 1930).
    Memoirs
    ———. *The Fiery Fountains* (New York: Hermitage House, 1951). *Memoirs*
Anderson, Sherwood. *France and Sherwood Anderson: Paris Notebook, 1921,*
    ed. by Michael Fanning (Baton Rouge: Louisiana State University Press,
    1976). *Memoirs*
Antheil, George. *Bad Boy of Music* (Garden City, N.Y.: Doubleday, 1945).
    Memoirs
Aragon, Louis. *Feu de Joie*, with a drawing by Pablo Picasso (Paris: Au Sans
    Pareil, 1920). *Poetry*
    ———. *Anicet; ou, Le Panorama* (Paris: Gallimard, 1921). *Fiction*
    ———. *Le Libertinage* (Paris: Gallimard, 1924). *Fiction*
    ———. *Le Paysan de Paris* (Paris: Gallimard, 1926). *Fiction*
    ———. *Le Mouvement Perpétuel, Poèmes (1920–1924)*, with 2 drawings by
    Max Morise (Paris: Gallimard, 1926). *Poetry*
    ———. *La Grande Gaîté*, with two drawings by Yves Tanguy (Paris: Gallimard,
    1929). *Poetry*
    ———. *Blanche ou l'Oubli* (Paris: Gallimard, 1967). *Fiction*

————. Tr., Lewis Carroll's *The Hunting of the Snark* as *La Chasse au Snark: Une Agonie en Huit Crises* (Paris: Hours Press, 1929). *Poetry*

Arlen, Michael. *The Green Hat* (New York: George H. Doran, 1924). *Fiction*

————. *Babes in the Wood: A Relaxation Intended for Those Who Are Always Travelling but Never Reaching a Destination* (Garden City, N.Y.: Doubleday, Doran, 1929). *Fiction*

Artaud, Antonin. *A la Grande Nuit, ou le Bluff Surréaliste (Paris: Chez l'Auteur, 1927). Fiction*

————. *L'Art et la Mort* (Paris: R. Denoel, 1929). *Commentary*

Asch, Nathan. "Paris Was Home," *Paris Review* (Summer 1954). *Memoir*

Atget, Eugène. *Atget, Photographe de Paris,* Preface by Pierre MacOrlan (New York: E. Weyhe, 1930). *Photographs*

Barnes, Djuna. *A Book* (New York: Boni and Liveright, 1923); expanded and reissued as *A Night Among the Horses* (New York: Liveright, 1929). *Miscellany: fiction, poems, short plays*

————. *The Ladies Almanack* (Dijon: n.p., printed for the author by M. Darantière, 1928). Note: The private printing became necessary when an original agreement with Titus and the Black Manikin Press fell through at the last minute; thus, some copies carry the Black Manikin logo and erroneously appear to have been published by Titus's press. *Parody*

————. *Ryder* (New York: Liveright, 1928). *Fiction*

————. *Nightwood* (London: Faber and Faber, 1936). *Fiction*

Barney, Natalie. *Pensées d'une Amazone* (Paris: Emile-Paul Frères, 1920). *Reflections*

————. *Poems et Poèmes; Autres Alliances* (Paris: Emile-Paul Frères; New York: George H. Doran, 1920). *Poetry*

————. *Aventures de l'Esprit* (Paris: Emile-Paul Frères, 1929). *Correspondence and reminiscences*

————. *The One Who Is Legion: or, A. D.'s After-Life,* with two illustrations by Romaine Brooks (London: 500 copies privately printed by E. Partridge, 1930). *Fiction*

Beach, Sylvia. *Shakespeare and Company* (New York: Harcourt, Brace, 1959). *Memoirs*

Beasley, Gertrude. *My First Thirty Years* (Paris: Contact Editions, 1925). *Memoirs*

Beckett, Samuel. "Dante . . . Bruno. Vico . . . Joyce," *transition* 16–17 (June 1929). *Criticism*

————. *Whoroscope* (Paris: Hours Press, 1930). *Fiction*

————. *Proust* (New York: Grove Press, 1931). *Criticism*

Bell, Julian. *Essays, Poems and Letters,* ed. by Quentin Bell, with contributions by J. M. Keynes, David Garnett, and others (London: Hogarth Press, 1938). *Memoirs and poetry*

Benét, Rosemary Carr (Mrs. Stephen Vincent). Tr., Colette, *The Gentle Libertine* (New York: Grosset and Dunlap, 1930). *Fiction*

————. Tr., Colette, *A Lesson in Love* (New York: Farrar and Rinehart, 1932). *Fiction*

Benét, Stephen Vincent. *Spanish Bayonet* (New York: George H. Doran, 1926). *Fiction*

————. *John Brown's Body* (Garden City, N.Y.: Doubleday, Doran, 1928). *Poetry*

————. *Ballads and Poems: 1915–1930* (Garden City, N.Y.: Doubleday, Doran, 1931). *Poetry*

————. "Epic on an American Theme: Stephen Vincent Benét and the Guggenheim Foundation," *The New Colophon* [New York] II, pt. 5 (1949). *Letters from Benét to the Foundation regarding the writing of "John Brown's Body"*

Benoist-Méchin, Jacques-Gabriel-Paul-Michel. *La Musique et l'Immortalité dans l'Oeuvre de Marcel Proust* (Paris: S. Kra, 1926). *Commentary*

Bernhardt, Sarah. *The Idol of Paris* (London: C. Palmer, 1921). *Reminiscence*

————. *The Art of the Theatre*, tr. by H. J. Stenning, Preface by James Agate (London: G. Bles, 1924). *Criticism*

————. *Sarah Bernhardt's Love Letters to Pierre Berton*, tr. by Sylvestre Dorian (Girard, Kan.: Haldeman-Julius Co., 1924). *Erotica (mild)*

————. *Sarah Bernhardt's Love Letters to [Victorien] Sardou*, ed. by Sylvestre Dorian (Girard, Kan.: Haldeman-Julius Co., 1924). *Erotica (mild)*

————. *Sarah Bernhardt's Philosophy of Love*, ed. by Sylvestre Dorian (Girard, Kan.: Haldeman-Julius Co., 1924). *Erotica (mild)*

Berry, Walter. *Devant la Mêlée* (Paris: Imprimerie Lahure, 1922). *Addresses to U.S. Chamber of Commerce*

————. *47 Unpublished Letters from Marcel Proust to Walter Berry* (Paris: Black Sun Press, 1930). *Correspondence*

Bibesco, Princess Marthe. *Isvor, the Country of Willows*, tr. by Hamish Miles (London: W. Heinemann, 1924). *Fiction*

————. *Au Bal avec Marcel Proust* (Paris: Gallimard, 1928). *Extracts of letters from Proust*

————. *Catherine-Paris*, tr. by Malcolm Cowley (New York: Harcourt, Brace, 1928). *Fiction*

————. *The Green Parrot*, tr. by Malcolm Cowley (New York: Harcourt, Brace, 1929). *Fiction*

Biddle, George. *The Yes and No of Contemporary Art: An Artist's Evaluation* (Cambridge: Harvard University Press, 1957). *Commentary*

————. *An American Artist's Story* (Boston: Little, Brown, 1939). *Memoirs*

Bird, William. Preface, *Les Années Vingt: Les Ecrivains Américains à Paris et Leurs Amis, 1920–1930* (Paris: Centre Culturel Américain, 1959). *Program notes for the 1959 exhibition*

Bishop, John Peale. *The Collected Essays*, ed. and intro. by Edmund Wilson (New York: Scribner's, 1948). *Commentary*

Bishop, Morris. *Paramount Poems*, drawings by Alison Mason Kingsbury (New York: Milton, Balch and Co., 1929). *Poetry*

Boulanger, Nadia. *Lectures on Modern Music* (Houston: Rice Institute Pamphlet, 1926). *Lectures*

Bourdelle, Emile-Antoine. *Bourdelle par Lui-Même; Se Pensée et Son Art*, ed. by Gaston Varenne (Paris: Fasquelle Editeurs, 1937). *Reflections*

Bowen, Stella. *Drawn from Life* (London: Collins, 1941). *Memoirs*

Bowles, Paul. *Without Stopping: An Autobiography* (New York: Putnam's, 1972). *Autobiography*

Boyle, Kay. "A Christmas Carol for Emanuel Carnevali" and "Madame Tout Petit," in *The New American Caravan* (1928); "Madame . . ." reprinted in *Wedding Day and Other Stories* (New York: J. Cape and H. Smith, 1930). *Poetry and fiction*

————. *Short Stories* (Paris: Black Sun Press, Editions Narcisse, 1929). *Fiction*

————. *Plagued by the Nightingale* (New York: J. Cape and H. Smith, 1931). *Fiction*

————, and Robert McAlmon. *Being Geniuses Together* (Garden City, N.Y.: Doubleday, 1968; San Francisco: North Point, 1984). *Memoirs*

Bradley, William Aspenwall, Tr., Louis Hémon, *My Fair Lady* (New York: Macmillan, 1923). *Fiction*

————. Tr., René Lalou, *Contemporary French Literature* (New York: Knopf, 1924). *Criticism*

————. Tr., Wanda Landowska, *Music of the Past* (New York: Knopf, 1924). *Fiction*

————. Tr., Louis Hémon, *Monsieur Ripois and Nemesis* (New York: Macmillan, 1925). *Fiction*

Breton, André. *Manifeste du Surréalisme; Poisson Soluble* (Paris: Editions du Sagittare, 1924). *Treatise*

————. *Les Pas Perdus* (Paris: Nouvelle Revue Française, 1924). *Surrealist anecdotal commentary*

————. *Légitime Défense* (Paris: Editions Surréalistes, 1926). *Treatise*

————. *Introduction au Discourse sur le Peu de Réalité* (Paris: Gallimard, 1927). *Commentary*

————. *Nadja* (Paris: Gallimard, Nouvelle Review Française, 1928). *Surrealist anecdotal commentary*

————. "Second Manifeste du Surréalisme," *La Révolution Surréaliste* 12:5 (December 1929); (Paris: Kra, 1930). *Treatise*

————, and Philippe Soupault. *Les Champs Magnétique* (Paris: Au Sans Pareil, 1920). *Dada graphics*

Bricktop (Ada Smith du Conge), with James Haskins. *Bricktop* (New York: Atheneum, 1983). *Autobiography*

Bromfield, Louis. *The Green Bay Tree* (New York: Frederick A. Stokes, 1924). *Fiction*

————. *Possession* (New York: Frederick A. Stokes, 1925). *Fiction*

————. *Early Autumn: A Story of a Lady* (New York: Frederick A. Stokes, 1926). *Fiction. The three novels above constitute a trilogy.*

———. *A Good Woman* (New York: Frederick A. Stokes, 1927). *Fiction*

———. *The Strange Case of Miss Annie Spragg* (New York: Frederick A. Stokes, 1928). *Fiction*

———. *Awake and Rehearse* (New York: Frederick A. Stokes, 1929). *Fiction*

Bryant, Louise. *Mirrors of Moscow* (New York: T. Seltzer, 1923). *Commentary*

Bryher (Winifred Ellerman). *Arrow Music* (London: J. and E. Bumpus, 1922). *Poetry*

———. *Two Selves* (Paris: Contact Editions, 1923). *Fiction*

———. *Civilians* (London: Territet, Pool, 1927). *"The characters and incidents in this story are not fictitious," according to Bryher.*

———. *Film Problems of Soviet Russia* (London: Pool, 1929). *Commentary*

———. *The Heart to Artemis: A Writer's Memoir* (New York: Harcourt, Brace and World, 1962). *Memoirs*

Bullitt, William. *It's Not Done* (New York: Harcourt, Brace, 1926). *Fiction*

Buñuel, Luis. *My Last Sigh* (New York: Knopf, 1983). *Memoirs*

Buss, Kate. *Studies in the Chinese Drama* (Boston: The Four Seas Co., 1922). *Criticism*

Butts, Mary. *Speed the Plow and Other Stories* (London: Chapman and Hall, 1923). *Fiction*

———. *Ashe of Rings* (Paris: Three Mountains Press, 1925). *Fiction*

———. *Imaginary Letters, with Engravings on Copper from the Original Drawings by Jean Cocteau* (Paris: E. W. Titus, 1928). *Fiction*

———. *Crystal Cabinet: My Childhood at Salterns* (London: Methuen, 1937). *Memoirs*

Calder, Alexander. *Animal Sketching* (Pelham, N.Y.: Bridgman Publishers, 1926). *Commentary*

———. *Calder: An Autobiography with Pictures* (New York: Pantheon Books, 1966). *Memoirs*

Callaghan, Morley. *That Summer in Paris: Memories of Tangled Friendships with Hemingway, Fitzgerald, and Some Others* (New York: Coward-McCann, 1963). *Memoirs*

Calmer, Edgar ("Ned"). *All the Summer Days* (Boston: Little, Brown, 1961). *Fiction*

Cannell, Kathleen ("Kitty"). *Jam Yesterday* (New York: W. Morrow, 1945). *Childhood memoirs*

Carnevali, Emanuel. *A Hurried Man* (Paris: Contact Publishing Co., 1925). *Commentary*

Cather, Willa. *One of Ours* (New York: Knopf, 1922). *Fiction*

Cendrars, Blaise. *L'Or; La Merveilleuse Histoire du Général Johann August Suter* (Paris: B. Grasset, 1925). *History*

———. *L'ABC du Cinéma* (Paris: Les Ecrivains Réunis, 1926). *Criticism*

———. *Moravagine* (Paris: B. Grasset, 1926). *Fiction*

———. Ed., *Anthologie Nègre* (Paris: Au Sans Pareil, 1927). *Fiction*

———. *Le Plan de l'Aiguille* (Paris: Au Sans Pareil, 1927). *Fiction*

————. *Petits Contes Nègres pour les Enfants des Blancs* (Paris: Editions des Portiques, 1928). *Fiction*

————. *Panama; or, The Adventures of My Seven Uncles*, tr. & illus. by John Dos Passos (New York: Harper, 1931). *Fiction*

Chagall, Marc. *Ma Vie*, tr. from the Russian by Bella Chagall, Preface by André Salmon, with 32 early drawings by the author (Paris: Stock, 1931). *Memoirs*

Charters, James ("Jimmy the Barman"). *This Must Be the Place*, ed. by Morrill Cody, introduction by Ernest Hemingway (London: Herbert Joseph, 1934). *Memoirs*

Chevalier, Maurice. *The Man in the Straw Hat: My Story*, tr. by Caroline Clark (New York: T. Y. Crowell, 1949). *Memoirs*

Chirico, Giorgio de. *Chirico, Avec des Fragments Littéraires de l'Artiste*, ed. by Waldemer George (Paris: Editions des Chroniques du Jour, 1928). *Commentary*

————. *Memorie della Mia Vita* (Roma: Astrolabio, 1945). *Memoirs*

Coates, Robert. *The Eater of Darkness* (Paris: Contact Editions, 1926). *Fiction*

Cocteau, Jean. *Vocabulaire* (Paris: Editions de La Sirène, 1922). *Poetry*

————. *Le Grand Ecart* (Paris: Stock, 1923); tr. by Lewis Galantière (New York: G. P. Putnam's Sons, 1929). *Fiction*

————. *L'Ange Heurtebise, Poèmes; Avec une Photographie de l'Ange par Man Ray* (Paris: Stock, 1925). *Poetry*

————. *Poésie, 1916–1923* (Paris: Nouvelle Revue Française, 1925) *Poetry*

————. *Le Rappel d'Ordre*; includes "Le Secret Professionel," "Autour de Thomas l'Imposteur," "Coq et Arlequin," and others (Paris: Stock, 1926). *Fiction*

————. *Opéra, Oeuvres Poétiques, 1925–1927* (Paris: Stock, 1927). *Poetry*

————. *Antigone. Les Mariés de la Tour Eiffel* (Paris: Editions de la Nouvelle Revue Française, 1928). *Fiction*

————. *Oedipe-Roi* and *Roméo et Juliette* (Paris: Plon, 1928). *Lyrics and choreography; Stravinsky's score and Roger Désormière's arrangements not included*

————. *Les Enfants Terribles* (Paris: B. Grasset, 1929). *Fiction*

————. *Opium: The Diary of an Addict*, tr. by Ernest Boyd, with 27 illustrations by the author (London: Longmans, Green, 1932). *Memoirs; previously published in France*

————. *Orphée: A Tragedy in One Act and an Interval*, tr. by Carl Wildman (London: Oxford University Press, 1933). *Drama; previously published in France*

Cody, Morrill. "Shakespeare and Company — Paris," *Publishers' Weekly* (12 April 1924). *Memoir*

————, and Hugh Ford. *The Women of Montparnasse* (New York: Cornwall Books, 1984). *Memoirs*

Coleman, Emily Holmes. *The Shutter of Snow* (New York: Viking, 1930). *Autobiographical fiction*

Colette, Sidonie-Gabrielle. *L'Envers du Music-Hall* (Paris: Flammarion, 1913). *Autobiographical fiction*

———. *Chéri* (Paris: A. Fayard, 1920). *Fiction*

———. *La Maison de Claudine* (Paris: J. Ferenczi, 1922). *Autobiographical fiction*

———. *Le Voyage Egoïste* (Paris: Edouard Pelletan, 1922). *Autobiographical fiction*

———. *Le Blé en Herbe* (Paris: E. Flammarion, 1923); tr. as *The Ripening Seed. Fiction*

———. *Aventures Quotidiennes* (Paris: E. Flammarion, 1924). *Autobiographical fiction*

———. *La Femme Cachée* (Paris: Flammarion, 1924). *Fiction*

———. *L'Enfant et les Sortilèges. Music de Maurice Ravel* (Paris: Duraud et Cie, 1925); tr. by Christopher Fry as *The Boy and the Magic. Libretto*

———. *La Fin de Chéri* (Paris: Flammarion, 1926). *Fiction*

———. *La Naissance du Jour* (Paris: Flammarion, 1928); tr. by Rosemary Carr Benét as *The Lesson of Love. Fiction*

———. *La Seconde* (Paris: J. Ferenczi, 1929). *Fiction*

Colum, Mary. *From These Roots: The Ideas that Have Made Modern Literature* (New York: C. Scribner's Sons, 1937). *Criticism*

Colum, Padraic. Ed., *Anthology of Irish Verse* (New York: Boni and Liveright, 1922). *Poetry collections*

———. *The Children Who Followed the Piper* (New York: Macmillan, 1922). *Fairy tales*

———. *Dramatic Legends and Other Poems* (New York: Macmillan, 1922). *Poetry*

———. *Castle Conquer* (New York: Macmillan, 1923). *Fiction*

———. *At the Gateways of the Day* (New Haven: Yale University Press, 1924). *Hawaiian folk legends*

———. *The Peep-Show Man* (New York: Macmillan, 1925). *Juvenile*

———. *The Voyagers: Being Legends and Romances of Atlantic Discovery* (New York: Macmillan, 1925). *Fiction*

———. *The Road Round Ireland* (New York: Macmillan, 1926). *Travel sketches and commentary*

———. *Creatures* (New York: Macmillan, 1927). *Poetry*

———. *The Fountain of Youth: Stories Retold* (New York: Macmillan, 1927). *Fiction*

———. *Balloon: A Comedy in Four Acts* (New York: Macmillan, 1929). *Drama*

Copland, Aaron. *Our New Music: The Leading Composers of Europe and America* (New York: McGraw-Hill, 1941). *Commentary*

Covarrubias, Miguel. *Negro Drawings* (New York: Knopf, 1927). *Cartoons and caricatures*

Cowley, Malcolm. *Blue Juniata* (New York: Jonathan Cape and Harrison Smith, 1929). *Poetry*

————. *Exile's Return: A Narrative of Ideas* (New York: W. W. Norton, 1934); rev. and reissued as *Exile's Return: A Literary Odyssey of the 1920s* (New York: Viking, 1951). *Memoirs*

————. Ed., *After The Genteel Tradition: American Writers Since 1910* (New York: W. W. Norton, 1937). *Collection of essays*

————. "The Twenties in Montparnasse," *Saturday Review* (11 March 1967). *Memoir*

————. *A Second Flowering* (New York: Viking, 1973). *Memoirs*

————. *—And I Worked at the Writer's Trade: Chapters of Literary History, 1918–1978* (New York: Viking, 1978). *Memoirs*

Crane, Hart. *White Buildings* (New York: Boni and Liveright, 1926). *Poetry*

————. *The Bridge* (Paris: Black Sun Press, 1930). *Poetry*

Crevel, René. *Mon Corps et Moi* (Paris: Aux Editions du Sagittaire, 1926). *Commentary*

————. *Babylone* (Paris: Simon Kra, 1927). *Fiction*

————. *Etes-Vous Fous?* (Paris: Gallimard, Editions de la Nouvelle Revue Française, 1929). *Fiction*

————. *Mr. Knife, Miss Fork*, tr. by Kay Boyle (Paris: Black Sun Press, 1931). *Fiction*

————. *Dali: ou, L'Anti-Obscurantisme* (Paris: Les Editions Surréaliste, 1931). *Commentary*

Crosby, Caresse. *Crosses of Gold* (Paris: A. Messein, 1925). *Poetry*

————. *Graven Images* (Boston: Houghton Mifflin, 1926). *Poetry*

————. *Painted Shores* (Paris: Black Sun Press, Editions Narcisse, 1927). *Poetry*

————. *The Stranger* (Paris: Black Sun Press, Editions Narcisse, 1927). *Poetry*

————. *Impossible Melodies* (Paris: Black Sun Press, Editions Narcisse, 1928). *Poetry*

————. *Poems for Harry Crosby* (Paris: Black Sun Press, 1931). *Poetry*

————. *The Passionate Years* (New York: Dial Press, 1953). *Memoirs*

Crosby, Harry. *Sonnets for Caresse* (Paris: privately printed by N. Trécult, 1925; reissued Paris: Albert Messein, 1926; reissued Paris: Black Sun Press, Editions Narcisse, 1927). *Poetry*

————. *Red Skeletons* (Paris: Black Sun Press, Editions Narcisse, 1927). *Poetry*

————. *Chariot of the Sun* (Paris: At the Sign of the Sundial, Cour du Soleil d'Or, 1928); reissued with Preface by D. H. Lawrence (Paris: Black Sun Press, 1931). *Poetry*

————. *Transit of Venus* (Paris: Black Sun Press, 1928). *Poetry*

————. *Mad Queen* (Paris: Black Sun Press, 1929). *Verse and prose "tirades"*

————. *Sleeping Together: A Book of Dreams* (Paris: Black Sun Press, 1929). *Poetry*

————. *The Sun* (Paris: Black Sun Press, 1929). *Poetry*

————. *Shadows of the Sun*, 3 vols., (Paris: Black Sun Press, 1928–30). *Poetry*

————. *Aphrodite in Flight* (Paris: Black Sun Press, 1930). *Poetry*

————. *Torchbearer* (Paris: Black Sun Press, 1931). *Poetry*

————. *Collected Poems* (Paris: Black Sun Press, 1931). *Poetry*

————. *Shadows of the Sun: The Diaries of Harry Crosby*, ed. by Edward Germain (Santa Barbara, Calif.: Black Sparrow, 1977). *Diaries*

Crowder, Henry. *Henry-Music;* includes poems by Nancy Cunard, Richard Aldington, Samuel Beckett, and others (Paris: Hours Press, 1930). *Poetry*

Crowley, Aleister (Edward Alexander). *The Diary of a Drug Fiend* (London: Collins, 1922). *Fiction; often thought to be an actual diary*

————. *Magick in Theory and Practice, by the Master Therion* (Paris: Lecram Press, 1929). *Commentary*

————. *Moonchild: A Prologue* (London: Mandrake Press, 1929). *Fiction*

————. *The Stratagem and Other Stories* (London: Mandrake Press, 1929). *Fiction*

————. *The Banned Lecture: "Gilles de Rais," To Have Been Delivered Before the Oxford University Poetry Society . . . on the Evening of February 3, 1930* (London: P. R. Stephenson, 1930). *Lecture*

————. *The Spirit of Solitude: An Autohagiography Subsequently Re-Antichristened. The Confessions of Aleister Crowley* (London: Mandrake Press, 1929). *Memoirs of a sort*

Cullen, Countee. *Color* (New York: Harper and Bros., 1925). *Poetry*

————. *Copper Sun* (New York: Harper and Bros., 1927). *Poetry*

————. *The Ballad of the Brown Girl* (New York: Harper and Bros., 1927). *Poetry*

————. *The Black Christ* (New York: Harper and Bros., 1929). *Poetry*

Cummings, E. E. *The Enormous Room* (New York: Boni and Liveright, 1922). *Fiction*

————. *Tulips and Chimneys* (New York: Thomas Seltzer, 1923). *Poetry*

————. *&* (New York: privately printed, 1925). *Poetry*

————. *XLI Poems* (New York: Dial Press, 1925). *Poetry*

————. *Is 5* (New York: Boni and Liveright, 1926). *Poetry*

————. *Him* (New York: Boni and Liveright, 1927). *Drama*

————. *[no title]* (New York: Covici-Friede, 1930). *Poetry*

Cunard, Nancy. *Outlaws* (London: E. Matthews, 1921). *Poetry*

————. *Sublunary* (London: Hodder and Stoughton, 1923). *Poetry*

————. *Parallax* (London: Hogarth Press, 1925). *Poetry*

————. *Poems (Two)* (London: Aguila Press, 1930). *Poetry*

————. *Negro Anthology. . . , 1931–1933* (London: Whishart and Co., 1934). *Collection*

Dahlberg, Edward. "The Expatriates: A Memoir," *Texas Quarterly* 6 (Summer 1963). *Memoir*

Dali, Salvador. *La Femme Visible* (Paris: Editions Surréalistes, 1930). *Commentary*

————. *L'Amour et la Mémoire* (Paris: Editions Surréalistes, 1931). *Poetry*

————. *The Secret Life of Salvador Dali*, tr. by Haakon M. Chevalier (New York: Dial Press, 1949). *Memoirs*

Damrosch, Walter. *My Musical Life* (New York: Scribner's, 1923). *Memoirs*

Darantière *[firm, printers, Dijon]. Sensvivent les Caractères et les Impressions de Maurice Darantière de Dijon, Imprimeur à Lensigne du Joïeux Laboureur* (Dijon, 1925). *Printing specimens*

————. *Recueil de Caractères de l'Imprimerie Darantière à Dijon* (Dijon: Imprimerie Darantière, 1929). *Printing specimens*

Davidson, Jo. *Between Sittings: An Informal Autobiography* (New York: Dial Press, 1951). *Memoirs*

Davis, George. *The Opening of a Door* (New York: Harper and Bros., 1931). *Fiction*

Desnos, Robert. *Deuil pour Deuil* (Paris: Editions du Sagittaire, 1924). *Poetic novel*

————. *C'est les Bottes de 7 Lieues Cette Phrase "Je Me Vois"* (Paris: La Galerie Simon, 1926). *Poetry*

————. *La Liberté ou l'Amour* (Paris: Editions du Sagittaire, 1927). *Poetic novel*

————. *Corps et Biens* (Paris: Gallimard, Editions du Sagittaire, 1924). *Poetry*

Donnelly, Honoria Murphy, with Richard N. Billings. *Gerald & Sara: Villa America and After* (New York: Times Books, 1982). *Memoirs*

Doolittle, Hilda (H. D.). *Hymen* (London: Egoist Press, 1921). *Poetry*

————. *Heliodora and Other Poems* (Boston: Houghton Mifflin, 1924). *Poetry*

————. *Collected Poems of H.D.* (New York: Boni and Liveright, 1925). *Poetry*

————. *Palimpsest* (Paris: Contact Editions, 1926). *Fiction*

————. *Hippolytus Temporizes* (Boston: Houghton Mifflin, 1927). *Drama*

————. *Hedylus* (Boston: Houghton Mifflin, 1927). *Poetry*

————. *The Usual Star* (Dijon: Imprimerie Darantière, 1928). *Fiction*

————. *Red Roses for Bronze* (New York: Random House, 1929). *Poetry*

Dos Passos, John. *Three Soldiers* (New York: George H. Doran, 1921). *Fiction*

————. "Seven Times Round the Walls of Jericho" (unpublished). *Fiction*

————. *Rosinante to the Road Again* (New York: George H. Doran, 1922). *Essays*

————. *A Pushcart at the Curb* (New York: George H. Doran, 1922). *Poetry*

————. *Manhattan Transfer* (New York: Harper, 1925). *Fiction*

————. *Orient Express* (New York: Harper, 1927). *Travel*

————. *The 42nd Parallel* (New York: Harcourt, Brace, 1930). *Fiction*

————. *1919* (New York: Harcourt, Brace, 1932). *Fiction*

————. *The Big Money* (Harcourt, Brace, 1936). *Completes the* USA *trilogy.*

————. *The Best Times: An Informal Memoir* (New York: New American Library, 1966). *Memoirs*

Duchamp, Marcel. *Salt-Seller: The Writings of Marcel Duchamp*, ed. by Michel Sanouillet and Elmer Peterson (New York: Oxford University Press, 1973). *Miscellaneous*

Duncan, Isadora. *Ecrits sur la Danse* (Paris: Editions du Grenier, 1927). *Commentary*

―――. *La Danse* (Paris: Editions R. Duncan, 1927). *Commentary*

―――. *My Life* (New York: Boni and Liveright, 1927).

―――. *The Art of the Dance*, ed. by Sheldon Chaney (New York: Theatre Arts Press, 1928). *Essays*

Duncan, Raymond. *La Beauté Eternelle* (Paris: Editions de l'Akadémia, 1921). *Poetry*

―――. *Oidipous* (Paris: Editions de l'Akadémia, 1927). *Drama*

―――. *De la Caverne au Temple: ou, De l'Architecture* (Paris: Editions R. Duncan, 1928). *Commentary*

―――. *Initiation aux Arts: De la Parole à l'Idéal; ou, De la Poésie* (Paris: Editions R. Duncan, 1928). *Commentary*

―――. *Poémes de Parole Torrentielle* (Paris: Editions R. Duncan, 1927). *Poetry*

Dunning, Ralph Cheever. *Rococo* (Paris: E. W. Titus, 1926). *Poetry*

―――. *Windfalls* (Paris: E. W. Titus, 1929). *Poetry*

Eastman, Max. *The Sense of Humor* (New York: C. Scribner's Sons, 1921). *Commentary*

―――. *Leon Trotsky: The Portrait of a Youth* (New York: Greenberg, 1925). *Commentary*

―――. *Since Lenin Died* (New York: Boni and Liveright, 1925). *Commentary*

―――. *Marx and Lenin: The Science of Revolution* (New York: A. and C. Boni, 1927). *Commentary*

―――. *Kinds of Love* (New York: C. Scribner's Sons, 1931). *Poetry*

―――. Tr., Alexander Pushkin, *Gabriel: A Poem in One Song* (New York: Covici-Friede, 1929). *Poetry*

Eisenstein, Sergei, and G. V. Alexandrov. *Der Kampf um die Erde (die Generallinie)*, tr. into German by Erwin Honig (Berlin: Schmidt and Co., 1929). *Screenplays and outlines*

Eliot, T. S. *The Sacred Wood: Essays on Poetry and Criticism* (London: Methuen and Co., 1920). *Criticism*

―――. *The Waste Land* (New York: Boni and Liveright, 1922). *Poetry*

―――. *Homage to John Dryden: Three Essays on Poetry of the Seventeenth Century* (London: Hogarth Press, 1924). *Criticism*

―――. *Poems, 1909–1925* (London: Faber and Gwyer, 1925). *Poetry*

―――. *Ash-Wednesday* (London: Faber and Faber, 1930). *Poetry*

Eluard, Paul. *Les Animaux et leurs Hommes. Les Hommes et leurs Animaux* (Paris: Au Sans Pareil, 1920). *Poetry*

―――. *Les Nécessités de la Vie et Les Conséquences des Rêves, Précedé d'Exemples* (Paris: Au Sans Pareil, 1921). *Poetic miscellany*

―――. *Répétitions* (Paris: Au Sans Pareil, 1922). *Poetry*

―――. *Mourir de ne pas Mourir* (Paris: Gallimard, Editions de la Nouvelle Revue Française, 1924). *Poetry*

————. *Les Dessous d'une Vie: ou, La Pyramide Humaine* (Marseilles: Cahiers du Sud, 1926). *Poetry*

————. *Capitale de la Douleur;* originally *L'Art d'Etre Malheureux* (Paris: Gallimard, Editions de la Nouvelle Revue Française, 1926). *Poetry*

————. *L'Amour la Poésie* (Paris: Gallimard, Editions de la Nouvelle Revue Française, 1929). *Poetry*

————. *A Toute Epreuve* (Paris: Editions Surréaliste, 1930). *Poetry*

———— and Max Ernst. *Les Malheurs des Immortels, Révélés par . . .* (Paris: Editions de la Revue Fontaine, 1922). *Poetic miscellany*

Ernst, Max. *Histoire Naturelle* (Paris: n.p., 1926). *Sketches*

————. *Das Arbeitszeitproblem* (Zurich: Rascher and Cie, 1929). *Commentary*

————. *La Femme — 100 Têtes; Avis au Lecteur par André Breton* (Paris: Editions du Carrefour, 1929). *Sketches*

Esenin, Sergei. *Confession d'un Voyou,* tr. by Marie Miloslawsky and Franz Hellens (Paris: J. Povolozky, 1922). *Poetry*

Faulkner, William. *Soldier's Pay* (New York: Boni and Liveright, 1926). *Fiction*

Fauset, Jessie. *There Is Confusion* (New York: Boni and Liveright, 1924). *Fiction*

————. *Plum Bun* (New York: Frederick A. Stokes, 1929). *Fiction*

Faÿ, [Marie-Louis] Bernard. *L'Esprit Révolutionnaire en France et aux Etats-Unis à la Fin du XVIII Siècle* (Paris: E. Champion, 1925); tr. by Ramon Guthrie (New York: Harcourt, Brace, 1927). *Historical analysis*

————. *Panorama de la Littérature Contemporaine* (Paris: Editions du Sagit-taire, 1925); tr. as *Since Victor Hugo* by Paul Rice Doolin (Boston: Little, Brown, 1927). *Criticism*

————. *L'Empire Américain et sa Démocratie en 1926* (Paris: L. de Soye, 1926). *Commentary*

————. *Bernard Faÿ's Franklin: The Apostle of Modern Times* (Boston: Little, Brown, 1929). *Commentary*

Fitzgerald, F. Scott. *This Side of Paradise* (New York: C. Scribner's Sons, 1920). *Fiction*

————. *Flappers and Philosophers* (New York: C. Scribner's Sons, 1920). *Fiction*

————. *The Beautiful and Damned* (New York: C. Scribner's Sons, 1922). *Fiction*

————. *Tales of the Jazz Age* (New York: C. Scribner's Sons, 1922). *Fiction*

————. *The Vegetable* (New York: C. Scribner's Sons, 1923). *Drama*

————. *The Great Gatsby* (New York: C. Scribner's Sons, 1925). *Fiction*

————. *All the Sad Young Men* (New York: C. Scribner's Sons, 1926). *Fiction*

————. *Tender Is the Night* (New York: C. Scribner's Sons, 1934). *Fiction*

————. *Taps at Reveille;* contains "Babylon Revisited," which first appeared in *The Saturday Evening Post,* 30 December/21 February 1931 (New York: C. Scribner's Sons, 1935). *Fiction*

————. *The Crack-Up,* ed. by Edmund Wilson (New York: New Directions, 1945). *Essays, letters, stories*

Fitzgerald, Zelda. *Save Me the Waltz* (New York: C. Scribner's Sons, 1932). *Fiction*

Flanner, Janet. *The Cubical City* (New York: G. P. Putnam's Sons, 1926). *Fiction*

————. *Paris Was Yesterday* (New York: Viking, 1972). *Extracts from her* New Yorker *columns*

————. Tr., Colette, *Chéri* (New York: Boni and Liveright, 1929). *Fiction*

Ford, Ford Madox. *The Marsden Case* (London: Duckworth, 1923). *Fiction*

————. *Mister Bosphorus and the Muses* (London: Duckworth, 1923). *Fiction*

————. *Women and Men* (Paris: Three Mountains Press, 1923). *Commentary*

————. *Some Do Not;* first of the Tietjens tetralogy (London: Duckworth, 1924). *Fiction*

————. *No More Parades;* second of the Tietjens tetralogy (London: Duckworth, 1925). *Fiction*

————. *A Man Could Stand Up;* third of the Tietjens tetralogy (London: Duckworth, 1926). *Fiction*

————. *A Mirror to France* (London: Duckworth, 1926). *Commentary*

————. *New Poems* (New York: W. E. Rudge, 1927). *Poetry*

————. *New York Essays* (New York: W. E. Rudge, 1927). *Commentary*

————. *New York Is Not America* (London: Duckworth, 1927). *Commentary*

————. "Some American Expatriates," *Vanity Fair* 28 (April 1927). *Commentary*

————. *Last Post;* fourth (and last) of the Tietjens tetralogy (London: Duckworth, 1928). *Fiction*

————. *A Little Less Than Gods* (London: Duckworth, 1928). *Fiction*

————. *No Enemy: A Tale of Reconstruction* (New York: Macauley, 1929). *Fiction*

————. *It Was the Nightingale* (Philadelphia: Lippincott, 1933). *Memoirs*

Foujita, Tsugouharu. *Légendes Japonaises Recueillies et Illustrées* (Paris: Editions de l'Abeille d'Or, 1923). *Fiction*

————. *Les Aventures du Roi Pausole* (Paris: A. Fayard, 1925). *28 woodcuts*

Fraenkel, Michael. *Werther's Younger Brother* (Paris: Carrefour Press, 1930). *Fiction*

————. "The Genesis of the *Tropic of Cancer*," in *The Happy Rock: A Book About Henry Miller* (Berkeley, Calif.: Bern Porter, 1945). *Commentary*

Friend, [Harold] Krebs. *The Herdboy* (Paris: Three Mountains Press, 1926). *Poetry*

Galantière, Lewis. *France Is Full of Frenchmen* (New York: Payson and Clark, 1928). *Commentary*

————. "There Is Never Any End to Paris," *New York Times Book Review* (10 May 1964). *Commentary*

————. Tr., Paul Morand, *Nothing But the Earth* (New York: R. M. McBride, 1927). *Travel and commentary*

————. Tr., Rémy de Gourmont, *Dream of a Woman* (New York: Boni and

Liveright, 1927). *Fiction* [Note: In the twenties Galantière also translated works by Jean Cocteau, Jeanne M. Pouguet, Joseph Delteil, Leon Daudet, Marcel Proust, and Jakob Wassermann.]

Geddes, Virgil. *Forty Poems* (Paris: Editions des "Meilleurs Livres," 1926). *Poetry*

———. *The Frog: A Play in Five Scenes* (Paris: E. W. Titus, 1926). *Drama*

———. *Poems 41 to 70* (Paris: Editions des "Meilleurs Livres," 1926). *Poetry*

Gilbert, Stuart. *James Joyce's "Ulysses": A Study* (New York: Knopf, 1930). *Criticism*

———, with Auguste Morel, overseen by Valéry Larbaud and James Joyce. Tr. into French, James Joyce, *Ulysses* (Paris: A. Monnier, 1929). *Fiction*

Glassco, John. *Memoirs of Montparnasse* (New York: Oxford University Press, 1970). *Memoirs*

Goldman, Emma. *The Crushing of the Russian Revolution* (London: Freedom Press, 1922). *Commentary*

———. *My Disillusionment in Russia* (Garden City, N.Y.: Doubleday, Page, 1923). *Commentary*

———. *Living My Life* (New York: A. A. Knopf, 1931). *Memoirs*

Goncharova, Natalia. *Les Ballets Russes: Serge de Diaghilew et la Décoration Théatrale* (Belvès, Dordogne: P. Vorms, 1955). *Commentary*

Gordon, Caroline. *Penhally* (New York: C. Scribner's Sons, 1931). *Fiction*

Green, Julien. *Mont-Cinère* (Paris: Plon-Nourrit, 1926); tr. as *Avarice House* (1927). *Fiction*

———. *Adrienne Mesurat* (Paris: Plon, 1927); tr. by Henry Longan Stuart as *The Closed Garden* (New York: Harper and Bros., 1928). *Fiction*

———. *Les Clefs de la Mort* (Paris: J. Schiffrin, 1927); tr. by Courtney Bruerton (London: W. Heinemann, 1931). *Fiction*

———. *Suite Anglais* (Paris: Les Cahiers de Paris, 1927). *Criticism*

———. *Le Voyage sur la Terre* (Paris: Nouvelle Revue Française, 1927); tr. as *The Pilgrim on the Earth* (1929). *Fiction*

———. *Un Puritain Homme de Lettres: Nathaniel Hawthorne* (Toulouse: Les Cahiers de Paris, 1928). *Criticism*

———. *Léviathan* (Paris: Plon, 1929); tr. by Vyvyan Holland as *The Dark Journey* (New York: Harper and Bros., 1929). *Fiction*

———. *Personal Record, 1928–1939*, tr. by Jocelyn Godefroi (New York: Harper and Bros., 1939). *Journals*

———. *Memories of Happy Days* (New York: Harper and Bros., 1942). *Memoirs*

Guggenheim, Marguerite ("Peggy"). *Out of This Century* (New York: Dial Press, 1946). *Memoirs*

———. Ed., *Art of This Century* (New York: Art of This Century, 1942). *Catalogue of paintings and sculptures owned by P.G.*

Gunther, John. *Eden for One* (New York: Harper and Bros., 1927). *Fiction: "An Amusement"*

————. *Peter Lancelot* (London: M. Secker, 1927). *Fiction: "An Amusement"*

————. *The Golden Fleece* (New York: Harper and Bros., 1929). *Fiction*

————. *Inside Europe* (New York: Harper and Bros., 1936). *Commentary*

Gurdjieff, Georgei Ivanovitch. *The Herald of Coming Good* (Paris: n.p., 1933). *Commentary*

Guthrie, Ramon. *Marcabrun: The Chronicle of a Foundling . . .* (New York: George H. Doran, 1926). *Fiction*

————. *A World Too Old* (New York: George H. Doran, 1927). *Poetry*

————. *Parachute* (New York: Harcourt, Brace, 1928). *Fiction*

Hall, Radclyffe. *The Forge* (London: J. Arrowsmith, 1924). *Fiction*

————. *The Unlit Lamp* (London: Cassell, 1924). *Fiction*

————. *A Saturday Life* (London: J. Arrowsmith, 1925). *Fiction*

————. *Adam's Breed* (Garden City, N.Y.: Doubleday, Page, 1926). *Fiction*

————. *The Well of Loneliness* (Paris: Obelisk Press, 1933). *Fiction*

Hamnett, Nina. *Laughing Torso* (London: Constable, 1932). *Memoirs*

————. *Is She a Lady: A Problem in Autobiography* (London: Wingate, 1925). *Memoirs/Letters*

Harmsworth, Alfred (Lord Northcliffe). *Newspapers and Their Millionaires: With Some Further Meditations About Us* (London: Associated Newspapers, Ltd., 1922). *Commentary*

Harris, Frank. *Undream'd of Shores* (New York: Brentano's, 1924). *Memoirs*

————. *Joan la Romée* (London: Fortune Press, 1926). *Drama*

————. *Latest Contemporary Portraits* (New York: Macaulay, 1927). *Commentary*

————. *My Life and Loves*, 3 vols. (Paris: the author, privately printed, 1922–1927). *Memoirs/Fiction*

Hartley, Marsden. *Adventures in the Arts: Informal Chapters on Painters, Vaudeville and Poets* (New York: Boni and Liveright, 1921). *Commentary*

————. *Twenty-Five Poems* (Paris: Contact Publishing Co., 1923). *Poetry*

Hastings, Beatrice. *The Old "New Age" — Orage and Others* (London: Blue Moon Press, 1936). *Memoirs/Commentary*

Hawkins, Eric, with Robert N. Sturdevant. *Hawkins of the Paris Herald* (New York: Simon and Schuster, 1963). *Memoirs*

Hemingway, Ernest. *Three Stories & Ten Poems* (Paris: Contact Editions, 1923). *Fiction/Poetry*

————. *in our time* (Paris: Three Mountains Press, 1924). *Fiction*

————. *In Our Time* (New York: Boni and Liveright, 1925). *Fiction*

————. *The Torrents of Spring* (New York: Scribner's, 1926). *Fiction*

————. *The Sun Also Rises* (New York: Scribner's, 1926). *Fiction*

————. *Men Without Women* (New York: Scribner's, 1927). *Fiction*

————. *Collected Poems* (Paris: n.p., 1929). *Poetry, "originally published in Paris, 1922–1929, in various periodicals and in* Three Stories and Ten Poems*"*

————. *A Farewell to Arms* (New York: Scribner's, 1929). *Fiction*

————. *A Moveable Feast* (New York: Scribner's, 1964). *Memoirs*

————. *By-Line: Ernest Hemingway: Selected Articles and Dispatches of Four Decades,* ed. by William White (New York: Scribner's, 1967). *Journalism*

Herrick, Myron T. *Myron T. Herrick: Friend of France: An Autobiographical Biography* by Col. T. Bentley Mott (Garden City, N. Y.: Doubleday, Doran, 1929). *Memoirs*

Herrmann, John. *What Happens* (Paris: Contact Editions, 1926). *Fiction*

Hiler, Hilaire (See also Arthur Moss). *From Nudity to Raiment* (New York: F. Weyhe, 1929). *Commentary*

Huddleston, Sisley. *France and the French* (New York: C. Scribner's Sons, 1927). *Commentary*

————. *France* (New York: C. Scribner's Sons, 1927). *Commentary*

————. *In and About Paris* (New York: George H. Doran, 1927). *Commentary*

————. *Mr. Paname: A Paris Fantasia* (New York: George H. Doran, 1927). *Fiction*

————. *Articles de Paris: A Book of Essays* (New York: Macmillan, 1928). *Commentary*

————. *Paris* (New York: R. M. McBride, 1928). *Commentary*

————. *Paris Salons, Cafés, Studios: Being Social, Artistic and Literary Memories* (Philadelphia: Lippincott, 1928). *Commentary*

————. *Europe in Zigzags: Social, Artistic, Literary and Political Affairs on the Continent* (Philadelphia: Lippincott, 1929). *Commentary*

————. *Back to Montparnasse: Glimpses of Broadway in Bohemia* (Philadelphia: Lippincott, 1931). *Memoirs*

Hughes, [James] Langston. *The Weary Blues* (New York: A. A. Knopf, 1926). *Poetry*

————. *Fine Clothes to the Jew* (New York: A. A. Knopf, 1927). *Poetry*

————. *Not Without Laughter* (New York: A. A. Knopf, 1930). *Fiction*

Hulme, Kathryn. *We Lived as Children* (New York: A. A. Knopf, 1938). *Fiction*

————. *Undiscovered Country: A Spiritual Adventure* (Boston: Little, Brown, 1966). *Memoirs*

Imbs, Bravig. *Eden: Exit This Way and Other Poems* (Paris: G. Fraser, 1926). *Poetry*

————. *Confessions of Another Young Man* (New York: Henkle-Yewdale House, 1936). *Memoirs*

Jacob, Max. *Cinématoma* (Paris: Editions de La Sirène, 1920). *Commentary/Memoir*

————. *Le Labatoire Central: Poésies . . .* (Paris: Au Sans Pareil, 1921). *Poetry*

————. *La Roi de Béotie* (Paris: Editions de la Nouvelle Revue Française, 1921). *Fiction and drama*

————. *Art Poétique* (Paris: Chez Emile-Paul Frères, 1922). *Poetry*

————. *Filbuth: Ou, La Montre en Or* (Paris: Editions de la Nouvelle Revue Française, 1922). *Portraits*

————. *Le Cabinet Noir* (Paris: Gallimard, Editions de la Nouvelle Revue Française, 1928). *Commentary*

————. *Visions de Souffrances et de la Mort de Jésus Fils de Dieu* (Paris: Aux Quatres Chemins, 1928). *40 pen and ink drawings*

————. *Tableaux de la Bourgeoisie* (Paris: Editions de la Nouvelle Revue Française, 1929). *Drawings and lithographs*

John, Augustus. *Autobiography* (London: J. Cape, 1975). *Memoirs*

Johnson, James Weldon. *Along This Way: The Autobiography of . . .* (New York: Viking, 1933). *Memoirs*

Jolas, Eugene. *Cinema* (New York: Adelphi, 1926). *Poetry*

————. *Secession in Astropolis* (Paris: Black Sun Press, 1929). *Commentary and fiction*

————. *I Have Seen Monsters and Angels* (Paris: Transition Press, 1938). *Memoirs*

————, et al. "Testimony against Gertrude Stein," *transition Pamphlet #1* (Supplement to *transition* 23, 1934–1935; issued February 1935). *Commentary of various lengths by Eugene and Maria Jolas, Georges Braque, Henri Matisse, Tristan Tzara, and others*

————. Ed., *Le Nègre Qui Chante* (Paris: Editions des Cahiers Libre, 1928). *Song lyrics*

————. Ed. and tr., *Anthologie de la Nouvelle Poésie Américaine* (Paris: Kra, 1928). *Poetry*

————, with Robert Sage. Eds., *transition Stories* (New York: W. V. McKee, 1929). *Fiction: 23 stories from* transition

Josephson, Matthew. *Zola and His Time* (New York: Macaulay, 1928). *History*

————. *Portrait of the Artist as an American* (New York: Harcourt, Brace, 1930). *Commentary*

————. *Life Among the Surrealists.* (New York: Holt, Rinehart and Winston, 1962). *Memoirs*

Joyce, James. *Ulysses* (Paris: Shakespeare and Co., 1922). *Fiction*

————. *Poems Penyeach* (Paris: Shakespeare and Co., 1927). *Poetry*

————. *Anna Livia Plurabelle;* from "Work in Progress", i.e., *Finnegans Wake* (New York: C. Gaige, 1928). *Fiction*

————. *Tales Told of Shem and Shaun: Three Fragments from Work in Progress [Finnegans Wake]* (Paris: Black Sun Press, 1929). *Fiction*

————. *Haveth Childers Everywhere;* from "Work in Progress," i.e., *Finnegans Wake* (Paris: Obelisk Press, 1930). *Fiction*

————. *Finnegans Wake* ["Work in Progress"] (New York: Viking, 1939). *Fiction*

Kahane, Jack. *Memoirs of a Booklegger* (London: Michael Joseph, 1939). *Memoirs*

Kiki (Alice Prin). *Les Souvenirs de Kiki* (Paris: Henri Broca, 1929). *Kiki's Memoirs*, tr. by Samuel Putnam, introduction by Ernest Hemingway (Paris: Black Manikin Press, 1930). *Memoirs*

Komroff, Manuel. *The Grace of Lambs* (New York: Boni and Liveright, 1925). *Fiction*

―――. *The Voice of Fire* (Paris: E. W. Titus, 1927). *Fiction*

―――. *The Great Fables* (New York: Coward-McCann, 1928). *Fiction*

―――. *Tales of the Monks: From the Gesta Romanorus* (New York: Coward-McCann, 1928). *Fiction*

―――. *Coronet* (New York: Coward-McCann, 1929). *Fiction*

―――. Ed., *The Apocrypha* (New York: L. MacVeagh, Dial Press, 1929). *Biblical*

Kreymborg, Alfred. *Less Lonely* (New York: Harcourt, Brace, 1923). *Poetry*

―――. *Puppet Plays* (New York: Harcourt, Brace, 1923). *Drama*

―――. *Troubador: An Autobiography* (New York: Boni and Liveright, 1925). *Memoirs*

―――. *There's a Moon Tonight* (New York: S. French, 1926). *Drama*

―――. *Funnybone Alley* (New York: Macaulay, 1927). *Children's drama*

―――. *Jane, Jean and John* (New York: S. French, 1927). *Drama*

―――. *Body and Stone* (New York: Random House, 1929). *Poetry*

Laney, Al. *Paris Herald: The Incredible Newspaper* (New York: Appleton-Century, 1947). *Memoirs*

Lanham, Edwin. *Sailors Don't Care* (Paris: Contact Editions, 1929). *Fiction*

Larbaud, Valéry. *Amants, Heureux Amants* (Paris: Nouvelle Revue Française, 1923). *Fiction*

―――. *Les Poésies de A. O. Barnabooth* [pseudonym] (Paris: Editions de la Nouvelle Revue Française, 1923). *Poetry*

―――. *Ce Vice Impuni, la Lecture: Domaine Anglais* (Paris: Messein, 1924). *Criticism*

―――. *Paul Valéry et la Méditerranée* (Maestricht: A. A. M. Stols, 1926). *Biographical miscellany*

―――. *Jaune, Bleu, Blanc* (Paris: Gallimard, 1927). *Commentary*

―――. *Notes Sur Antoine Héroët et Jean de Lingendes* (Paris: Editions Lapina, 1927/28). *Historical commentary*

―――. *Allen* (Paris: Editions de la Chronique des Lettres Française, 1929). *Fiction*

―――. *Journal, 1912–1935* (Paris: Gallimard, 1955). *Journal*

―――. Tr., Samuel Butler, *Erewhon* (Paris: Editions de la Nouvelle Revue Française, 1920). *Fiction*

Laurencin, Marie. *Eventail: Dix Gravures de Marie Laurencin, Accompagnées de Poésies Nouvelles de Louis Codet. . . , André Breton. . . , Max Jacob. . . , Valéry Larbaud, A. Salmon* (Paris: Editions de la Nouvelle Revue Française, 1922). *Sketches and poetry*

―――. *Petit Bestiaire* (Paris: F. Bernouard, 1926). *Poetry*

―――. Charles Lutwidge Dodgson [Lewis Carroll] *Alice in Wonderland*, with 6 colored lithographs by Marie Laurencin (Paris: Black Sun Press, 1930). *Lithographs*

Lawson, John Howard. *Roger Bloomer* (New York: T. Seltzer, 1923). *Drama*
——. *Processional: A Jazz Symphony of American Life in Four Acts* (New York: T. Seltzer, 1925). *Drama*
——. *International* (New York: Macaulay, 1927). *Drama*
——. *Loud Speaker: A Farce* (New York: Macaulay, 1927). *Drama*
Leblanc, Georgette. *Souvenirs (1895–1918)* (Paris: B. Grasset, 1931); tr. by Janet Flanner as *Souvenirs: My Life with Maeterlinck* (New York: E. P. Dutton, 1932). *Memoirs*
——. *La Machine à Courage* (Paris: J. B. Janin, 1947). *Memoirs*
Le Gallienne, Eva. *At 33* (New York: Green, 1934). *Memoirs/Letters*
——. *With a Quiet Heart* (New York: Viking, 1953). *Memoirs*
Le Gallienne, Julia (Norregard). Tr., Peter Nansen, *Marie: A Book of Love* (Boston: J. W. Luce, 1924). *Fiction*
Le Gallienne, Richard. *The Junkman, and Other Poems* (Garden City, N.Y.: Doubleday, Page, 1920). *Poetry*
——. *The Quest of the Golden Girl* (New York: John Lane, 1920). *Fiction*
——. *A Jongleur Strayed: Verses on Love and Other Matters Sacred and Profane* (Garden City, N.Y.: Doubleday, Page, 1922). *Poetry*
——. *The Le Gallienne Book of American Verse* (New York: Boni and Liveright, 1922). *Poetry*
——. *The Romantic '90s* (Garden City, N.Y.: Doubleday, Page, 1925). *Commentary and memoirs*
——. *From a Paris Garret* (New York: I. Washburn, 1936). *Commentary*
——. *From a Paris Scrapbook* (New York: I. Washburn, 1938). *Commentary*
Leiris, Michel. *Le Point Cardinal* (Paris: S. Kra, 1927). *Poetic miscellany*
——, and André Masson. *Simulacre: Poèmes et Lithographies* (Paris: Editions de la Galerie Simon, 1925). *Poetry and lithographs*
Levy, Julien. *Surrealism* (New York: Black Sun Press, 1936). *Commentary*
Lewis, Sinclair. *Main Street: The Story of Carol Kennicott* (New York: Harcourt, Brace and Howe, 1920) *Fiction*
——. *Babbitt* (New York: Harcourt, Brace, 1922). *Fiction*
——. *Our Mr. Wrenn* (New York: Harcourt, Brace, 1923). *Fiction*
——. *Arrowsmith* (New York: Harcourt, Brace, 1925). *Fiction*
——. *Elmer Gantry* (New York: Harcourt, Brace, 1927). *Fiction*
——. *The Man Who Knew Coolidge: Being the Soul of Lowell Schmaltz, Constructive and Nordic Citizen* (New York: Harcourt, Brace, 1928). *Fiction*
——. *Dodsworth* (New York: Harcourt, Brace, 1929). *Fiction*
——. *The American Fear of Literature: Nobel Address Delivered in Stockholm, December 12, 1930* (Stockholm: P. A. Norstedt, 1931). *Address*
——. *From Main Street to Stockholm: The Letters of Sinclair Lewis, 1919–1930*, ed. by Harrison Smith (New York: Harcourt, Brace, 1952). *Letters*
Lewis, Wyndham. *Time and Western Man* (London: Chatto and Windus, 1927). *Commentary*

————. *Blasting and Bombardiering* (London: Eyre and Spottiswoode, 1937). *Memoirs*

Lewisohn, Ludwig. *The Creative Life* (New York: Boni and Liveright, 1924). *Commentary*

————. *The Case of Mr. Crump* (Paris: E. W. Titus, 1926). *Fiction*

————. *The Island Within* (New York: Harper and Bros., 1928). *Fiction*

————. *Adam* (New York: Harper and Bros., 1929). *Drama*

————. *Mid-Channel: An American Chronicle* (New York: Harper and Bros., 1929). *Memoirs*

Liebling, A. J. *Between Meals: An Appetite for Paris,* reprinted in *Liebling Abroad: Four Complete Classics in One Volume* (New York: Playboy Press, 1981) and reprinted again by itself (San Francisco: North Point Press, 1987). *Memoirs*

Longstreet, Stephen. *We All Went to Paris: Americans in the City of Light: 1776–1971* (New York: Macmillan, 1972). *Memoirs and history*

Loving, Pierre. *Indian Summer* in *Ten Minute Plays,* ed. and foreword by Pierre Loving (New York: Brentano's, 1923). *Drama*

Lowenfels, Walter. *Episodes and Epistles* (New York: T. Seltzer, 1923). *Poetry*

————. *Apollinaire, An Elegy* (Paris: Hours Press, 1930). *Poetry*

————. *U.S.A. With Music: An Operatic Tragedy* (Paris: Carrefour Editions, 1930). *Opera*

Loy, Mina. *Psycho-Democracy: A Movement to Focus Human Reason on the Conscious Direction of Evolution* (Firenze: Tipografià Peri and Rossi, 1920). *Commentary*

————. *Lunar Baedecker* (Paris: Contact Publishing Co., 1923). *Poetry*

MacLeish, Archibald. *The Happy Marriage, and Other Poems* (Boston: Houghton Mifflin, 1924). *Poetry*

————. *The Pot of Earth* (Boston: Houghton Mifflin, 1925). *Poetry*

————. *Nobodaddy* (Cambridge, Mass.: Dunster House, 1926). *Drama*

————. *Streets in the Moon* (Boston: Houghton Mifflin, 1926). *Poetry*

————. *Einstein* (Paris: Black Sun Press, 1929). *Poetry*

————. *New Found Land* (Paris: Black Sun Press, 1930). *Poetry*

————. *Poems, 1924–1933* (Boston: Houghton Mifflin, 1933). *Poetry*

————. "There Was Something about the Twenties," *Saturday Review* (31 December 1966). *Memoirs*

————. "Autobiographical Notes," *Riders on the Earth: Essays and Recollections* (Boston: Houghton Mifflin, 1978). *Commentary and memoirs*

Mansfield, Katherine. *The Garden Party, and Other Stories* (New York: A. A. Knopf, 1922). *Fiction*

————. *The Dove's Nest, and Other Stories* (New York: A. A. Knopf, 1923). *Fiction*

————. *Journal of Katherine Mansfield,* ed. by J. Middleton Murry (New York: A. A. Knopf, 1927). *Journal*

Masson, André. *L'Eglise Abbatiale Saint-Ouen de Rouen . . . , Etude sur les Vitraux par Jean Lafond . . .* (Paris: H. Laurens, 1920). *Commentary*

———. *Hanoi Pendant la Période Héroïque 1873–1888)* (Paris: P. Geuthner, 1929). *History and commentary*

Matisse, Henri. *Henri Matisse* by Roger Fry (New York: E. Weyhe, 1930). *Reproductions and commentary*

Maxwell, Elsa. *R.S.V.P. — Elsa Maxwell's Own Story* (Boston: Little, Brown, 1954). *Memoirs*

McAlmon, Robert. *Exploration* (London: Egoist Press, 1921). *Poetry and prose sketches*

———. *A Hasty Bunch* (Paris: Contact Publishing Co., 1921). *Fiction*

———. *A Companion Volume* (Paris: Contact Publishing Co., 1923). *Fiction*

———. *Post-Adolescence* (Paris: Contact Publishing Co., 1923). *Fictionalized autobiography*

———. *Village: As It Happened Through a Fifteen Year Period* (Paris: Contact Publishing Co., 1924). *Fiction*

———. *The Portrait of a Generation* (Paris: Contact Editions, 1926). *Poetry*

———. *Distinguished Air: Grim Fairy Tales* (Paris: Three Mountains Press, 1925). *Fiction*

———. *North America: Continent of Conjecture* (Paris: Contact Editions, 1929). *Poetry*

———. *Unfinished Poem*, with decorations by Hilaire Hiler (Paris: Contact Editions, 1929). *Poetry*

———. *Indefinite Huntress, and Other Stories* (Paris: Crosby Continental Editions, 1932). *Fiction*

———. *McAlmon and the Lost Generation: A Self-Portrait*, ed. with commentary by Robert E. Knoll (Lincoln: University of Nebraska Press, 1962). *Journal*

———. *Being Geniuses Together* (London: Secker and Warburg, 1938). *Memoirs*

———. Ed., *Contact Collection of Contemporary Writers* (Paris: Contact Publishing Co., 1925). *Miscellany*

McBride, Mary Margaret, and Helen Josephy. *Paris Is a Woman's Town* (New York: Coward-McCann, 1929). *Commentary/Travel*

McKay, Claude. *Home to Harlem* (New York: Harper and Bros., 1928). *Fiction*

———. *Banjo: A Story Without a Plot* (New York: Harper and Bros., 1929). *Fiction*

———. *A Long Way from Home* (New York: L. Furman, 1937). *Memoirs*

Milhaud, Darius. *Notes Without Music: An Autobiography*, tr. by Donald Evans (New York: Knopf, 1953). *Memoirs*

Millay, Edna St. Vincent. *A Few Figs from Thistles: Poems and Four Sonnets* (New York: F. Shay, 1921). *Poetry*

———. *Second April* (New York: M. Kennerley, 1921). *Poetry*

———. *The Harp-Weaver, and Other Poems* (New York: Harper and Bros., 1923). *Poetry*

————. *Poems* (London: M. Secker, 1923). *Poetry*

————. *Three Plays;* all previously published: *The Lamp and the Bell, Aria da Capo,* and *Two Slatterns* (New York: Harper and Bros., 1926). *Drama*

————. *The Buck in the Snow, and Other Poems* (New York: Harper and Bros., 1928). *Poetry*

Miller, Henry. *Tropic of Cancer* (Paris: Obelisk Press, 1934). *Fiction*

Miró, Joan. Lise Hirtz. *"Il Etait une Petit Pie": 7 Chansons et 3 Chansons pour Hyacinthe avec 8 Dessins en Couleur par Joan Miró* (Paris: J. Bucher, 1928). *Graphics*

Mondrian, Piet. *Le Néo-Plasticisme: Principe Général de l'Equivalence Plastique* (Paris: Editions de l'Effort Moderne, 1920). *Commentary*

Monnier, Adrienne. *La Figure* (Paris: La Maison des Amis des Livres, 1923). *Poetry*

————. *Les Vertus* (Paris: La Société Général d'Imprimerie ed d'Edition, 1926). *Poetry*

————. *The Very Rich Hours of Adrienne Monnier,* tr., intoduction, and commentary by Richard McDougall (New York: Scribners, 1976). *Memoirs*

Monroe, Harriet. "The Editor in France," *Poetry: A Magazine of Verse* 23:2 (November 1923). *Commentary*

————. *Poets and Their Art* (New York: Macmillan, 1926). *Commentary*

————. *A Poet's Life: Seventy Years in a Changing World* (New York: Macmillan, 1938). *Memoirs*

Moore, George. *Peronnick the Fool* (Paris: Hours Press, 1928). *Fiction*

Moore, Grace. *You're Only Human Once* (Garden City, N.Y.: Doubleday, Doran, 1944). *Memoirs*

Moorhead, Ethel. *See* Ernest Walsh.

Morand, Paul. *Tendres Stocks* [tr. as *Green Shoots*], Preface by Marcel Proust (Paris: Editions de la Nouvelle Revue Française, 1921). *Fiction*

————. *Ouvert la Nuit* [tr. as *Open All Night*] (Paris: Editions de la Nouvelle Revue Française, 1922). *Fiction*

Moss, Arthur, and Hiler Harzberg [a.k.a. Hilaire Hiler]. *Slapstick and Dumbbell: A Casual Survey of Clowns and Clowning* (New York: J. Lawren, 1934). *Commentary*

Mowrer, Paul Scott. *The Good Comrade and Fairies* (New York: E. P. Dutton, 1923). *Poetry*

————. *Our Foreign Affairs: A Study in National Interest and the New Diplomacy* (New York: E. P. Dutton, 1924). *Commentary*

————. *Red Russia's Menace: How the Communist Dictators of Moscow Have Constructed a Militant Monster for Armed Aggression and Are Plotting World Conquest* (Chicago: Chicago Daily News Co., 1925). *Commentary and then some*

Munson, Gorham. *Destinations: A Canvass of American Literature Since 1900* (New York: J. H. Sears, 1928). *Criticism*

————. *The Awakening Twenties: A Memoir-History of a Literary Period* (Baton Rouge: Louisiana State University Press, 1985). *Memoirs*

Murphy, Honoria. *See* Honoria Murphy Donnelly.

Neagoe, Peter. Ed., *Americans Abroad: An Anthology* (The Hague: Servire Press, 1932). *Literary collection*

Nin, Anaïs. *D. H. Lawrence: An Unprofessional Study* (Paris: E. W. Titus, 1932). *Criticism*

————. *The Early Diary of Anaïs Nin,* Volumes III (1923–27) and IV (1927–32) (New York: Harcourt, Brace, Jovanovich, 1983, 1985). *Diaries*

Olivier, Fernande. *Picasso et Ses Amis* (Paris: Stock, 1933); tr. by Jane Miller as *Picasso and His Friends* (New York: Appleton-Century, 1965). *Memoirs*

O'Neill, Eugene. *Dynamo* (New York: Liveright, 1929). *Drama*

————. *Mourning Becomes Electra* (New York: Liveright, 1931). *Drama*

Osborn, Richard Galen. "No. 2 Rue Auguste Bartholdi," in *The Happy Rock: A Book About Henry Miller* (Berkeley, Calif.: Bern Porter, 1945). *Memoirs*

Paul, Elliot. *The Amazon* (New York: Liveright, 1930). *Fiction*

————. *The Mysterious Mickey Finn: or, Murder at the Café du Dôme, an International Mystery* (New York: Modern Age Books, 1939). *Fiction*

————. *The Last Time I Saw Paris* (Garden City, N.Y.: Sun Dial Press, 1942). *Memoirs*

————. *A Narrow Street* (London: Cresset Press, 1942). *Memoirs*

————. *Springtime in Paris* (New York: Random House, 1950). *Memoirs*

————. *Murder on the Left Bank: A Homer Evans Mystery* (New York: Random House, 1951). *Fiction*

Picabia, Francis. *Unique Eunuque,* with a self-portrait by the author and a Preface by Tristan Tzara (Paris: Au Sans Pareil, 1920). *Dada commentary*

Picasso, Pablo. *Pablo Picasso,* by Christian Zervos (Paris: Editions Cahiers d'art, 1942), vol. 4 *Oeuvres de 1920 à 1922;* vol. 5 *Oeuvres de 1923 à 1925;* vol. 6 *Supplément* aux volumes 1 à 5; vol. 7 *Oeuvres de 1926 à 1932. Illustrated commentary*

Piston, Walter. *Principles of Harmonic Analysis* (Boston: E. C. Shirmer Music Co., 1933). *Commentary*

Poiret, Paul. *107 Recettes ou Curiosités Culinaires* (Paris: H. Jonquières, 1928). *Commentary*

————. *En Habillant l'Epoque* (Paris: B. Grasset, 1930). *Commentary*

————. *King of Fashion: The Autobiography of Paul Poiret,* tr. by Stephen Haden Guest (Philadelphia: Lippincott, 1931). *Memoirs*

————. *My First Fifty Years,* tr. by Stephen Haden Guest (London: V. Gollancz, 1931). *Memoirs*

Pound, Ezra. *Hugh Selwyn Mauberley* (London: Ovid Press, 1920). *Poetry*

————. *Indiscretions; or, Une Revue de Deux Mondes* (Paris: Three Mountains Press, 1923). *Autobiographical fragment*

————. *Antheil and the Treatise on Harmony* (Paris: Three Mountains Press,

1924); expanded with "Supplementary Notes" and reissued (Chicago: Covici, 1927). *Criticism*

————. *A Draft of XVI Cantos* (Paris: Three Mountains Press, 1925). *Poetry*

————. *Imaginary Letters* (Paris: Black Sun Press, 1930). *Commentary*

Prévost, Jean. *Plaisirs des Sports; Essais sur le Corps Humaïn* (Paris: Gallimard, 1926). *Commentary*

————. *Brûlures de la Prière* (Paris: Editions de la Nouvelle Revue Française, 1926). *Commentary*

————. *La Pensée de Paul Valéry* (Nimes: A. Chastanier, 1926). *Commentary*

————. *La Vie de Montaigne* (Paris: Gallimard, 1926). *Commentary*

————. *Merlin: Petites Amours Profanes* (Paris: Gallimard, Editions de la Nouvelle Revue Française, 1927). *Poetry*

————. *Agrippa d'Aubigné: Sa Vie à Ses Enfants* (Paris: Gallimard, 1928). *History*

————. *Le Chemin de Stendahl* (Paris: P. Hartmann, 1929). *Biography*

————. *Dix-Huitième Année* (Paris: Gallimard, Editions de la Nouvelle Revue Française, 1929). *Memoirs*

————. *Eiffel* (Paris: Rieder, 1929). *Commentary*

————. *Les Frères Bouquinquant* (Paris: Gallimard, Editions de la Nouvelle Revue Française, 1930). *Fiction*

Prokofiev, Serge. *Autobiography, Articles, Reminiscences* (Moscow: Foreign Languages Publishing House, n.d.). *Memoirs*

Proust, Marcel. *Remembrance of Things Past;* 4-volume American edition, tr. by C. K. Scott Moncrieff (New York: Random House, 1934). *Fiction*

Putnam, Samuel. *Paris Was Our Mistress: Memoirs of a Lost and Found Generation* (New York: Viking, 1947). *Memoirs*

Radiguet, Raymond. *La Diable au Corps* (Paris: B. Grasset, 1923); tr. by Kay Boyle as *The Devil in the Flesh* (New York: H. Smith, "Crosby Continental Editions, Paris," 1932). *Fiction*

————. *Le Bal du Comte d'Orgel* (Paris: B. Grasset, 1924); tr. by Malcolm Cowley as *The Count's Ball* (New York: W. W. Norton, 1929). *Fiction*

————. *Les Joues en Feu* (Paris: B. Grasset, 1929). *Poetry*

————. *Denise,* illustrated with lithographs by Juan Gris (Paris: Editions de la Galérie Simon, 1926). *Fiction*

Rascoe, Burton. *Before I Forget* (Garden City, N.Y.: Doubleday, Doran, 1937). *Memoirs*

————. *We Were Interrupted* (Garden City, N.Y.: Doubleday, 1947). *Memoirs*

Ray, Man. *Les Champs Délicieux* (Paris, Société Général d'Imprimerie et d'Edition, 1922). *Photography*

————. *Revolving Doors, 1916–1917* (Paris: Editions Surréalistes, 1926). *Photography*

————. *Photographs, 1920–1934, Paris* (Hartford, Conn.: James Thrall Soby, 1934). *Photography*

————. *Self-Portrait* (Boston: Little, Brown, 1963). *Autobiography*

Rhys, Jean (Ella Gwendoline Rees Williams). *The Left Bank and Other Stories* (New York: Harper and Bros., 1927). *Fiction*
————. *Quartet* (a.k.a. *Postures*) (New York: Simon & Schuster, 1929). *Fiction*
————. *After Leaving Mr. Mackenzie* (New York: A. A. Knopf, 1931). *Fiction*
Rice, Elmer. *The Adding Machine* (Garden City, N.Y.: Doubleday, Page, 1923). *Drama*
————. *Street Scene* (New York: S. French, 1929). *Drama*
————. *The Subway* (New York: S. French, 1929). *Drama*
————. *See Naples and Die* (New York: S. French, 1930). *Drama*
————. *The Left Bank* (New York: S. French, 1931). *Drama*
Riding, Laura. *Love as Love, Death as Death* (London: Seizin Press, 1928). *Poetry*
————. *Four Unposted Letters to Catherine* (Paris: Hours Press, 1930). *Fiction*
————. *Though Gently* (Dejá, Majorca: Seizin Press, 1930). *Prose and poetry*
————. *Twenty Poems Less* (Paris: Hours Press, 1930). *Poetry*
Rodker, John. *The Future of Futurism* (New York: E. P. Dutton, 1927). *Commentary*
————. *Collected Poems 1912–1925* (Paris: Hours Press, 1930). *Poetry*
————. *Memoirs of Other Fronts* (London: Putnam, 1932). *Memoirs*
Root, Waverley. "King of the Jews," *transition* 9 (December 1927). *Commentary regarding Roth's piracy of Joyce's* Ulysses
————. *The Paris Edition: The Autobiography of Waverley Lewis Root, 1927–1934*, edited and with an introduction by Samuel Abt (San Francisco: North Point Press, 1987). *Memoirs*
Sage, Robert. *See* Eugene Jolas.
Salmon, André. *La Négresse du Sacré-Coeur* (Paris: Editions de la Nouvelle Revue Française, 1920); tr. by Slater Brown as *The Black Venus* (New York: Macaulay, 1929). *Fiction*
————. *L'Age de l'Humanité* (Paris: Editions de la Nouvelle Revue Française, 1921). *Poetry*
————. *Natchalo (Le Commencement): Scènes de la Révolution Russe* (Paris: Impr. de l'Illustration, 1922). *Drama*
————. *Archives du Club des Onze* (Paris: Chez Mornay, 1923). *Fiction*
————. *Cézanne* (Paris: Stock, 1923). *Commentary*
————. *André Derain: Vingt-Six Reproductions de Peintures Précédées d'une Etude Critique* . . . (Paris: Nouvelle Revue Française, 1924). *Reproductions and commentary*
————. *Henri Rousseau, Dit le Douanier* (Paris: G. Crès, 1927). *Commentary*
————. *Max Jacob: Poète, Peintre, Mystique, et Homme de Qualité* (Paris: R. Girard, 1927). *Commentary*
————. *Tout l'Or du Monde* (Paris: Kra, 1927). *Poetry*
————. *Art Russe Moderne* (Paris: Editions Laville, 1928). *Collection and commentary*
————. *Chagall* (Paris: Editions des Chroniques du Jour, 1928). *Commentary*

————. *Kisling* (Paris: Editions des Chroniques du Jour, 1928). *Commentary*

Sato, Ken. Tr., *Quaint Tales of Samurais* by Saikaku Ibara, 1641–1693 (Paris: Contact Publishing Co., 1929). *Fiction*

Schiaparelli, Elsa. *Shocking Life* (New York: Dutton, 1954). *Memoirs*

Schlumberger, Jean. *Un Homme Heureux* (Paris: Editions de la Nouvelle Revue Française, 1920). *Fiction*

————. *Le Mort de Sparte* (Paris: Editions de la Nouvelle Revue Française, 1921). *Drama*

————. *Le Camarade Infidèle* (Paris: Editions de la Nouvelle Revue Française, 1922). *Fiction*

————. *Le Lion Devenu Vieux* (Paris: Editions de la Nouvelle Revue Française, 1924). *Fiction*

————. *Césaire; ou, La Puissance de l'Esprit* (Paris: Gallimard, 1927). *Drama*

————. *Les Yeux de Dix-Huit Ans* (Paris: Editions de la Nouvelle Revue Française, 1928). *Fiction*

Schwerke, Irving. *Kings Jazz and David* (Paris: Les Presses Modernes, 1927). *Commentary*

Scudder, Janet. *Modeling My Life* (New York: Harcourt, Brace, 1925). *Memoirs*

Seabrook, William. *The Magic Island* (New York: Harcourt, Brace, 1929); tr. into French by Gabriel Hons as *L'Ile Magique*, with Preface by Paul Morand (Paris: Firmin-Didot, 1929). *Commentary*

————. *Air Adventure: Paris — Sahara — Timbuctoo* (New York: Harcourt, Brace, 1933). *Commentary*

————. *No Hiding Place* (Philadelphia: Lippincott, 1942). *Memoirs*

Seldes, Gilbert. *The Seven Lively Arts* (New York: Harper and Bros., 1924). *Commentary*

————. "Uneasy Chameleons," *Saturday Evening Post* (1 January 1927). *Commentary*

————. *Him and the Critics: A Collection of Opinions on E. E. Cummings' Play. . .* , with an Introduction by Gilbert Seldes (Provincetown, Mass.: Provincetown Playhouse, 1928). *Commentary*

Sert, Misia. *Misia* (Paris: Gallimard, 1952). *Letters and memoirs*

Service, Robert W. *Ploughman of the Moon: An Adventure Into Memory* (New York: Dodd, Mead, 1945). *Memoirs*

Sheean, Vincent. *Personal History* (Garden City, N.Y.: Doubleday, Doran, 1935). *Memoirs*

Shirer, William. *20th Century Journey: A Memoir of a Life and Times* (New York: Simon and Schuster, 1976). *Memoirs*

Skinner, Cornelia O. *Family Circle* (Boston: Houghton Mifflin, 1948). *Memoirs*

Slocombe, George. *Paris in Profile* (Boston: Houghton Mifflin, 1929). *Commentary*

————. *The Tumult and the Shouting* (New York: Macmillan, 1936). *Memoirs*

Solano, Solita. *The Uncertain Feast* (New York: G. P. Putnam's Sons, 1924). *Fiction*

————. *The Happy Failure* (New York: G. P. Putnam's Sons, 1925). *Fiction*

————. *This Way Up* (New York: G. P. Putnam's Sons, 1927). *Fiction*

————. *Paris Between the Wars: An Unpublished Memoir by Solita Solano*, ed. and commentary by John C. Broderick. *Quarterly Journal of the Library of Congress* (October 1977). *Memoirs*

Soupault, Philippe. *Le Bon Apôtre* (Paris: Editions du Sagittaire, 1923). *Fiction*

————. *A la Dérive* (Paris: J. Ferenczi, 1923). *Fiction*

————. *Les Frères Durandeau* (Paris: B. Grasset, 1924). *Fiction*

————. *En Joue!* (Paris: B. Grasset, 1925). *Fiction*

————. *Corps Perdu* (Paris: Au Sans Pareil, 1926). *Fiction*

————. *Guillaume Apollinaire; ou, Reflets de l'Incendie* (Marseille: Les Cahiers du Sud, 1927). *Commentary*

————. *Henri Rousseau, le Douanier* (Paris: Editions des Quatre Chemins, 1927). *Commentary*

————. *Histoire d'un Blanc* (Paris: San Pareil, 1927). *Memoirs*

————. *Le Dernières Nuits de Paris* (Paris: Calmann-Lévy, 1928); tr. by William Carlos Williams as *Last Nights of Paris* (New York: Macaulay, 1929). *Fiction*

————. *William Blake*, tr. by J. Lewis May (New York: Dodd, Mead, 1928). *Commentary*

————. *Le Grand Homme* (Paris: Editions Kra, 1929). *Fiction*

Soutine, Chaim. *See* Monroe Wheeler.

Spear, Thelma. *First Fruits* (Paris: E. W. Titus, 1927). *Poetry*

Stearns, Harold. *America and the Young Intellectual* (New York: George H. Doran, 1921). *Commentary*

————. "Apologia of an Expatriate," *Scribner's Magazine* (March 1929). *Commentary*

————. *Rediscovering America* (New York: Liveright, 1934). *Commentary*

————. *The Street I Know* (New York: Lee Furman, 1935). *Memoirs*

————. Ed., *Civilization in the United States* (New York: Harcourt, Brace, 1922). *Commentary*

Steffens, Lincoln. *The Autobiography* (New York: Harcourt, Brace, 1931). *Memoirs*

Stein, Gertrude. *Geography and Plays* (Boston: Four Seas, 1922). *Commentary and fiction*

————. *The Making of Americans: Being a History of a Family's Progress* (Paris: Contact Editions, 1925). *Fiction*

————. *Composition as Explanation* (London: Hogarth Press, 1926). *Commentary*

————. *A Book Concluding with as a Wife Has a Cow a Love Story* (Paris: Editions de la Galerie Simon, 1926). *Fiction*

————. "An Elucidation," *transition* 1 (April 1927). *Criticism. Because the text was garbled, Stein insisted that the entire article be reprinted as a monograph and inserted in the magazine for its subscribers.*

————. *A Village: Are You Ready Yet Not Yet* (Paris: Editions de la Galerie Simon, 1928). *Drama*

————. *An Acquaintance with Description* (London: Seizin Press, 1929). *Commentary*

————. *Before the Flowers of Friendship Faded Friendship Faded* (Paris: Plain Edition, 1931). *Poetry*

————. *How to Write* (Paris: Plain Edition, 1931). *Commentary*

————. *Lucy Church Amiably: A Novel of Romantic Beauty and Nature which Looks Like an Engraving* (Paris: Plain Edition, 1931). *Fiction*

————. *Autobiography of Alice B. Toklas* (New York: Harcourt, Brace, 1933). *Memoirs*

————. *Four Saints in Three Acts: A Lyrical Opera* in *Operas and Plays* (Paris: Plain Edition, 1932); issued separately as *Four Saints in Three Acts: An Opera to Be Sung*, intro. by Carl Van Vechten, music by Virgil Thomson (New York: Random House, 1934). *Libretto*

————. *Everybody's Autobiography* (New York: Random House, 1937). *Fiction*

Stein, Leo. *The A-B-C of Aesthetics* (New York: Boni and Liveright, 1927). *Commentary*

————. *Journey into the Self: Being the Letters, Papers and Journals of Leo Stein*, ed. by Edmund Fuller (New York: Crown, 1950). *Letters, etc.*

Stephens, James. *Irish Fairy Tales* (New York: Macmillan, 1920). *Fiction*

————. *Collected Poems* (London: Macmillan, 1926). *Poetry*

————. *Etched in Moonlight* (New York: Macmillan, 1928). *Poetry*

————. *Julia Elizabeth* (New York: C. Gaige, 1929). *Drama*

Stewart, Donald Ogden. *Mr. and Mrs. Haddock Abroad* (New York: George H. Doran, 1924). *Fiction*

————. *Mr. and Mrs. Haddock in Paris, France* (New York: Harper and Bros., 1926). *Fiction*

————. *By a Stroke of Luck* (New York: Paddington Press, 1975). *Memoirs*

Stravinsky, Igor. *Stravinsky: An Autobiography* (New York: Simon and Schuster, 1936). *Autobiography*

Symons, Arthur. *Mes Souvenirs* (Paris: Hours Press, 1929). *Reminiscences*

Tate, Allen. *Poems 1928–1931* (New York: C. Scribner's Sons, 1932). *Poetry*

————. "Random Thoughts on the 1920s," *Minnesota Review* (Fall 1960). *Memoir*

Thomson, Virgil. *Virgil Thomson* (New York: Knopf, 1966). *Autobiography*

Thurber, James. "The First Time I Saw Paris" and "Exhibit X," in *Alarms and Diversions* (New York: Harper and Bros., 1957). *Fiction and reminiscences*

Toklas, Alice. *What Is Remembered* (New York: Holt, Rinehart and Winston, 1963). *Memoirs*

Toomer, Jean. *Cane* (New York: Boni and Liveright, 1923). *Fiction*

Tree, Iris. *The Traveller, and Other Poems* (New York: Boni and Liveright, 1927). *Poetry*

Tzara, Tristan. *Anthologie Dada* (Zurich: Mouvement Dada, 1919). *Dada commentary*

———. *Sept Manifestes Dada*, with some drawings by Francis Picabia (Paris: J. Budry, 1920). *Commentary*

———. *Mouchoir de Nuages*, decorated with etchings by Juan Gris (Paris: Editions de la Galerie Simon, 1925). *Drama*

———. *De Nos Oiseaux, Poèmes*, illustrated by Hans Arp (Paris: Kra, 1929). *Poetry*

Vail, Laurence. *Piri and I* (New York: Lieber and Lewis, 1923). *Autobiographical fiction*

Vitrac, Roger. *Les Mystères de l'Amour* (Paris: Editions de la Nouvelle Revue Française, 1926). *Drama*

———. *Connaissance de la Mort* (Paris: Nouvelle Revue Française, 1926). *Poetry*

———. *Cruautés de la Nuit* (Marseille: Les Cahiers du Sud, 1927). *Poetry*

———. *Victor; ou, Les Enfants au Pouvoir* (Paris: R. Denoel, 1929). *Drama*

Walrond, Eric. *Tropic Death* (New York: Boni and Liveright, 1926). *Fiction*

Walsh, Ernest. *Poems and Sonnets*, with a Memoir by Ethel Moorhead (New York: Harcourt, Brace, 1934). *Poetry*

Wescott, Glenway. *Good-Bye Wisconsin* (New York: Harper and Bros., 1928). *Fiction*

———. *The Babe's Bed* (Paris: Harrison, 1930). *Fiction*

West, Nathanael. *The Dream Life of Balso Snell* (Paris and New York: Contact Editions, 1931). *Fiction*

Wheeler, Monroe. *Soutine* (New York: Museum of Modern Art, 1950). *Commentary*

White, Walter. *A Man Called White* (New York: Viking, 1948). *Memoirs*

Wilder, Thornton. *The Cabala* (New York: A. and C. Boni, 1926). *Fiction*

——— *The Bridge at San Luis Rey* (New York: A. and C. Boni, 1927). *Fiction*

———. *The Angel That Troubled the Waters, and Other Plays* (New York: Coward-McCann, 1928). *Drama*

Williams, William Carlos. *The Great American Novel* (Paris: Three Mountains Press, 1923). *Fiction*

———. *Spring and All* (Paris: Contact Publishing Co., 1923). *Poetry*

———. "Robert McAlmon's Prose," *transatlantic review* 1:5 (May–June 1924). *Commentary*

———. *In the American Grain* (New York: A. and C. Boni, 1925). *Commentary*

———. *A Voyage to Pagany* (New York: Macaulay, 1928). *Memoirs and commentary*

———. *Autobiography* (New York: Random House, 1951). *Autobiography*

Wilson, Edmund. *The Shores of Light: A Literary Chronicle of the Twenties and Thirties* (New York: Farrar, Straus and Young, 1952). *Commentary*

———. *The American Earthquake: A Documentary of the Twenties and Thirties* (Garden City, N.Y.: Doubleday, 1958). *Commentary*

————. *The Twenties: From Notebooks and Diaries of the Period*, ed. by Leon Edel (New York: Farrar, Straus and Giroux, 1975). *Memoirs and commentary*

Wilson, Robert Forrest. *Paris on Parade* (Indianapolis: Bobbs Merrill, 1924). *Commentary*

————. *How to Wine and Dine in Paris* (Indianapolis: Bobbs Merrill, 1930). *Commentary*

Windeler, B. Cyril. *Elimus*, woodcuts by Dorothy Shakespear (Paris: Three Mountains Press, 1923). *Fiction*

Wolfe, Thomas. *Look Homeward, Angel* (New York: Scribner's, 1929). *Fiction*

————. *Of Time and the River* (New York: Scribner's, 1935). *Fiction*

Wylie, Elinor Hoyt. *Collected Poems* (New York: A. A. Knopf, 1932). *Poetry*

INDEX OF STREETS, AVENUES, BOULEVARDS, ETC.

Page numbers printed in **boldface** indicate a street heading, with addresses listed, as opposed to a textual reference. The map on which the street appears is provided in parentheses.

INDEX OF NOTEWORTHY PLACES, INFAMOUS EVENTS, AND SUNDRY THINGS

INDEX OF PERSONS MENTIONED